A HANDBOOK

OF CRITICAL APPROACHES

TO LITERATURE

A HANDBOOK OF CRITICAL APPROACHES TO LITERATURE

Wilfred L. Guerin

Earle G. Labor

Lee Morgan

CENTENARY COLLEGE OF LOUISIANA

John R. Willingham

THE UNIVERSITY OF KANSAS

HARPER & ROW, PUBLISHERS

NEW YORK AND LONDON

A HANDBOOK OF CRITICAL APPROACHES TO LITERATURE
Copyright © 1966 by Harper & Row, Publishers, Incorporated. Printed
in the United States of America. All rights reserved. No part of this book
may be used or reproduced in any manner whatsoever without written
permission except in the case of brief quotations embodied in critical
articles and reviews. For information address Harper & Row, Publishers,
Incorporated, 49 East 33rd Street, New York, N.Y. 10016.

Library of Congress Catalog Card Number: 66–14168

To our first critics—

Carmel Cali Guerin

Rachel Higgs Morgan

Sylvia Kirkpatrick Steger

Grace Hurst Willingham

CONTENTS

PREFACE

This book originated like many college-level textbooks: for several years the collaborators had been concerned about the problems connected with the teaching of literary analysis and had concluded that students urgently needed a more formalized and up-to-date introduction to a serious study of literature than was then available. We had found that most freshmen and a surprisingly large number of upperclassmen were entering and emerging from courses in literature still unenlightened about the most rewarding critical techniques that a keen reader could apply to good imaginative writing. Even students in whom the exposure to literature could be said to have "taken" often had only a narrow and fragmented concept of such interpretive approaches. One of our first aims in this book, therefore, has been to help establish a sound balance in the student's critical outlook. We see no reason why any college or university student—or, for that matter, any advanced high school student—should not have at hand the main lines of the most useful approaches to literary criticism.

Our aims in this book are specific (they may seem modest). The book is intended to provide a basic introduction to the major critical-interpretive perspectives which a reader just beginning a serious study may bring to bear on literature. It describes and demonstrates to the uninitiated student the critical tools that have come to be regarded as indispensable for the sensitive reader; these tools we call "approaches."

This is a *handbook* of critical approaches; therefore we have tried to make it suggestive rather than exhaustive and flexible rather than dogmatic. An incredible amount of critical jargon exists, but we have preferred to use the simplest, most accurate, most expressive terms and definitions. Once the student has mastered the basic techniques of critical reading, he can easily enough learn the sophisticated terminology.

Each of the five main chapters begins with an introduction to and definition of a particular interpretive approach, followed usually by a detailed practical application of its approach to four major works, one each from the genres of the novel, the short story, poetry, and drama. Each chapter also cites many other literary works for occasional illustrations. There is no rigid sequence from chapter to chapter, nor are all major works treated in the same degree of detail in each chapter, for not all works lend themselves equally well to a given approach. Moreover, one important by-product of our treatment of critical reading should be the student's recognition of the most suitable "approach" for a given literary work.

Chapter 1 considers the cluster of perspectives generally accepted as "traditional," for example, the biographical, the historical, and the moralistic; it points out both the advantages and the limitations of these approaches. Chapter 2 deals with the formalistic approach, which has come to be especially associated with the "New Criticism." Chapter 3 is a treatment of psychology in literature, concentrating on Freudian criticism. Chapter 4 moves into the realm of Jungian archetypal patterns and cultural myths as they are manifested in literature. Chapter 5 demonstrates a sophisticated application of several of the preceding approaches as they may be fused and expanded into another perspective, a perspective that gives further insight into patterns of image-metaphor-symbol. In conclusion, Chapter 6 reviews briefly the special concerns of such other approaches as the sociological, the linguistic, and the genetic.

This *Handbook* is directed toward the student beginning a serious study of literature and to both students and teachers unfamiliar with the dramatic changes and refinements that have taken place in literary analysis over the last four decades or so. Indeed, we undertook this primer of definition and illustration because we realized that some of these approaches—long taken for granted by literary critics and theorists—had not filtered down to the high schools, the colleges, and often the graduate schools themselves. Thus, we have not tried to be particularly original; we have simply tried to demonstrate in one handy volume—and, as far as we can discover, for the first time in this fashion—a significant portion of the spectrum of interpretive approaches to literature that have long existed but up to now have not been used by many students of literature.

We sincerely hope that one who studies this book will develop a sharper critical acumen, a greater appreciation of the richness of literature, and a sense of joy whenever he undertakes that most characteristic act of the truly cultivated person—reading. Moreover, we anticipate that the student who has explored conscientiously the implications and techniques outlined will possess a heightened confidence in his own critical perceptions.

This *Handbook* lends itself particularly well to introductory literature courses on either the freshman or sophomore college level. Two of the major works analyzed at length, *Huckleberry Finn* and *Hamlet,* are easily available in inexpensive paperback editions. The other two works, "To His Coy Mistress" and "Young Goodman Brown," are included in this book. But, helpful as we believe the *Handbook* will be in the interpretation of these works, we trust that it will be primarily a model or guidebook for the interpretation of other literary works. In short, the *Handbook* may serve as a supplementary text, best used with an anthology or set of paperbacks.

This book also, however, should have a validity in its own right for anyone who enjoys literature. It spells out methods that can be employed in analyzing a Hemingway novel, a Fitzgerald short story, a Shaw play, or a Browning poem. The subsections in the various chapters are designed to call specific attention to the genres as treated in the several approaches and in some cases to provide easily perceived steps that may be followed in analysis. The glossary at the end of the *Handbook* is not intended as a substitute for the longer dictionaries of critical terms, but it does define the technical terms that have special relevance for the present discussions. The bibliography lists some of the most helpful books related to the respective interpretive approaches, books that are generally available in any academic library. (Publication details are given in the text for books not listed in the bibliography.)

The *Handbook* may be read as a continuous unit, of course, but it has both flexibility and adaptability. For example, although it is primarily organized by "approaches" rather than by "genres," the instructor may assign at the beginning of a course the introductory section of each chapter and later the section of each chapter that deals with a certain genre. Thus the instructor who decides to begin with the short story may assign the introductory section of each chapter and then the five discussions of "Young Goodman Brown." In another possible use of the *Handbook*, students could read several literary works early in the term and discuss them in class without immediate recourse to the *Handbook*. Then they might read the *Handbook* or pertinent sections of it and bring their resulting new insights to bear on the literature read earlier, as well as on subsequent reading. This "double exposure" would have the advantage of creating the sense of discovery that awaits the perceptive reader.

Finally, our debt to the canon of literary criticism and scholarship is fairly obvious, and we acknowledge it with gratitude. Our bibliography only suggests the breadth and depth of critical scholarship and teaching from which this volume derives. We wish especially to thank those who have made many helpful suggestions in the preparation of this book: William B. Allmon, James A. Gowen, and Donald F. Warders, all of The University of Kansas; Laurence Perrine of Southern Methodist University; Arthur Schwartz of the University of Missouri; Richard Coanda of the University of Southern California; and James Wilcox of Adrian College. For their assistance in penetrating the maze of

reference materials, we wish to express our appreciation to Kath-
leen Owens and Czarena Stuart of the Centenary College Library.
And for undertaking the burden of typing the manuscript, let us
register our deep gratitude to Irene Winterrowd, Yvonne B.
Willingham, Mildred B. Smith, Melinda M. Carpenter, Alyce
Palpant, and Jeanette DeLine. Adrian College graciously made
available two summer-study grants to one of the collaborators.
And our wives stoically endured the whole project.

W.L.G.
E.G.L.
L.M.
J.R.W.

A HANDBOOK

OF CRITICAL APPROACHES

TO LITERATURE

CHAPTER

1

Traditional approaches

Some years ago, a story was making the rounds in academic circles, where it was received in good humor by all the enlightened teachers of literature. A professor of English in one of our great Eastern universities, so the story goes, entered the classroom one day and announced that the poem under consideration for that hour was to be Andrew Marvell's "To His Coy Mistress." He then proceeded to discuss Marvell's politics, religion, and career. He described Marvell's character, mentioned that he was respected by friend and foe alike, and speculated on whether he was married. At this point the bell rang. The professor closed

1

his sheaf of notes, looked up, smiling, and concluded, "Damn fine poem, men. Damn fine."

The story was told to ridicule the type of analysis that dominated the study of literature until the 1930s. In this approach, the work of art frequently appeared to be of secondary importance, something that merely illustrated "background." Such an approach often—many would say inevitably—led to the study of literature as essentially biography or history, rather than art.

Well on in the twentieth century, however, a new type of literary analysis emerged in which the literary work per se— that is, as a separate entity divorced from "extrinsic" considerations—became the dominant concern of scholars. The "New Critics," as the proponents of this position were called, insisted that scholars concentrate on the work itself, on the text, and examine it as an aesthetic creation—that is, as art. This method has revolutionized the study of literature. It has frequently divided critics and teachers into opposing factions—those of the older school, for whom literature provides primarily an opportunity for exercising the "really relevant" scholarly and cultural disciplines like history, linguistics, and biography, and the New Critics, who maintain that literature has an intrinsic worth, that it is not just one of the media of transmitting biography and history. Now that the controversy has lessened, the rationale of the New Criticism seems to have put into clearer focus what a poem or play or piece of fiction is trying to do; it has unquestionably corrected many wrongheaded interpretations resulting from an unwise use of the older method. To this extent, it has expanded our perceptions and appreciations of literary art.

Nevertheless, in their zeal to avoid the danger of interpreting a literary work solely as biography and history—the end result of the traditional method, they thought—many twentieth-century scholars have been guilty of what may well be a more serious mistake: ignoring any information not in the work itself, however helpful or necessary it might be. Happily, the most astute critics have espoused a more eclectic approach—they have fused a variety of techniques. They have certainly insisted on treating literature as literature, but they have not ruled out the possibility of further aesthetic illumination from traditional quarters.

In any event, while we may grant the basic position that literature is primarily art, it needs to be affirmed also that art does not exist in a vacuum. It is a creation by someone at some time in history, and it is intended to speak to other human beings about some idea or issue that has human relevance. Any piece of literature, or any work of art for that matter, will always be more meaningful to knowledgeable people than to uninformed ones. Its greatness comes from the fact that when the wisest, most cultivated, most sensitive minds bring all of their information, experience, and feeling to contemplate it, they are moved and impressed by its beauty, by its unique kind of knowledge, and even by its nonaesthetic values. It is surely dangerous to assume that a work of art must always be judged or looked at or taught as if it were disembodied from all experience except the strictly aesthetic. Many literary classics are admittedly autobiographical, propagandistic, or topical (that is, related to contemporary events).

Thus, while we have not yet elaborated these critical methods, let us be aware from the outset that we shall be dealing with some widely divergent interpretive approaches to literature. And, however much newer modes of analysis may be in the ascendant, the traditional methods retain much of their originally acknowledged validity.

TYPES OF TRADITIONAL APPROACHES

Textual-linguistic

Strictly speaking, the textual-linguistic approach is not precisely a method of criticism; it is nonetheless an extremely important tool in literary analysis. It concentrates on the authenticity of the text and the correct meaning of words in their historical context. One of the first things the traditional scholar does is to establish a text based on these principles. This is actually a problem not only in the case of older works, where defects in the manuscript or printers' idiosyncrasies may confuse, but also in contemporary literature, which often makes use of a cryptic, onomatopoeic, highly allusive language. The reader frequently assumes that the text before him has come down unchanged from its original form. More often than not, the reverse is the case, and what he sees is the result of painstaking emendation and collation of textual variants. The student beginning a serious study of literature is often indebted to a significant tradition of textual scholarship, a branch of literary studies necessary before any other type of critical analysis is possible. The object of such scholarship is the establishment of the most authentic text, the text as the original author had it, free of scribes' and publishers' errors. For example, the student who uses the eight-volume Chicago edition of *The Canterbury Tales,* a collation of scores of medieval manuscripts, will certainly appreciate the efforts of these precomputer scholars. Similarly, the studies of W. W. Greg, A. W. Pollard, and a host of others have gone far toward the establishment of a satisfactory Shakespearean text. This type of precritical scholarship should create in the student a healthy respect for the printed word, the evolution of its denotations and connotations, and the impact of its position in a given context. A quotation from Poe's "To Helen" will suffice to illustrate this last point. In the original version, Poe wrote:

> To the beauty of fair Greece
> And the grandeur of old Rome.

His revision is a happier combination:

> To the glory that was Greece
> And the grandeur that was Rome.

Here, the suggestion of the past-ness and ideality of classical Greece and the magnificence and pomp of imperial Rome are more nearly approximated in the revised "metaphors" than in the earlier "statement."

HISTORICAL-BIOGRAPHICAL

The historical-biographical approach has been evolving for at least two and a half centuries. Its basic tenets are perhaps most clearly articulated in the writings of the nineteenth-century French critics, Sainte-Beuve and Taine. Put simply, this approach sees a literary work chiefly, if not exclusively, as a reflection of its author's life and times or the life and times of the characters in the work. Furthermore, some handbooks of literature define additional approaches, for example, the expressive (a product of the Romantics), which sees literature as a source of unique knowledge deriving from the artist's *imagination* and therefore glorifies "self-expression" as the true function of art; and the impressionist, which focuses on what the critic *feels* in the presence of a work of art. Since these are related to the biographical approach generally, however, perhaps we can dispense with extended treatments of them individually in this introductory book. Indeed, the terms are more conventionally used in the terminology of painting than of literature. In any event, by the twentieth century, all these approaches had coalesced, and the "traditional" teacher or critic was likely to combine them in his analysis.

At the risk of laboring the obvious, we will mention the historical implications of *Piers Plowman,* which is, in addition to being a magnificent allegory, a scorching attack on the corruption in every aspect of fourteenth-century English life—social, political, and religious. So timely, in fact, were the poet's phrases that they became "electrifying watchwords" in the Peasants' Revolt. Similarly, John Milton's sonnet, "On the Late Massacre in Piedmont," illustrates the topical quality that great literature may and often does possess. This poem commemorates the slaughter in 1655 of the Waldenses, members of a Protestant sect living in the valleys of northern Italy. A knowledge of this background clarifies at least one rather factual reference and two allusions in the poem. Several of Milton's other sonnets also reflect events in his life or times. Two such are "On His Blindness," best understood when one realizes that the poet became totally blind when he was forty-four, and "On His Deceased Wife," a tribute to his second wife, Katherine Woodcock. Milton was already blind when he married her, a fact that explains the passage, "Her face was veiled."

An historical novel is likely to be more meaningful when either its milieu or that of its author is understood. James Fenimore Cooper's *The Last of the Mohicans,* Sir Walter Scott's *Ivanhoe,* and Charles Dickens' *A Tale of Two Cities* are certainly better understood by readers familiar with the French and Indian War (and the frontier experience generally), Anglo-Norman Britain, and the French Revolution. And, of course, there is a very real sense in which these books are *about* these great historical events, in which the author is interested in the characters only to the extent that they are molded by these events.

What has just been said will apply even more to ideological or propagandist novels. Harriet Beecher Stowe's *Uncle Tom's Cabin,* Frank Norris' *The Octopus,* and Upton Sinclair's *The Jungle* ring truer (or falser as the case may be) to those who know about the antebellum South, railroad expansion in the late nineteenth century, and scandals in the American meatpacking industry in the early twentieth century. And Sinclair Lewis' satires take on added bite and fun for those who have lived in or observed the cultural aridity of *Main Street,* who have been treated by shallow and materialistic physicians like some of those in *Arrowsmith,* who have sat through the sermons and watched the shenanigans of religious charlatans like Elmer Gantry, or who have dealt with and been in Lions Clubs with all-too-typical American businessmen like Babbitt. Novels may lend themselves somewhat more readily to this particular interpretive approach; they usually treat a broader range of experience than poems do and thus are affected more by extrinsic factors.

It is a mistake, however, to think that poets do not concern themselves with social themes or that good poetry cannot be written about such themes. Actually, poets have from earliest times been the historians, the interpreters of contemporary culture, and the prophets of their people. Take, for example, a poet as mystical and esoteric as William Blake. Many of his best poems can be read meaningfully only in terms of Blake's England. His "London" is an outcry against the oppression of man by society: he lashes out against child labor in his day and the Church's indifference to it, against the Government's indifference to the indigent soldier who has served his country faithfully, and against the horrible and unnatural consequences of a social code that represses sexuality. His "Preface to Milton" is at once a denunciation of the "dark Satanic Mills" of the Industrial Revolution and a joyous battle cry of determination to build "Jerusalem / In England's green and pleasant Land." It has been arranged as an anthem for church choirs, is widely used in a hymn setting, and was sung in London in the 1945 election by the victorious Labor Party. Obviously, then, even some lyric poems are susceptible to historical-biographical analysis.

Political and religious verse satires like Dryden's in the seventeenth century and personal satires like Pope's in the eighteenth century have as one of their primary purposes the ridiculing of contemporary situations and persons. Dryden propounds his own Anglican faith and debunks that of Dissenters and Papists in *Religio Laici*. Later, when he had renounced Anglicanism and embraced Roman Catholicism, he again defended his position, and in *The Hind and the Panther* he attacked those who differed. His *Absalom and Achitophel* is a verse allegory using the Biblical story of Absalom's rebellion against his father, King David, to satirize the Whig attempt to replace Charles II with his illegitimate son, the Duke of Monmouth. Pope's *Dunciad* is certainly a satire against all sorts of literary stupidity and inferiority, but it is also directed against particular literary people who had had the ill fortune to offend Pope. All of these works may be understood and appreciated without extensive historical or biographical background, but most readers would probably agree with T. S. Eliot, in his essay "Tradition and the Individual Talent," that "No poet, no artist of any art, has his complete meaning alone," and with Richard D. Altick, in his book *The Art of Literary Research* (W. W. Norton and Company, Inc., 1963), that ". . . almost every literary work is attended by a host of outside circumstances which, once we expose and explore them, suffuse it with additional meaning."

The triumph of such verse satires as those of Dryden and Pope is that they possess considerable merit as poems, merit that is only enhanced by their topicality. That they should ever have had to be defended because they were topical or "unpoetic" is attributable to what Professor Ronald S. Crane, in *A Collection of English Poems, 1660–1800* (Harper & Row, 1932), calls the tyranny of certain Romantic and Victorian "presuppositions about the nature of poetry" and the "inhibitions of taste which they have tended to encourage." He mentions among such presuppositions the notions that "true poetry is always a direct outpouring of personal feeling; that its values are determined by the nature of the emotion which it expresses, the standards being naturally set by the preferences of the most admired poets in the nineteenth-century tradition; that its distinctive effort is 'to bring unthinkable thoughts and unsayable sayings within the range of human minds and ears'; that the essence of its art is not statement but suggestion" (p. v).

Thus, even topical poetry can be good when not limited by the presuppositions that assume that poetry (and, by extension, all imaginative literature) is narrow; they make poetry a precious thing, something primarily personal, even esoteric. And, it might be added, such a view of poetry is much too limited and dogmatic for an area of literature that has continued to challenge definition.

MORAL-PHILOSOPHICAL

The moral-philosophical approach is as old as classical Greek and Roman critics. Plato, for example, emphasized moralism and utilitarianism, and Horace *dulce et utile,* delight and instruction. Among its most famous exemplars, perhaps, are the commentators of the Age of Neoclassicism in English literature (1660–1800), particularly Dr. Samuel Johnson. The basic position of such critics is that the larger function of literature is to teach morality. Sometimes such teaching is religiously oriented, sometimes philosophically. Fielding's *Tom Jones,* for example, illustrates the moral superiority of a hot-blooded young man like Tom, whose sexual indulgences are decidedly atoned for by his humanitarianism, tenderheartedness, and honor. Serving as foils to Tom are the real sinners in the novel—the vicious and the hypocritical. Hawthorne's *The Scarlet Letter* is likewise seen essentially as a study of the effects of secret sin on a human soul, that is, sin unconfessed before both God and man, as the sin of Arthur Dimmesdale with Hester Prynne, or, even more, the sin of Chillingworth. Robert Frost's "Stopping by Woods on a Snowy Evening" teaches that duty and responsibility take precedence over beauty and pleasure. And so on.

In each instance, the critic is not unaware of form, figurative language, and other purely aesthetic considerations, but they are for him secondary. The important thing is the moral or philosophical teaching. This is not on its highest plane Sunday-Schoolish (in the bad sense), though it may at first sound so. All great literature teaches—in the larger sense. The critic who employs the moral-philosophical approach insists on ascertaining and stating *what* is taught. If the work is in any degree significant or intelligible, this meaning will be there.

It seems reasonable, then, to employ historical-biographical, textual-linguistic, or moral-philosophical analyses among other methods in getting at the total meaning of a literary work when the work seems to call for them. Such approaches are less likely to err on the side of overinterpretation than are more esoteric methods. And Laurence Perrine warns in his very fine introduction to poetry, *Sound and Sense* (Harcourt, Brace, 1956), that overinterpretation is a particularly grievous critical error. In discussing Frost's "The Road Not Taken," a poem which does not require extrinsic background, Perrine maintains that the person who sees this poem "as being only about a choice between two roads in a wood has at least gotten part of the experience that the poem communicates, but the reader who reads into it anything he chooses might as well discard the poem and simply daydream" (p. 70).

If, then, the traditional approach to literary analysis may have tended to be somewhat deficient in imagination and may have neglected the newer sciences, if it may have been too content with a "common-sense" interpretation of material, it has performed this valuable service: in avoiding cultism and faddism, it has preserved scholarly discipline and balance in literary criticism. We do not mean that we favor the traditional criticism over more aesthetic interpretive approaches. We do suggest, however, that any knowledge or insight (with special reference to scholarly disciplines like history, philosophy, theology, sociology, art, and music) that can help to explain or clarify a literary work ought to be given the fullest possible chance to do so.

The reader who intends to employ the traditional approaches to a literary work will almost certainly employ them simultaneously. That is, he will bring to bear on the poem, for instance, all the information and insights these respective disciplines can give him in seeing just what the poem means and does.

TRADITIONAL APPROACHES TO MARVELL'S "TO HIS COY MISTRESS"

TEXTUAL-LINGUISTIC

Andrew Marvell's "To His Coy Mistress" contains several words that require some kind of textual validation. One is the last word in this couplet:

> Now therefore, while the youthful hue
> Sits on thy skin like morning dew.

The first edition of the poem has "glew," a variant spelling of "glue." But this would not make good sense in the context. "Lew" (dialectal "warmth") has been suggested as a possible reading, but some editors have conjectured "dew," apparently so happy an emendation that virtually all textbooks print it without any explanation. Two other words in the poem that must be explained are "transpires" and "instant" in the couplet.

> And while thy willing soul transpires
> At every pore with instant fires.

In each case, the word is much nearer to its Latin original than to its twentieth-century meaning. "Transpires" thus means literally "breathes forth," and "instant" means "now present" and "urgent." Admittedly, this sort of linguistic information borders on the technical, but an appreciation of the meaning of the words is imperative for a full understanding of the poem.

Genre and Paraphrasable Content

Most critics are careful to ascertain what literary genre (type) they are dealing with, whether a poem (and if so, what particular kind), a drama, a novel, or a short story. This first "what are we dealing with?" step is highly necessary, since different literary genres are judged according to different standards. We do not expect, for example, the sweep and grandeur of an epic in a love lyric, nor do we expect the degree of detail in a short story that we find in a novel. The lyric, the genre to which "Coy Mistress" belongs, is a fairly brief poem characterized primarily by emotion, imagination, and subjectivity. Having ascertained the genre and established the text, the employer of traditional methods of interpretation next determines what the poem says on the level of statement or, as John Crowe Ransom has expressed it, "paraphrasable content." The reader discovers that the poem is a proposition, a scheme or offer suggesting sexual intercourse. At first it contains, however, nothing of the coarseness or crudity usually implied in the word "proposition." On the contrary, though impassioned it is graceful, sophisticated, even philosophical. The speaker, a man, has evidently urged an unsuccessful suit on his sweetheart. Finding her reluctant, he now, as the poem opens, is making use of his most eloquent "line." But it is a "line" that reveals him no common lover. It is couched in the form of an argument in three distinct parts, which go something like this: (1) If we had all the time in the world, I could have no objection to even an indefinite postponement of your acceptance of my suit. (2) But the fact is we do not have much time at all; and once this phase of existence (that is, life) is gone, all our chances for love are gone. (3) Therefore, the only conclusion that can logically follow is that we should love one another now, while we are young and passionate, and thus seize what pleasures we can in a world where time is all too short. After all, we know nothing about any future life and have only the grimmest observations of the effects of death.

HISTORICAL-BIOGRAPHICAL

We know, of course, several facts about Marvell and his times that may help to explain this framework of logical argument and at the same time the learned allusions and the tone that pervade the poem. First, Marvell was an educated man (Cambridge B.A., 1639), the son of an Anglican priest with Puritan leanings. Since both he and his father had received a scholastic education, the poet was undoubtedly steeped in classical literature and modes of thought. Moreover, the emphasis on classical logic and polemics in his education was probably kept strong in his mind by his political actions (he was a Puritan, a Parliamentarian, an admirer of Cromwell, a writer of political satires, and an assistant to Milton in the Latin Secretaryship of the Government). That it should occur, therefore, to Marvell to have the speaker plead his suit logically should surprise no one.

There is, however, nothing pedantic or heavy-handed in this disputatious technique. Rather, it is playful and urbane, as are the allusions to Greek mythology, courtly love, and the Bible. When the speaker begins his argument, he establishes himself in a particular tradition of love poetry, that of courtly love. No one would mistake this poem for love in the manner of "Frankie and Johnny," or "O my luve's like a red, red rose," or "Sonnets from the Portuguese." It is based on the elevation of the beloved to the status of a goddess, hence a virtually unattainable object, one to be idolized. Yet this goddess is capable of cruelty, and in the first couplet the speaker accuses her of a "crime," the crime of withholding her love from him. But because she is a goddess, she is capricious and whimsical, and the worshipper must humor her by following the conventions of courtly love: he will "complain" (of her cruelty and his subsequent pain and misery) by the Humber; he will "serve" her through praise, adoration, and faithful devotion from the fourth millennium B.C. (the time of Noah's Flood) to the conversion of the Jews to Christianity, an event prophesied to take place just before the end of the world. Doubtless, this bit of humor is calculated to make the lady smile and to put her off her guard for the ulterior motive of the speaker. However pronounced courtly love may be in the opening portion of the poem (argument), by the time the speaker has arrived at his conclusion, he has stripped the woman of all pretense of modesty or divinity by his accusation that her "willing soul" literally exudes or breathes forth ("transpires") urgent ("instant") passion and by his direct allusion to kinesthetic ecstasy: "sport us," "roll all our strength," "tear our pleasures with rough strife / Thorough the iron gates of life:" (the virginal body).

Many allusions in the poem that have to do with the passage of time show Marvell's religious and classical background. Two have been mentioned: the Flood and the conversion of the Jews. But there are others that continue to impress the reader with the urgency of the speaker's plea. "Time's wingèd chariot" is the traditional metaphor for the vehicle in which the sun, moon, night, and time are represented as pursuing their course. At this point, the speaker is still in the humorous vein, and the image is, despite its serious import, a pleasing one. The humor grows increasingly sardonic, however, and the images become in the second stanza downright repulsive. And the allusions in the last stanza (the conclusion to the argument or case) do not suggest playfulness or a Cavalier attitude at all. Time's "slow-chapped [slow-jawed] power" alludes to the cannibalism of Chronos (Time), chief of the gods, who devoured all his children until Rhea hid Zeus, who later seized the power. The last couplet,

> Thus, though we cannot make our sun
> Stand still, yet we will make him run,

suggests several possible sources, both Biblical and classical.

Joshua commanded the sun to stand still so that he could win a battle against the Amorites (Joshua 10:13). Phaeton took the place of his father, the sun, in a winged chariot and had a wild ride across the sky culminating in his death (Ovid, *The Metamorphoses*). Zeus bade the sun to stand still in order to lengthen his night of love with Alcmene, the last mortal woman he embraced. In this example, it is, of course, easy to see the appropriateness of the figures to the theme of the poem. Marvell's speaker is saying to his mistress that they are human, hence mortal. They do not have the ear of God as Joshua had so that God will intervene miraculously and stop time. Nor do they possess the power of the pagan deities of old. They must instead cause time to pass quickly by doing what is pleasurable.

In addition to Marvell's classical and Biblical background, further influences on the poem are erotic literature, Metaphysical poetry, and *vers de société*. Erotic poetry is, broadly speaking, simply love poetry, but it must emphasize the sensual. In "Coy Mistress" this emphasis is evident in the speaker's suit through the references to his mistress' breasts and "the rest" of her charms and in the image of the lovers rolled up into "one ball." The poem is Metaphysical in its similarities to other seventeenth-century poems that deal with the psychology of love and religion and employ bizarre, grotesque, shocking, and often obscure figures to enforce their meaning. Such lines as "My vegetable love should grow," the warning that worms may violate the mistress' virginity and that corpses do not make love, the likening of the lovers to "amorous birds of prey," and the allusion to Time's devouring his offspring ("slow-chapped")—all help identify the poem as a product of the seventeenth-century revolt against the romantic and saccharine conventions of Elizabethan love poetry.

Furthermore, a common theme was *carpe diem*, "seize the day," a philosophy of "eat and drink, for tomorrow we shall die." Many of Marvell's contemporaries treated this idea —for example, Robert Herrick in "To the Virgins, To Make Much of Time" and Edmund Waller in "Go, Lovely Rose." As for its relation to *vers de société*, "To His Coy Mistress" partakes more of the tone than the subject matter of such poetry, manifesting for the most part wit, gaiety, charm, polish, sophistication, and ease of expression—all of these despite some rough Metaphysical imagery. This type of poetry naturally exhibits certain fundamental attitudes toward the main issue this poem treats— sex. These attitudes reflect an essentially pagan view. They depict sexual intercourse as strictly dalliance ("Now let us sport us while we may"), as solely a means of deriving physical sensations. Although not a Cavalier poet, Marvell is here letting his speaker express a typically Cavalier idea.

One more aspect of the historical background of the composition of the poem may be helpful in understanding its paradoxically hedonistic and pessimistic character. The seventeenth century, it should be remembered, was not only a period of intense religious and political struggle; it was also a period of revolutionary scientific and philosophical thought. It was the century when Sir Francis Bacon's inductive method was establishing itself as the most reliable way of arriving at scientific truth; it was the century when the Copernican theory tended to minimize the uniqueness and importance of the earth, hence of man, in the universe; and it was the century when Thomas Hobbes's materialism and degrading view of human nature tended to outrage and disturb the orthodox or reflective Christian. Given this kind of intellectual milieu, readers may easily see how the poem might be interpreted as the impassioned utterance of a man who has lost anything resembling a religious or philosophical view of life (excluding, of course, pessimism). The paradox of the poem consists in the question of whether the speaker is honestly reflecting his view of life—pessimism—and advocating sensuality as the only way to make the best of a bad situation; or whether he is simply something of a cad—typically male, conceited, and superior, employing eloquence, argument, and soaringly passionate poetry merely as a "line," a kind of devious means to a sensual end. If the former is the case, there is something poignant in the way the man must choose the most exquisite pleasure he knows, sensuality, as a way of spitting in the face of his grand tormentor and victorious foe, Time.

TRADITIONAL APPROACHES TO *HAMLET*

To attempt a complete analysis of *Hamlet* in the scope of this chapter would be not only presumptuous but also contrary to the very intention of this book, which is to demonstrate methods of literary interpretation—in the case of this chapter, from the "traditional" approach.

GENRE AND PARAPHRASABLE CONTENT

Hamlet is, of course, a drama, that is, a literary work that recounts a story on a stage where actors impersonate the characters of the story. Specifically, it is a tragedy, a play depicting the downfall of a central figure, traditionally a person of high rank or stature. In *Hamlet,* it seems more practical, owing to the length of the play and the numerous textual questions, to look first at the paraphrasable content and then to tackle other interpretive problems.

The main lines of the plot of *Hamlet* are clear. Hamlet, Prince of Denmark and heir presumptive to the Danish throne, is grief-stricken and plunged into melancholy by the recent death of his father and the "o'erhasty" remarriage of his mother to her late husband's brother, who has succeeded to the throne. The Ghost of the prince's father appears to him and reveals that he was murdered by his brother, who now occupies the throne and whom he describes as "incestuous" and "adulterate." Enjoining young Hamlet not to harm his mother, the Ghost exhorts him to take revenge on the murderer. In order to ascertain beyond question the guilt of his uncle and subsequently to plot his revenge, Hamlet feigns madness. His sweetheart Ophelia and his former schoolfellows Rosencrantz and Guildenstern attempt to discover from him the secret of his "antic behavior"—Ophelia because her father, Polonius, has ordered her to do so, Rosencrantz and Guildenstern because the King has ordered them to do so. All are unsuccessful. Before actually initiating his revenge, Hamlet wants to be sure it will hit the guilty person. To this end, he arranges for a company of traveling players to present a drama in the castle which will depict the murder of his father as the Ghost has described it. When the King sees the crime re-enacted, he cries out and rushes from the assembly. This action Hamlet takes to be positive proof of his uncle's guilt, and from this moment he awaits only the right opportunity to kill him. After the play, Hamlet visits his mother's apartment, where he mistakes Polonius for the King and kills him. The killing of Polonius drives Ophelia mad and also convinces the King that Hamlet is dangerous and should be gotten out of the way. He therefore sends Hamlet to England, accompanied by Rosencrantz and Guildenstern, ostensibly to collect tribute, in reality to be murdered. But Hamlet eludes this trap by substituting the names of his erstwhile schoolfellows on his own death warrant and escaping through the help of pirates. He reaches Denmark in time for the funeral of Ophelia, who has apparently drowned herself. Laertes, her brother, has returned from Paris vowing vengeance on Hamlet for the death of his father. The King helps Laertes by arranging a fencing match between the two young men and seeing to it that Laertes' weapon is naked and poisoned. To make doubly sure that Hamlet will not escape, the King also poisons a bowl of wine from which Hamlet will be sure to drink. During the match, Laertes wounds Hamlet, the rapiers change hands, and Hamlet wounds Laertes; the Queen unwittingly drinks the poisoned wine; and Laertes confesses his part in the treachery to Hamlet, who then stabs the King to death. All of the principals are thus dead, and young Fortinbras of Norway becomes King of Denmark.

TEXTUAL-LINGUISTIC

Few literary works have received the amount and the degree of textual study that Shakespeare's *Hamlet* has. There are some obvious reasons for this. To begin with, even the earliest crude printings, shot through with the grossest errors, revealed a story and a mind that excited and challenged viewers, producers, readers, critics, and scholars—so much so that the scholars decided not to let the matter drop but rather to do everything possible to ascertain what Shakespeare actually wrote. The other reasons are all related to this one. Shakespearean editors ever since have realized the importance of establishing an accurate text if students and audiences are to come at the meaning of *Hamlet.*

It is difficult at this remove in time for the college freshman or sophomore embarking on a serious reading of *Hamlet* to realize that the beautiful anthology or the handy paperback before him, each edited by an eminent authority, contains the product of over three hundred years of scholarly study of four different versions of *Hamlet* and nevertheless still includes some moot and debatable readings. Also, besides questionable readings, there are a number of words whose meanings have changed over the years but which must be understood in their Elizabethan senses if the play is to be properly interpreted. To be sure, modern editors explain the most difficult words, but occasionally they let some slip by or fail to note that reputable scholars differ. Obviously, it is not possible here to point out all of the variants of a given passage or to give the seventeenth-century meaning of every puzzling construction, but the student can catch at least a glimpse of the multiplicity and the richness of interpretations by examining some of the more famous ones.

One of the best known examples of such textual problems occurs in Act I, scene ii, "O that this too too solid flesh would melt." This is perhaps the most common rendering of this line. The word "solid" appears in the first folio edition (1623) of Shakespeare's complete works. Yet the second quarto edition (1604–1605), probably printed from Shakespeare's own manuscript, has "sallied," a legitimate sixteenth-century form of "sully" (to dirty, or make foul). These words pose two rather different interpretations of the line: if one reads "solid," the line seems to mean that Hamlet regrets the corporeality of the flesh and longs for bodily dissolution in order to escape the pain and confusion of fleshly existence. If, on the other hand, one reads "sullied," the line apparently reveals Hamlet's horror and revulsion upon contemplating the impurity of life and, by extension, his own involvement in it through the incest of his mother. J. Dover Wilson in *What Happens in "Hamlet"* sees "sullied flesh" as the clue to many significant passages in the play (for example, to Hamlet's imaginations "foul as Vulcan's stithy"), to his preoccupation with sexuality—particularly with the sexual nature of his mother's crime—and to his strange conduct toward Ophelia and Polonius. This view becomes even more credible when one considers Hamlet's seemingly incomprehensible remark to Polonius in II, ii, where he calls the old man a "fishmonger" (Elizabethan slang for "pimp"), implies that Ophelia is a prostitute by referring in the same speech to "carrion" (Elizabethan "flesh" in the carnal sense), and warns Polonius not to let her "walk i' the sun" (that is, get too close to the "son" of Denmark, the heir apparent, him of the "sullied flesh" and "foul" imaginations). Wilson explains Hamlet's ambiguous remark as obscene because Hamlet is angry that Polonius would stoop to "loose" his daughter to him (as stockmen "loose" cows and mares to bulls and stallions to be bred) in order to wheedle from him the secret of his behavior, and he is angry and disgusted that his beloved would consent to be used in this way. Hence, his later obscenities to her, as in III, i, when he tells her repeatedly to go to a "nunnery" (Elizabethan slang for "brothel").

One final example must suffice to illustrate the importance of textual accuracy in interpreting literature. In Quarto Two the speeches of the officiant at Ophelia's funeral are headed "Doct." This is probably "Doctor of Divinity," the term which a recent editor of *Hamlet,* Cyrus Hoy (Norton Critical Edition, 1963), inserts in the stage directions. The "Doctor of Divinity" reading was one reason for J. Dover Wilson's asserting positively that Ophelia's funeral was a Protestant service, contrary to the way directors often stage it. Indeed, the point seems to be a relevant one since it affects one's interpretation of the play. Although Shakespeare used anachronisms whenever they suited his purpose, a careless disregard of facts and logic was not typical of him. For example, both Hamlet and Horatio are students at Wittenberg. That this university was founded several hundred years after the death of the historical Hamlet is beside the point. What does seem important is that Wittenberg was the university of Martin Luther and a strong center of Protestantism. It is not unreasonable to assume then that Shakespeare wanted his audience to think of Denmark as a Protestant country (it was so in his day)— indeed that he wanted the entire drama to be viewed in contemporary perspective, a point that will be elaborated later in this chapter.

HISTORICAL-BIOGRAPHICAL

It will doubtless surprise most students to know that *Hamlet* is considered by some authorities—especially the Oxford historian A. L. Rowse, in his recent *William Shakespeare, A Biography* (Harper & Row, 1963)—to be highly topical and highly autobiographical. In view of the recent death of Elizabeth I and the precarious state of the succession, Shakespeare's decision to mount a production of *Hamlet,* with its usurped throne and internally disordered state, comes as no surprise. Indeed, the timeliness of such a play must have struck Shakespeare even earlier (*Hamlet* was probably written between 1598 and 1602) as Queen Elizabeth's advanced age and poor health called increasing attention to the problem of the succession. There is some ground for thinking that Ophelia's famous characterization of Hamlet may be intended to suggest the Earl of Essex, formerly Elizabeth's favorite, who had incurred her severe displeasure, been tried for treason, and executed:

> The courtier's, soldier's, scholar's, eye, tongue, sword,
> The expectancy and rose of the fair state,
> The glass of fashion and the mould of form,
> The observed of all observers. . . . (III, i)

Also, something of Essex may be seen in Claudius' observation on Hamlet's madness and his popularity with the masses.

> How dangerous it is that this man goes loose!
> Yet must we not put the strong law on him:
> He's loved of the distracted multitude,
> Who like not in their judgment but their eyes;
> And where 'tis so, the offender's scourge is weighed,
> But never the offence. (IV, iii)

Yet another contemporary historical figure, the Lord Treasurer Burghley, may be seen in the character of Polonius. Rowse points out that Shakespeare had probably often heard his patron, the young Henry Wriothesley, Earl of Southampton, express contempt for Elizabeth's old Lord Treasurer; indeed, this was the way many of the gallants of Southampton's generation felt. Burghley possessed most of the shortcomings Shakespeare gave to Polonius: he was boring, meddling, and given to wise old adages and truisms—he left a famous set of pious yet shrewd precepts for his son, Robert Cecil. Moreover, he had an elaborate spy system that kept him informed about both friend and foe. One is reminded of Polonius' assigning Reynaldo to spy on Laertes in Paris (II, i). This side of Burghley's character was so well known that it might have been dangerous for Shakespeare to portray it on stage while the old man was alive (since in fact Burghley had died in 1598, Shakespeare could with safety do so in this general way).

Other topical references include Shakespeare's opinion (II, ii, 35 ff.) about the revival of the private theater, which would employ children and which would constitute a rival for the adult companies of the public theater, for which Shakespeare wrote. It is also reasonable to assume that Hamlet's instructions to the players (III, ii) contain Shakespeare's criticisms of contemporary acting, just as Polonius' description of the players' repertoire and abilities (II, ii) is Shakespeare's satire on dull people who profess preferences for rigidly classified genres. Scholars have also pointed out Shakespeare's treatment of other stock characters of the day: Osric, the Elizabethan dandy; Rosencrantz and Guildenstern, the boot-licking courtiers; Laertes and Fortinbras, the men of action; Horatio, the "true Roman" friend; and Ophelia, the anemic courtly love heroine.

The historical critic in looking at *Hamlet* might be expected to ask, "What do we need to know about eleventh-century Danish court life or about Elizabethan England to understand this play?" Similar questions are more or less relevant to the traditional interpretive approach to any literary work, but they are particularly germane to analysis of *Hamlet*. For one thing, most twentieth-century American students, largely unacquainted with the conventions, let alone the subtleties, of monarchical succession, wonder—unless they are aided by notes—why Hamlet does not automatically succeed to the throne after the death of his father. He is not just the oldest son; he is the only son. Such students need to know that in Hamlet's day the Danish throne was an elective one. The royal council, composed of the most powerful nobles in the land, named the next king. The custom of the throne's descending to the oldest son of the late monarch had not yet crystallized into law.

As true as this may be in fact, however, Dover Wilson maintains that it is not necessary to know it for understanding *Hamlet* because Shakespeare intended his audiences to think of the entire situation as English—characters, customs, and plot—as he apparently did in most of his plays even though they were set in other countries. Wilson's theory is based upon the assumption that an Elizabethan audience could have but little interest in the peculiarities of Danish government, whereas the problems of royal succession, usurpation, and potential revolution in a contemporary English context would be of paramount concern. He thus asserts that Shakespeare's audience conceived Hamlet to be the lawful heir to his father and Claudius to be a usurper and the usurpation to be one of the main factors in the play, important both to Hamlet and Claudius. Whether one accepts Wilson's theory or not, it is certain that Hamlet thought of Claudius as a usurper, for he describes him to Gertrude as

A cutpurse of the empire and the rule,
That from a shelf the precious diadem stole
And put it in his pocket!   (III, iv)

and to Horatio as one

>   . . . that hath killed my king and whored my mother,
>   Popped in between th' election and my hopes; . . .   (V, ii)

This last speech suggests strongly that Hamlet certainly expected to succeed his father by election if not by primogeniture.

Modern students are also likely to be confused by the charge of incest against the Queen. While her second marriage to the brother of her deceased husband would not be considered incestuous today by many civil and religious codes, it was so considered in Shakespeare's day. Some dispensation or legal loophole must have accounted for the popular acceptance of Gertrude's marriage to Claudius. That Hamlet considered the union incestuous, however, cannot be emphasized too much, for it is this repugnant character of Gertrude's sin, perhaps more than any other factor, that plunges Hamlet into the melancholy of which he is a victim. And here it is necessary to know what "melancholy" was to Elizabethans and to what extent it is important in understanding the play. A. C. Bradley tells us that it meant to Elizabethans a condition of the mind characterized by nervous instability, rapid and extreme changes of feeling and mood, and the disposition to be for the time absorbed in a dominant feeling or mood, whether joyous or depressed. Modern psychologists might diagnose Hamlet's malady as manic-depressive psychosis. If Hamlet's actions and speeches are examined closely, they seem to indicate symptoms of this disease. Hamlet is by turns cynical (I, ii), idealistic (II, ii), hyperactive, lethargic, averse to evil, disgusted at his uncle's drunkenness and his mother's sensuality, convinced he is rotten with sin. To appreciate his apparent procrastination, his vacillating from action to contemplation, and the other superficially irreconcilable features in his conduct, readers need to realize that at least a part of Hamlet's problem is that he is a victim of extreme melancholy. (For more detailed discussions of Hamlet's melancholy, see A. C. Bradley's *Shakespearean Tragedy,* J. Dover Wilson's *What Happens in "Hamlet,"* and Weston Babcock's *Hamlet, A Tragedy of Errors* [Purdue, 1961].)

One reason for *Hamlet's* popularity with Elizabethan

audiences was that it dealt with a theme they were familiar with and fascinated by—revenge. *Hamlet* is in the grand tradition of revenge tragedies and contains virtually every stock device observable in vastly inferior plays of this type. Thomas Kyd's *The Spanish Tragedy* (ca. 1585) was the first successful English adaptation of the Latin tragedies of Seneca. The typical revenge tragedy began with a crime (or the recital of it) ; continued with an injunction by some agent (often a Ghost) to the next of kin to avenge the crime; grew complicated by various impediments to the revenge such as identifying the criminal and hitting upon the proper time, place, and mode of the revenge; and concluded with the death of the criminal, the avenger, and frequently all of the principals in the drama.

One additional fact about revenge may be noted. When Claudius asks Laertes to what lengths he would go to avenge his father's death, Laertes answers that he would "cut [Hamlet's] throat i' th' church" (IV, vii). It is probably no accident that Laertes is so specific about the method by which he would willingly kill Hamlet. In Shakespeare's day it was popularly believed that repentance had to be vocal to be effective. By cutting Hamlet's throat, presumably before he could confess his sins, Laertes would deprive Hamlet of this technical channel of grace. Thus, Laertes would destroy both Hamlet's soul and his body and risk his own, a horrifying illustration of the measure of his hatred. Claudius' rejoinder to this,

No place indeed should murder sanctuarize;
Revenge should have no bounds . . . ,   (IV, vii)

indicates the desperate state of the King's soul. He is condoning murder in the church, traditionally a haven of refuge, protection, and legal immunity for murderers.

Elizabethan audiences were well acquainted with these conventions. They thought there was an etiquette, almost a ritual, about revenge; they believed that it was in fact a fine art and that it required a consummate artist to execute it.

Moral-philosophical

Any discussion of *Hamlet* should acknowledge the enormous body of excellent commentary that sees the play as primarily valuable for its moral and philosophical insights. Little more can be done here than to summarize the most famous of such interpretations. They naturally center around the character of Hamlet. Some explain Hamlet as an idealist temperamentally unsuited for life in a world peopled by fallible creatures. He is therefore shattered when he discovers that some humans are so ambitious for a crown that they are willing to murder for it and that others are so highly sexed that they will violate not only the laws of decorum (for example, by remarrying within a month of a spouse's death) but also the civil and ecclesiastical laws against incest. He is further crushed when he thinks that his fiancée and his former schoolfellows are tools of his murderous uncle. Other critics see Hamlet's plight as that of the essentially moral and virtuous intellectual man, certainly aware of the gentlemanly code that demands satisfaction for a wrong, but too much the student of philosophy and the Christian religion to believe in the morality or the logic of revenge. Related to this is the view of Hamlet as a kind of transitional figure, torn between the demands and the values of the Middle Ages and the modern world. The opposed theory maintains that Hamlet *is* a man of action, thwarted by such practical obstacles as how to kill a king surrounded by a bodyguard. Many modern critics emphasize what they term Hamlet's psychoneurotic state, a condition that obviously derives from the moral complexities with which he is faced.

Hamlet fulfills the technical requirements of the revenge play as well as the salient requirements of a classical tragedy; that is, it shows a person of heroic proportions going down to defeat under circumstances too powerful for him to cope with. For most readers and audiences, the question of Hamlet's tragic flaw will remain a moot one. But this will not keep them from recognizing the play as one of the most searching artistic treatments of the problems and conflicts that form so large a part of the human condition.

TRADITIONAL APPROACHES TO *ADVENTURES OF HUCKLEBERRY FINN*

There are few works of literature that lend themselves to so many interpretive analyses as *Huckleberry Finn.* Bernard De Voto has written that the novel contains "God's plenty"; in that verdict lies the key to the traditional critical approach. The phrase "God's plenty" was also applied by Dryden to Chaucer's *Canterbury Tales;* so we should remember those attributes of Chaucer's art that elicited such praise—narrative and descriptive power, keen knowledge of human nature, high comedy, biting satire, and lofty morality. All of these are also in *Huckleberry Finn.*

GENRE AND PARAPHRASABLE CONTENT

Huckleberry Finn is a novel, an extended prose narrative dealing with characters within the framework of a plot. Such a work is usually fictitious, but both characters and situations or events may be drawn from real life. It may emphasize action or adventure (for example, *Treasure Island* or mystery stories); or it may concentrate on character delineation, that is, the way people grow or deteriorate or remain static in the happenings of life (*The Rise of Silas Lapham* or *Pride and Prejudice*); or it may illustrate a theme either aesthetically or propagandistically (*Wuthering Heights* or *Uncle Tom's Cabin*). It can, of course, do all three of these, as *Huckleberry Finn* does, a fact which accounts for the multiple levels of interpretation.

In genre, *Huckleberry Finn* is a direct descendant of the Spanish picaresque tale that arose in the sixteenth century as a reaction against the chivalric romance. In the latter type, pure and noble knights customarily rescued virtuous and beautiful heroines from enchanted castles guarded by fire-breathing dragons or wicked knights. In an attempt to debunk the artificiality and insipidity of such tales, Spanish writers of the day (notably the anonymous author of *Lazarillo de Tormes*) introduced into fiction a kind of antihero, the picaro—a rogue or rascal of low birth, who as the central figure lived by his wits and his cunning rather than by exalted chivalric ideals. (Although not a pure picaro, Cervantes' Don Quixote is involved in a plot more rambling and episodic than unified and coherent.) Indeed, except for the fact that the picaro is *in* each of the multitude of adventures, all happening "on the road," the plot is negligible by modern standards. In these stories, we simply move with this new type of hero from one wild and sensational experience to another, involving many pranks and much trenchant satire. Later treatments of the theme have occasionally minimized and frequently eliminated the roguish or rascally qualities of the picaro. Dickens' picaros, for example, are usually model little poor boys.

Many of the classics of world literature are much indebted to the picaresque tradition, among them René Le Sage's *Gil Blas,* Henry Fielding's *Tom Jones,* and Charles Dickens' *David Copperfield,* to mention only a few. *Huckleberry Finn* is an obvious example of the type. The protagonist is a thirteen- or fourteen-year-old boy living in the American antebellum South. He is a member by birth of the next-to-the-lowest stratum of Southern society, white trash—one who has a drunkard father who alternately abandons him and then returns to persecute him, no mother, no roots, and no background or breeding in the conventionally accepted sense. He is the town bad boy who smokes, chews, plays hooky, and stays dirty, and whom two good ladies of St. Petersburg, Missouri, have elected to civilize.

The narrative moves onto "the road" when Huck, partly to escape the persecution of his drunken father and partly to evade the artificially imposed restrictions and demands of society, decides to accompany Nigger Jim, the slave of his benefactors, in his attempt to run for his freedom. The most immediate reason for Jim's deciding to run away is the fact that Miss Watson, his owner, has decided to sell him "down the river"—that is, into the Deep South, where instead of making a garden for nice old ladies or possibly being a house servant, he will surely become a field hand and work in the cane or cotton fields. These two, the teen-aged urchin and the middle-aged slave, defy society, the law, and convention in a daring escape on a raft down the dangerous Mississippi River. A point about Jim's escape that needs clarification is his attempt to attain his freedom by heading *south;* actually, however, Cairo, Illinois, free territory and Jim's destination, is farther south on the river than St. Petersburg, Missouri, where he is escaping from. Thus when the fugitives miss Cairo in the fog and dark, they have lost their only opportunity to free Jim by escaping southward. Still another point is that if it had been Jim's object simply to get to *any* free territory, he might as easily have crossed the river to Illinois right at St. Petersburg, his home. But this was not his aim. Although a free state, Illinois had a law requiring its citizens to return runaway slaves. Jim therefore wanted particularly to get to *Cairo,* Illinois, a junction of the underground railroad system where he could have been helped on his way north and east on the Ohio River by abolitionists.

Continually in fear of being captured, Huck and Jim travel mostly at night. They board an abandoned steamboat which has run onto a snag in the river and find on it a gang of robbers and cutthroats, whom they manage to elude without detection. They find a vacant house floating down the river which contains the body of a man shot in the back, who, Jim later reveals, is Huck's father. They become involved in a blood feud between two aristocratic pioneer families. They witness a cold-blooded murder and an attempted lynching on the streets of an Arkansas village. They acquire two disreputable traveling companions who force them to render menial service and to take part in burlesque Shakespearean performances, bogus revival meetings, and attempted swindles of orphans with newly inherited wealth. Finally, after some uneasy moments when Jim is captured, they learn that Jim has been freed by his owner, and Huck decides to head west—away from civilization.

HISTORICAL-BIOGRAPHICAL

Thus, in genre and at the surface narrative level, the novel is something of a thriller. The sensationalism may seem to make the story improbable, if not incredible, but we should consider its historical and cultural context. This was part of frontier America in the 1840s and 1850s, a violent and bloody time. It was the era of Jim Bowie and his murderous knife, of gunslingers like Jack Slade, of Indian fighters like Crockett and Houston. Certainly there is a touch of the frontier, South or West, in the roughness, the cruelty, the lawlessness, and even the humor of *Huckleberry Finn*. Indeed, Mark Twain was very much in the tradition of such Southwestern humorists as Thomas Bangs Thorpe and such professional comedians as Artemus Ward and Josh Billings; he employed dialect for comedy, burlesque, the "tall tale," bombast, the frontier brag. *Huckleberry Finn,* of course, far transcends this type.

Furthermore, we know from Mark Twain's autobiographical writings and from scholarly studies of him, principally those of Bernard De Voto, A. B. Paine, and Dixon Wecter, that the most sensational happenings and colorful characters in *Huckleberry Finn* are based on actual events and persons Twain saw in Hannibal, Missouri, where he grew up, and in other towns up and down the Mississippi. For example, the shooting of Old Boggs by Colonel Sherburn was drawn from the killing of one "Uncle Sam" Smarr by William Owsley on the streets of Hannibal on January 24, 1845. The attempted lynching of Sherburn was also an echo of something that Mark Twain saw as a boy, for he declared in later life that he once "saw a brave gentleman deride and insult a [lynch] mob and drive it away." During the summer of 1847 Benson Blankenship, older brother of the prototype of Huck, secretly aided a runaway slave by taking food to him at his hide-out on an island across the river from Hannibal. Benson did this for several weeks and resolutely refused to be enticed into betraying the poor devil for the reward offered for his capture. This is, undoubtedly, the historical source of Huck's loyalty to Jim that finally resulted in his electing to "go to Hell" in defiance of law, society, and religion rather than turn in his friend.

The obscene performance of the "Royal Nonesuch" in Bricksville, Arkansas, where the King prances about the stage on all fours as the "cameleopard," naked except for rings of paint, was based on some of the bawdier male entertainments of the old Southwest. This particular type featured a mythical phallic beast called the "Gyascutus." There were variations, of course, in the manner of presentation, but the antics of the King illustrate a common version. (Both Mark Twain and his brother Orion recorded performances of this type, Orion in an 1852 newspaper account of a Hannibal showing, Mark in a notebook entry made in 1865 while he was in Nevada.)

The detailed description of the Grangerford house with its implied yet hilarious assessment of nineteenth-century culture may be traced to a chapter from *Life on the Mississippi* entitled "The House Beautiful." Here may be observed the conformity to the vogue of sentimentalism, patriotism, and piousness in literature and painting and the general garishness in furniture and knickknacks.

One pronounced theme in *Huckleberry Finn* that has its origin in Twain's personality is his almost fanatical hatred of aristocrats. Indeed, aristocracy was one of his chief targets. *A Connecticut Yankee in King Arthur's Court* is less veiled than *Huckleberry Finn* in its attack on the concept. But it was not only British aristocracy that Twain condemned; elsewhere he made his most vitriolic denunciations of the American "Southern aristocrat." Though more subtle, *Huckleberry Finn* nevertheless is the more searching criticism of aristocracy. For one thing, aristocracy is hypocritical. Aristocrats are not paragons of true gentleness, graciousness, courtliness, and selflessness. They are trigger-happy, inordinately proud, implacable bullies. But perhaps Twain's antipathy to aristocracy, expressed in virtually all of his works, came from the obvious misery caused to all involved, perpetrators as well as victims. The most significant expression of this in *Huckleberry Finn* is, of course, in the notion of race superiority. Clinging as they did to this myth, aristocrats could justify any kind of treatment of Negroes—callous, heartless, cal- culated, neglectful. They could separate families, as in the case of Jim and the Wilks slaves; they could load them with chains, forget to feed them, hunt them like animals, curse and cuff them, exploit their labor, even think of them as subhuman, and then rationalize the whole sordid history by affirming that the slaves ought to be grateful for any contact with civilization and Chris- tianity.

Moreover, not only aristocrats but every section of white society subscribed to this fiction; thus a degenerate wretch like Pap Finn could shoulder a free Negro college professor off the sidewalk and later deliver an anti-government, racist tirade to Huck replete with the party line of the Know-Nothings, a semi- secret, reactionary political group that flourished for a brief period in the 1850s. (Its chief tenet was hostility to foreign-born Americans and the Roman Catholic Church. It derived its name from the answer its oath-bound members made to any question about it, "I don't know.") We thus sense the contempt Twain felt for Know-Nothingism when we hear its chief doctrines mouthed by a reprobate like Pap Finn.

Closely related to this indictment of aristocracy and racism and their concomitant evils are Twain's strictures on romanticism, which he thought largely responsible for the harmful myths and cultural horrors that beset the American South of his day. In particular, he blamed the novels of Sir Walter Scott and their idealization of a feudal society. In real life this becomes on the adult level the blood feud of the Grangerfords and Shepherdsons and on the juvenile level the imaginative "high jinks" of Tom Sawyer with his "robber gang" and his "rescue" of Jim.

There are many other examples of historical and biographi- cal influences on the novel. Mark Twain's vast knowledge of Negro superstitions was acquired from slaves in St. Petersburg and on the farm of his beloved uncle, John Quarles, prototype of Silas Phelps. Nigger Jim himself is modeled after Uncle Dan'l, a slave on the Quarles place. These superstitions and examples of folklore are not mere local color, devoid of rhyme or reason, but, as Daniel Hoffman has so clearly pointed out in chapter 15 of

Form and Fable in American Fiction (Oxford University Press, 1961), they are "of signal importance in the thematic development of the book and in the growth toward maturity of its principal characters." Huck was in real life Tom Blankenship, a boyhood chum of Twain's who possessed most of the traits Twain gave him as a fictional character. Although young Blankenship's real-life father was ornery enough, Twain modeled Huck's father on another Hannibal citizen, Jimmy Finn, the town drunk. Years spent as a steamboat pilot familiarized Mark Twain with every snag, sandbar, bend, or other landmark on the Mississippi, as well as the more technical aspects of navigation.

Some similarity between Twain and Chaucer, "the father of English literature," has been mentioned; it will not be inappropriate to examine one of the more obvious points of relationship. Like *The Canterbury Tales, Huckleberry Finn* gives its readers a portrait gallery of the times. Scarcely a class is omitted. The aristocracy is represented by the Grangerfords, the Shepherdsons, and Colonel Sherburn. They are hardly Randolphs and Lees of tidewater Virginia—their homes reveal that. The Grangerford parlor, for example, shows more of philistinism and puritanism than of genuine culture. These people are, nevertheless, portrayed as recognizable specimens of the traditional aristocrat, with their dignity, their courage, their devotion to principle, their graciousness, their preserving of ceremonious forms, and their Calvinistic piety. Colonel Sherburn, in particular, illustrates another aspect of the "traditional" aristocrat—his contempt for the common man—in his cold-blooded shooting of Old Boggs, his cavalier gesture of tossing the pistol on the ground afterwards, and his single-handedly facing down the lynch mob.

The towns of any size contain the industrious, respectable, conforming bourgeoisie. In this class are the Widow Douglas and her old maid sister Miss Watson, the Peter Wilks family, and Judge Thatcher. The Phelpses, too, although they own slaves and operate a "one-horse cotton plantation," belong to this middle class. Mrs. Judith Loftus, whose canniness undoes Huck when he is disguised as a girl, is, according to De Voto, the best drawn pioneer wife in any of the contemporary records. The host of anonymous but vivid minor characters reflects and improves upon the many eyewitness accounts. These minor characters include the ferryboat owner, the boatmen who fear smallpox as they hunt Jim, the raftsmen heard from a distance joking in the stillness of the night. The Bible Belt poor white, whether whittling and chewing and drawling on the store front benches of an Arkansas village or caught up in the fervor of a camp meeting or joining his "betters" in some sort of mob action, is described with an undeniable authenticity.

Criminals like the robbers and cutthroats on the "Walter Scott" and those inimitable confidence men, the King and the Duke, play their part. Pap Finn is surely the earliest instance of many of Faulkner's Snopes types—filthy, impoverished, ignorant, disreputable, bigoted, thieving, pitifully sure of only one thing, his superiority as a white man. Then we observe the Negroes themselves, convincing because they include not just stereotyped minstrel characters or "moonlight and magnolia good darkies," but interesting human beings, laughable, sullen, honorable, trifling, dignified, superstitious, illiterate, wise, pathetic, loyal, victimized. Most make only brief appearances, and yet we feel that we have known almost firsthand a group of engaging, complex, and gifted people.

Textual-linguistic

To Twain's good ear and appreciation of the dramatic value of dialect we owe not only these authentic and subtle shadings of class, race, and personality, but also, as Lionel Trilling has said, "a classic prose" which moves with "simplicity, directness, lucidity, and grace." T. S. Eliot called this "an innovation, a new discovery in the English language," an entire book written in the natural prose rhythms of conversation. This linguistic innovation is certainly one of the features to which Ernest Hemingway referred when he said that "all modern American literature comes from one book by Mark Twain called *Huckleberry Finn*." If we agree with Hemingway, therefore, we can think of Twain as "the father of modern American literature."

MORAL-PHILOSOPHICAL

But the chief impact of *Huckleberry Finn* is its morality. This is, indeed, the *meaning* of the novel. All other aspects are subservient to this one. "Man's inhumanity to man" (as Huck says, "Human beings *can* be awful cruel to one another") is the major theme of this work, and it is exemplified in both calm and impassioned denunciation and satire. Every major event and most of the minor ones are variations on this theme. The cruelty may be manifested in attempts to swindle young orphans out of their inheritance or con village yokels with burlesque shows or fleece religion-hungry frontier folk with camp meetings or tar and feather malefactors extralegally. Cruelty can and often does have more serious consequences, for example, the brutal and senseless slaughter of the aristocratic Grangerfords and Shepherdsons and the murder of a harmless old windbag by another proud and arrogant aristocrat.

The ray of hope that Mark Twain reveals is Huck himself, whose ultimate salvation comes when of his own choice he rejects the values of the society of his time (he has all along had misgivings about them) and decides to treat Jim as a fellow human being. The irony is that Huck has made the right decision by scrapping the "right" reasons, that is, the logic of conventional theology, and by following his own conscience. He is, probably, too young to have intellectualized his decision and made it apply to the Negro race as a whole. Doubtless it applies only to Jim as an individual. But this is a tremendous advance for a boy of Huck's years. It is a lesson that is stubbornly resisted, reluctantly learned. But it is *the* lesson of *Huckleberry Finn*.

Huckleberry Finn is a living panorama of a country at a given time in history. It also provides insights, and it makes judgments that are no less valid in the larger sense today than they are about the period Mark Twain chronicled. This fidelity to life in character, action, speech, and setting; this personal testament; this encyclopedia of human nature; this most eloquent of all homilies—all of these are what cause this book to be not only a supreme artistic creation, but also, in the words of Lionel Trilling, "one of the central documents of American culture."

TRADITIONAL APPROACHES TO "YOUNG GOODMAN BROWN"

"Young Goodman Brown," universally acclaimed as one of Hawthorne's best short stories, presents the student searching out its meaning with not only several, but several rather ambiguous, possibilities. D. M. McKeithan (*Modern Language Notes,* LXVII, 93) has listed the suggestions that have been advanced as "the theme" of the story: "the reality of sin, the pervasiveness of evil, the secret sin and hypocrisy of all persons, the hypocrisy of Puritanism, the results of doubt or disbelief, the devastating effects of moral scepticism, . . . the demoralizing effects of the discovery that all men are sinners and hypocrites." Admittedly, these themes are not as diverse as they might at first appear; they are, with the possible exception of the one specifically mentioning Puritanism, quite closely related. But meaning is not restricted to theme, and there are other ambivalences in the story that make its meanings both rich and elusive. In the rest of this chapter, we will look at "Young Goodman Brown" from our traditional approaches.

Textual-linguistic

Textually and linguistically, "Young Goodman Brown" presents relatively few problems. By 1835, when the tale was first published in the *New England Magazine,* printing was a well-established business and vocation. Proofreading and typesetting were done much more carefully than in Shakespeare's day. Obsolete words in the story like "wot'st" (know), "Goody" (Goodwife, or Mrs.), "Goodman" (Mr.) are defined in most desk dictionaries, and none of the other words has undergone radical semantic change. Nevertheless, although a literary work may have been written in a day when printing had reached a high degree of accuracy, a perfect text is not a foregone conclusion, and, of course, scholars are constantly working today on more accurate texts. We have mentioned stylistic and typographical innovations in modern literature that can sometimes make the establishment of a text a painstaking chore. Furthermore, we must never forget that authors frequently *revise* their work and that their revisions may well affect their meaning, more likely in a subtle than in a radical way. (Henry James, for example, almost constantly revised and polished, as did Poe, Whitman, and Frost.)

GENRE AND PARAPHRASABLE CONTENT

Initially, then, the work is a short story, that is, a relatively brief narrative of prose fiction (its length may range from 500 to 20,000 words) characterized by considerably more unity and compression in all of its parts—theme, plot, structure, character, setting, mood—than the novel. In the story we are considering, the situation is this: One evening near sunset sometime in the late seventeenth century, Goodman Brown, a young man who has been married only three months, prepares to leave his home in Salem, Massachusetts, and his pretty young bride, Faith, to go into the forest and spend the night on some mission which he will not disclose other than to say that it must be performed between sunset and sunrise. Although Faith has strong forebodings about his journey and pleads with him to postpone it, Brown is adamant and sets off. His business is evil by his own admission; he does not state what it is specifically, but it becomes apparent to the reader that it involves attending a witches' Sabbath in the forest, a somewhat remarkable action in view of the picture of Brown, drawn early in the story, as a professing Christian who admonishes his wife to pray and who intends to lead an exemplary life after this one night.

The rising action begins when Brown, out of the village, enters the dark, gloomy, and probably haunted forest. He has not gone far before he meets the Devil in the form of a middle-aged, respectable-looking man whom Brown has made a bargain to meet and accompany on his journey. Perhaps the full realization of who his companion is and what the night may hold in store for him now dawns on Brown, for he makes an effort to return to Salem. It is only a feeble attempt, however, for, though the Devil does not try to detain him, Brown continues walking with him deeper into the forest.

As they go, the Devil shocks Goodman Brown by telling him that his (Brown's) ancestors were religious bigots, cruel exploiters, and practitioners of the black art—in short, full-fledged servants of the Devil. Further, the young man is told that the very pillars of New England society, church, and state are witches (creatures actually in league with the Devil), lechers, blasphemers, and collaborators with the Devil. Indeed, he sees his childhood Sunday School teacher, now a witch, and overhears the voices of his minister and a deacon of his church as they ride past conversing about the diabolical communion service to which both they and he are going.

Clinging to the notion that he may still save himself from this breakup of his world, Goodman Brown attempts to pray, but stops when a cloud suddenly darkens the sky. A babel of voices seems to issue from the cloud, many recognizable to Brown as belonging to godly persons, among them his wife. After the cloud has passed, a pink ribbon such as Faith wears in her cap flutters to the ground. Upon seeing it, Goodman Brown is plunged into despair and hastens toward the witches' assembly. Once there, he is confronted with a congregation made up of the wicked and those whom Brown had always assumed to be righteous. As he is led to the altar to be received into this fellowship of the lost, he is joined by Faith. The climax of the story comes just before they receive the sacrament of baptism: Brown cries to his wife to look heavenward and save herself. In the next moment, he finds himself alone.

The denouement (resolution, unraveling) of the plot comes

quickly. Returning the next morning to Salem, Goodman Brown is a changed man. He now doubts that anyone is good—his wife, his neighbors, the officials of church and state—and he remains in this state of cynicism until he dies.

HISTORICAL-BIOGRAPHICAL

So much for the paraphrasable content. What kind of historical or biographical information do we need in order to get the full impact of this story, aesthetically and intellectually? Obviously, some knowledge of Puritan New England is necessary. We can place the story in time rather easily, since Hawthorne mentions that it takes place in the days of King William—that is, William III, who reigned from 1688 to 1702. Other evidences of the time of the story are the references to persecution of the Quakers by Brown's grandfather (the 1660s) and King Philip's War (primarily a massacre of Indians by colonists, 1675–1676), in which Brown's father participated. Specific locales like Salem, Boston, Connecticut, and Rhode Island are mentioned, as are terms used in Puritan ecclesiasticism and government, such as ministers, elders, meetinghouses, communion tables, saints (in the Protestant sense of *any* Christian), selectmen, and lecture days.

But it is not enough for us to visualize a sort of "First Thanksgiving" picture of steeple-crowned Pilgrims with Bibles and blunderbusses. For one thing, we need to know something of Puritan religion and theology. This means at least a slight knowledge of Calvinism, the main source of Puritan religious doctrine. A theology as extensive and complex as Calvinism and one that has been the victim of so many misconceptions cannot be described adequately in a handbook of this type. But at the risk of perpetuating some of these misconceptions, let us mention three or four tenets of Calvinism that will illuminate to some degree the story of Goodman Brown. Calvinism stresses the sovereignty of God—in goodness, power, and knowledge. Correspondingly, it emphasizes the helplessness and sinfulness of man. Man has been, since the Fall of Adam, *innately* and *totally* depraved. His only hope is in the grace of God, for God alone is powerful enough (sovereign enough) to save him. And the most notorious, if not the chief, doctrine is predestination, the belief that God has, before their creation, selected certain people for eternal salvation, others for eternal damnation. Appearances are therefore misleading; an outwardly godly man might not be one of the elect. Thus, it is paradoxical that Goodman Brown was so shocked to learn that there is evil among the apparently righteous. It was one of the most strongly implied teachings of his church.

In making man conscious of his absolute reliance on God alone for salvation, Puritan clergymen dwelt long and hard on the pains of hell and the powerlessness of mere men to escape them. Brown mentions to the Devil that the voice of his pastor "would make me tremble both Sabbath day and lecture day." This was a typical reaction. In Calvinism, nobody "had it made." Introspection was mandatory. Christians had to search their hearts and minds constantly to purge themselves of sin. Goodman Brown is hardly expressing a Calvinistic concept when he speaks of clinging to his wife's skirts and following her to Heaven. Calvinists had to work out their own salvation in fear and trembling, and they were often in considerable doubt about the outcome. The conviction that sin was an ever-present reality that destroyed the unregenerate kept it before them all the time and made its existence an undoubted, well-nigh tangible fact. We must realize that aspects of the story that strike modern readers as fantastic, like belief in witches and an incarnate Devil, were entirely credible to New Englanders of this period. Indeed, on one level, "Young Goodman Brown" may be read as a witch story. Hawthorne describes at length a concoction with which witches were popularly believed to have anointed themselves and a satanic worship service attended by witches, devils, and lost souls.

It is a matter of historical record that a belief in witchcraft and the old pagan gods existed in Europe side by side with Christianity well into the modern era. There was an analogous prevalent belief in Puritan New England. Clergymen, jurists, statesmen—educated people generally, as well as uneducated folk, were convinced that witches and witchcraft were realities. Cotton Mather, one of the most learned men of the period, attests eloquently to his own belief in these phenomena in *The Wonders of the Invisible World,* his account of the trials of several people executed for witchcraft. Some of the headings in the table of contents are instructive: for example, "A True Narrative, collected by Deodat Lawson, related to Sundry Persons afflicted by Witchcraft, from the 19th of March to the 5th of April, 1692," and "The Second Case considered, viz. If one bewitched be cast down with the look or cast of the Eye of another Person, and after that recovered again by a Touch from the same Person, is not this an infallible Proof that the party accused and complained of is in Covenant with the Devil?" Hawthorne's great-grandfather, John Hathorne (Nathaniel added the "w"), was one of the judges in the infamous Salem witch trials of 1692, during which many people were tortured and hanged and one was crushed to death (a legal technicality was responsible for this special form of execution). Commentators have long pointed to "Young Goodman Brown," *The Scarlet Letter,* and many other of Hawthorne's stories to illustrate his obsession with the guilt of his Puritan forebears for their part in these crimes. In his introduction to *The Scarlet Letter,* Hawthorne wrote of these ancestors who were persecutors of Quakers and witches and of his feeling that he was tainted by their crimes. The Devil testified that he helped young Goodman Brown's grandfather, a constable, lash a "Quaker woman . . . smartly through the streets of Salem," an episode undoubtedly related to Hawthorne's reference in *The Scarlet Letter* to his great-grandfather's "hard severity towards a woman of [the Quaker] sect."

Hawthorne's notebooks are also a source in interpreting his fiction. They certainly shed light on his preoccupation with the "unpardonable sin" and his particular definition of that sin. It is usually defined as blasphemy against the Holy Ghost or continued conscious sin without repentance or refusing to acknowledge the existence of God although the Holy Spirit has actually proved it. The notebooks, however, and stories like "Ethan Brand," "Young Goodman Brown," and *The Scarlet Letter* make it clear that for

Hawthorne, the Unpardonable Sin was to probe, intellectually and rationally, the human heart for depravity without tempering the search by a "human" or "democratic" sympathy.

The supernaturalism and horror of "Young Goodman Brown" mark the story as one variant of the Gothic tale, a type of glorified ghost story originating formally in late eighteenth-century England and characterized by spirit-haunted habitations, diabolical villains, secret doors and passageways, terrifying and mysterious sounds and happenings, and the like. Obviously, "Young Goodman Brown" bears only the slightest resemblance to these artificial creations, the aesthetic value of which is surely negligible. What is much more significant is that here is a variation of the Faust legend, the story of the man who makes a bargain with the Devil (frequently the sale of his soul) in exchange for some desirable thing. In this instance, Goodman Brown did not go nearly so far in the original indenture, but it was not necessary from the Devil's point of view. One glimpse of evil unmasked was enough to wither the soul of Brown forever.

Moral-Philosophical

The terror and suspense in the Hawthorne story function as integral parts of the allegory that defines the story's theme. In allegory (a narrative containing a meaning beneath the surface one), there is usually a one-to-one relationship, that is, one idea or object in the narrative stands for only one idea or object allegorically. A story from the Old Testament illustrates this. The Pharaoh of Egypt dreamed that seven fat cows were devoured by seven lean cows. Joseph interpreted this dream as meaning that seven years of plenty (good crops) would be followed by seven years of famine. "Young Goodman Brown" may occasionally rise above allegory (that one-to-one relationship) to become symbolic, that is, richer and possibly more ambiguous in meaning. Nevertheless, it seems reasonable to assume from the plot and the diction that "Young Goodman Brown" is not about just one Salem citizen of the late seventeenth century. Brown seems rather to typify mankind, to be in a sense Everyman, in that what he does and why he does it appear very familiar to most people, based on their knowledge of others and on honest appraisal of their own behavior.

For example, Goodman Brown, like most people, wants to experience evil, not perpetually, of course, for he is by and large a decent chap, a respectably married man, a member of a church, but he desires to "taste the forbidden fruit" ("have one last fling") before settling down to the business of being a solid citizen and attaining "the good life." He feels that he can do this because he means to retain his religious faith, personified in his wife, who, to reinforce the allegory, is even named Faith. But in order to encounter evil, he must part with his Faith at least temporarily, something he is either willing or compelled to do. It is here that he makes his fatal mistake, for evil turns out to be not some abstraction nor something that can be played with for a while and then put down, but the very pillars of Goodman Brown's world—his ancestors, his earthly rulers, his spiritual overseers, and finally his Faith. In short, so overpowering is the fact and the universality of evil in the world that Goodman Brown comes to doubt the existence of any good. By looking upon the very face of evil, he is transformed into a cynic and a misanthrope whose "dying hour was gloom."

Thomas E. Connolly (*American Literature*, XXVIII, 370–375) has remarked that Goodman Brown has not *lost* his faith; he has *found* it. That is, Goodman Brown believes that he understands the significance of the Calvinistic teaching of the depravity of man; this realization makes him doubt and dislike his fellow man and in effect paralyzes his moral will so that he questions the motivation of every apparently virtuous act. But this is surely a strange conclusion for Brown to reach, for he has violated the cardinal tenets of Calvinism. If Calvinism stressed anything, it stressed the practical and spiritual folly of placing hope or reliance on human beings and their efforts, which by the very nature of things are bound to fail, whereas God alone never fails. Therefore all trust should be reposed in Him. It is just this teaching that Brown has not learned. On the practical plane, he cannot distinguish between appearance and reality. He takes things and people at face value. If a man *looks* respectable and godly, Brown assumes that he is. And if the man turns out to be a scoundrel, Brown's every standard crumbles. He is in a sense guilty of a kind of idolatry: human institutions in the forms of ministers, church officers, statesmen, and wives have, as it were, been his god. When they are discredited, he has nothing else to place his trust in and thus becomes a cynic and a misanthrope.

Thus, rather than making a frontal attack on Calvinism, Hawthorne indicted certain reprehensible aspects of Puritanism— the widespread "holier-than-thou" attitude; the spiritual blindness which led many Puritans to mistake a pious front for genuine religion; the latent sensuality in the apparently austere and disciplined soul (the very capstone of hypocrisy since sins of the flesh were particularly odious to Puritan orthodoxy).

It will perhaps be argued that Calvinism at its most intense, with its dim view of human nature, is quite likely to produce cynicism and misanthropy. But historically, if paradoxically, Calvinists have been dynamic and full of faith; they have been social and political reformers, educators, enterprisers in business, explorers, foes of tyranny. The religious furnace in which these men's souls were tempered is too hot for Goodman Brown, however. He is of a weaker breed, and the sum of his experience with the hard realities of life is disillusion and defeat. He has lost his faith, whether because his faith was false or because he wished for an objectively verifiable certainty which is the antithesis of faith, Hawthorne does not say. He does not even say whether the whole thing was a dream or reality. Actually, it does not matter. The result remains: faith has been destroyed and supplanted by total despair because Brown is neither a good Calvinist, a good Christian, nor, in the larger sense, a good Man.

As we have seen in our analyses of these works, the traditional approach in literary interpretation is neither rigidly dogmatic nor unaesthetic. It is eclectic. And, while it has its rationale in the methods discussed in this chapter, it does not eschew insights from any other critical approach; it does, however, insist on its own fundamental validity. Imaginative literature is for and about the most complex being in creation, man. It is therefore altogether probable that whatever relates to him will in some degree benefit those seeking to analyze his thoughts and actions.

CHAPTER

2

The formalistic approach

As its name suggests, the object of "formalistic" criticism is to find the key to the structure and meaning of the literary work— a key that inevitably reveals itself as necessary to the experience of the work as an art *form*. This approach is based on the idea that, although extra-literary considerations (such as the author's life, his times, and sociological phenomena) may be interesting and sometimes quite helpful, the heart of the matter ought to be, quite simply: What *is* the literary work, what are its *shape* and *effect*, and *how* do these come about? In short, we search for the *form*, necessary for a real understanding of the work.

45

We discovered in Chapter 1 that we can consider a Dickens novel, for example, as a commentary on the social and economic conditions of its period; or we can try to understand Joseph Conrad's inner feelings about having left Poland for England, as shown in his fiction. Nevertheless, it is hardly for these reasons that we read and reread a great novel or a good poem. There may be value in the sociological or historical revelations of a literary work, but these do not really justify our calling the work an art form. We find that we must try again and again to put together faint clues and hints until finally we discover a unifying pattern. This is the pattern that, as modern critics say, *informs* or shapes the work inwardly and gives its parts a relevance to the whole and vice versa.

The formalistic approach may very well lead us to various levels of understanding and meaning, but the basic informing device remains the basic key to all levels. For example, *Adventures of Huckleberry Finn* may certainly be read as (1) a picaresque novel of the road, in which the essentially innocent Huck and Jim, although they must suffer from the rogues and impostors who compose most of society, finally emerge triumphant over all forces that seek to destroy or corrupt individualism; (2) a myth of passage from youth and innocence to initiation and adulthood; (3) a testing of the built-in American dilemma between individualism and the mass; (4) the story of a young, inexperienced nation painfully growing from innocence into awareness. Some critics have even insisted that the novel is an attack on slavery and racial discrimination. How much all these "meanings" are interwoven with and complementary to each other is suggested by the repetition of words like "innocent," "innocence," and "youth." But the meanings are all linked in the river journey that lies between two blocks of narrative (the beginning and the end), both experiences on land and "at home." It is the *form* of the novel, given its special quality by the presence of Huck as narrator and by his special point of view and by the relentless alternation of shocking catastrophe on land and peaceful interlude on water, that finally becomes the means for revelation to the reader—a revelation the good critic is always trying to express or explain. Ultimately, however, we must narrow our attention to *what* the literary work says, and to do that, we must first consider *how* it is said. We could say that the plot of a story, the content of a sonnet, the movement of a play are symbols for a theme. To understand more specifically how these concepts can be applied, however, we should consider the background of this kind of literary analysis.

The formalistic approach is usually associated with the rise of the New Criticism in the 1930s and 1940s. Coming together originally (at Vanderbilt University) in the years following the First World War, the New Critics included the poet-scholar-teacher, John Crowe Ransom, and bright young students like Allen Tate, Robert Penn Warren, and Cleanth Brooks. Associated at first in an informal group to discuss literature, they later called themselves the "Fugitives" and published a literary magazine in Nashville. At first they were all primarily interested in their own study and writing of lyric poetry; later they seemed equally absorbed by the economic, historic, social, and cultural pressures on the agrarian South. As they read and criticized each other's work, as well as that of other poets, they gradually came to agree on the primacy of certain principles and methods of analysis which, by the 1950s, had come to be more influential in American critical circles and in college classes in literature than any others.

The New Critics generally approved of precision and tightness in a literary work; they favored a style and tone that tended toward irony; they insisted upon a work's containing everything necessary for its interpretation; they believed that teachers of English and literary critics had too long concerned themselves with matters outside the work itself—for example, the life of the writer or the history of his times or the sociological and economic import of the work. Most important of all, they turned the attention of readers and students to the heart of the matter—what the work *says*. One notable effect of their labor has been to make one generation of serious college students much more careful and capable readers. The words of a poem, for example, may properly be mined for all their denotative and connotative values; even their etymology as revealed in a dictionary may offer significant guidelines to what the poem is saying. But the question of how a poem reveals the love life of the poet (for example, was Emily Dickinson revealing her feelings about the Reverend Charles Wadsworth in "If You Were Coming in the Fall"?) or the influence of contemporary events (for example, what does Keats's "Ode on a Grecian Urn" tell us of British interests in classical archeology in the nineteenth century?) is entirely irrelevant to a consideration of the work *as literature*. It may be interesting to know the circumstances of Coleridge's being interrupted in the midst of writing "Kubla Khan," of Poe's instinctive drive to find a mother-figure among his female acquaintances, of Whitman's possible homosexuality, of Shakespeare's relationship to the "dark lady" of the sonnets, of Rossetti's drug addiction, of Twain's boyhood along the river in frontier Missouri. But essentially, insisted the New Critics, such questions are irrelevant to the experience of the literary work itself *as an art form.* They urged the reader to do his own reading —always to look at a literary work freshly and to put aside the biographical, historical, and sociological trivia found in abundance in literary histories and "introductory essays" in anthologies. Always, they pointed out, the work—poem, short story, novel, play—is first of all *a structure of words,* words which, if the writer is careful, *mean in a rather precise way.* In short, they have suggested that the reader see what is *in* the poem, the novel, or the play, rather than what is *outside* it. It is the careful reader's responsibility to find the *principle that allows the work to reveal itself*—the way in which the words have been fitted together to form an organism, a separate, unique thing. An analysis of the work's text (the words, phrases, sentences, stanzas, as we move from smaller to larger elements), done carefully, rigorously, intensively, should lead to total experience of the work. Thus, no matter how interesting extraliterary considerations may be, they must not be allowed to get in the way of careful textual analysis. To perceive how the words of a literary work fit into a pattern of statement and suggestion is to begin to see the emergence of the form and structure of the organic whole.

Another important consideration for the New Critics was the recognition that a prose paraphrase of a poem is no more a proper equivalent for the poem itself than a plot summary can be considered the essence of a novel or play. Nor can mere prose summary of a work ever be considered an adequate critical performance. The summary may be one of the tools the critical reader chooses to use as he studies the text; but it must never be confused with the totality of the literary piece. More to the point is the discovery of a principle by which content and form are shown to be inseparable—and such a principle can be discovered only from the language, the imagery, the tone, the stanzaic patterns, the meters and rhymes (or lack of meters and rhymes), in short, the whole edifice of words and their arrangement within the work. Concentration upon *form* keeps us within the realm of art (which, after all, always implies *artful arrangement* of a given content), whereas concentration upon *content alone* tends to take us away from art into philosophy, morals, or dogma.

Mark Schorer has emphasized the distinction: "Modern criticism has shown that to speak of content as such is not to speak of art at all, but of experience; and that it is only when we speak of the *achieved* content, the form, the work of art as a work of art, that we speak as critics. The difference between content, or experience, and achieved content, or art, is technique" ("Technique as Discovery," *Hudson Review*, I [Spring, 1948], 67). He goes on to say that "technique is the only means [an author] has of discovering, exploring, developing his subject, of conveying its meaning, and, finally, of evaluating it." It then follows that the reader who would read as a critic will grant that the literary artifact is, first of all, an artful arrangement of language—an arrangement that sets it off markedly from the loose, often imprecise language of our everyday, mundane experience. One may speak in the language of cliché in saying, "Imagination is certainly a wonderful thing!" But it takes the technique, the artful arrangement of the artist to make the reader actually experience the nature of the imagination. Thus, Emily Dickinson writes,

I never saw a Moor—
I never saw the Sea—
Yet know I how the Heather looks
And what a Billow be.

I never spoke with God
Nor visited in Heaven—
Yet certain am I of the spot
As if the Checks were given—†

A logical first step in explaining the literary work is to *dis-cover what the words actually mean* in all their full denotative (literal, dictionary meaning) and connotative (suggestive) value. Obviously, for the careful analysis of a literary text, one needs a good dictionary always at hand. And sometimes he may need to go beyond the limitations of the abridged dictionary (such as *The American College Dictionary, Webster's New World Dictionary*, or *Webster's Seventh New Collegiate Dictionary*) to one of the larger unabridged dictionaries that give full accounts and even archaic meanings of older or less common words. To repeat a point made in Chapter 1, we can see, for example, that much of the concrete imagery of Shakespeare's song on winter is lost unless we know that "keel" in the line, "While greasy Joan doth keel the pot" means "to cool, by skimming." Moreover, we must be alert to any allusion (reference to or suggestion of) to mythology, history, or other words of literature. For example, Eliot's *The Waste Land* and Joyce's *Ulysses* are scarcely comprehensible (or at least might hardly seem worth the trouble) without some understanding of the many allusions in them. The full meaning of each word and each allusion, then, must be discovered by the thorough textual critic.

More than an exact interpretation of the words of the text, however, is required for its complete explanation. The *context*— for example, the nature and the personality of the speaker in a

† Emily Dickinson, #1052. Reprinted by permission of the publishers from Thomas H. Johnson, editor, *The Poems of Emily Dickinson* (Cambridge, Mass.: The Belknap Press of Harvard University Press, Copyright, 1951, 1955, by The President and Fellows of Harvard College).

poem—must be determined. In Browning's "My Last Duchess," we must understand not only the personality of the Duke, who is speaking, but we must sense something of the nature of the man to whom he addresses his remarks. Only to the extent that we understand *what* the Duke is saying as revealed largely by *how* he says it can we really comprehend the full implications of the Duchess' story; one of the beautiful ironies of the poem, after all, is the reader's awareness of implications that the Duke is not aware of. In Eliot's *The Waste Land,* we must always be alert to the presence of the Tiresias-figure, from whom all other characters in the poem take their being, as the ironically disposed commentator on the many situations that arise within the poem. When we begin to see in this poem the intricate links among the many pieces and bits of situations drawn from both the modern and the ancient worlds (and they are linked by the pervasive presence of Tiresias), we are beginning to see much of the way in which the form of the poem shows itself.

In fiction, we must find out the *point of view* used by the author: (1) the narrator who tells the story (Huck in *Adventures of Huckleberry Finn,* Marlow in *Lord Jim,* Nick Carraway in *The Great Gatsby,* Frederick Henry in *A Farewell to Arms*); (2) a character from whose vantage point the story is told (Charley Wales in Fitzgerald's "Babylon Revisited"); or (3) the *omniscient narrator* (the familiar pattern of narrative told by the all-knowing author in the third person). In Melville's *Moby-Dick,* the nature of Ishmael, who at least starts the telling of the story, must always be kept in mind; it is important that we get the journey of the *Pequod* framed within the sensibility of an outcast who longs to be reinstated within the human race but who instinctively distrusts those who make conciliatory gestures toward him. Holden Caulfield of J. D. Salinger's *The Catcher in the Rye* supplies the angle through which the "phonies" of his world are seen; that world must be understood in terms of Holden's attitude toward it, the impact of incidents and people on him, the kind of language with which he supports his narrative, and his age and consequent limitations (consider how different *The Catcher* would be if the narrator were a thirty-five-year-old man who had graduated from The University of Kansas and spent twelve years in his father's brokerage firm in Topeka). In F. Scott Fitzgerald's *The Great Gatsby,* the impact of the story would be completely different if it were told by someone other than the curiously complex and in many respects naive narrator, Nick Carraway, who, like Gatsby himself in a number of ways, is not always all that he seems to be or should be. Nick's Midwestern origins qualify his responses to his experiences, just as Huck Finn's adolescent frontier background determines his speech, his ironic turn of mind, his frequent use of the tall tale with all its hyperbole and romantic inventiveness, and his skill in getting out of trouble. Marlow, the narrator of *Lord Jim,* imposes upon the framework of the novel a kind of detachment which enables the reader to see Jim with a wholeness that transcends Jim's own romantic conception of himself.

In drama, also, the characters comment upon themselves and others in such a way that we can establish a tone peculiar to each and can evaluate speeches against a kind of yardstick supplied by the play as a whole. Of course, the way the playwright poses his characters against each other (the kind of conflict established is the real essence of the dramatic situation) and the kind of dialogue he puts in their mouths become keys to his attitude. Early in *Hamlet* we discover Hamlet's tendency toward poetic comment upon his situation and his world and his characteristic preference for thought over action.

With such principles of formalistic criticism as these in mind, let us now turn to a specific application of them.

A FORMALISTIC READING OF "TO HIS COY MISTRESS"

Since the New Critics and their followers have tended to concentrate on lyric poetry by both precept and example (though they by no means have ignored fiction or the drama), it is perhaps appropriate to look first at Andrew Marvell's "To His Coy

Mistress." Here the title helps somewhat (it often does!), for it tells the reader that the poem is probably an address by a male speaker to a reluctant (or to quote a standard dictionary definition for "coy," "shy, bashful, retiring, demure") female. We can forget about trying to figure out the identity of the woman or speculating about seventeenth-century standards of courtship and seduction; we can concentrate instead on what this poem says and how it says it. We need not even remember that the poem fits into the classical tradition of *carpe diem* (literally, "seize the day"; more freely, "make hay while the sun shines, girlie").

A first reading of the poem suggests that the hint in the title is indeed helpful: a male speaker importunes his mistress (today's equivalent is probably more like "girl friend") to cease being "coy" or reluctant in the face of his offered love. Certain key words begin to call attention to themselves in this first reading and may be underlined with pencil for easy recall when a more intensive second or third reading takes place. Thus, words like "time," "love's long day," references to an event in Biblical history ("the Flood"), the "slow" growth of "vast" empires (line 12), "an hundred years" and "two hundred [years]" and "thirty thousand [years]," "an age," "the last age," "lower rate [of time]," "Time's wingèd chariot hurrying near," "deserts of vast eternity," images of the inevitable death of the lady (a process of time) in lines 25–30, "now," "at once," "our time," "the iron gates of life," and the final references to the movement of the sun—all suggest a preoccupation on the speaker's part with the passing of time *and* the consequent brevity of life and youth *and* the importance of experiencing all the delights of young love in the proper season.

The first twenty lines of the poem present a series of conditions ("Had we but world enough and time," "if you please") and use only the subjunctive mood ("this coyness, lady, *were* no crime") and the closely related conditional verb forms of *should* and *would*. The emphasis is fairly obviously placed upon the qualification *if things were somehow or other different* or, more specifically, *if men and women were not imprisoned within fleeting time.* The elaborate conditions attached to the lady's coyness are yoked rather grotesquely and bitingly with vast exaggerations, a device known as hyperbole; thus the speaker and the lady *could* be separated by the distance between the Ganges River of India and the Humber River of England; the speaker's love *would* extend from before the famous Biblical flood in the story of Noah (the beginnings of orthodox Hebraic-Christian chronology) to the conversion of the Jews (which presumably will not take place until just before the Last Judgment)—in effect, throughout all time; his love is compared to a vast vegetable which *would* grow as large and as slowly as empires; he *would* expend a hundred years in praising her eyes and gazing raptly at the lady's forehead, two hundred years in adoration of each of her breasts, and thirty thousand years for the celebration of the rest of her body; and, after these rather specific periods of time, he adds that "an age at least" *should* be devoted to the celebration of each physical part, the last of which *should* reveal the lady's heart (that is, she *would* now presumably be ready to return his love after he had conducted such an elaborate and virtually endless courtship). This section is summed up by the concluding and apparently elaborate compliment,

> For, Lady, you deserve this state,
> Nor would I love at lower rate.

Probably we must search the dictionary for a fairly uncommon meaning of the word "state" in these lines, since the usual twentieth-century meanings are not quite suitable; in this case, it is better to read the rare or obsolete meaning of "high rank or position" (which has been attributed to her by the apparently tireless lover of the hypothetical situation suggested by "Had we but world enough, and time"). Since these twenty lines postulate a series of extravagantly impossible situations, all of which are connected grammatically with the opening conditional lines, we can see that the speaker is no irresponsible romantic dreamer who would prefer to exchange the limited human state for a condition less restricted by the clock and the calendar; he is, instead, a militant realist who recognizes *and accepts* the brevity of life, and who, through his extravagant conditional situations, points up the folly of unrealistic coyness by the female in the face of the even greater transience of youth and its biological drives.

With the beginning of the next twelve lines, the *tone* (attitude or feeling of the speaker as conveyed by the language and its artful arrangement) seems to shift from the seemingly expansive, genial, more conventional, exaggerated praise of the beloved female by the ardent lover. Instead, the speaker now turns away from idle concern with "what might be if human life were not so relentlessly limited" to say the kind of thing we do not conventionally say in love songs, love letters, or declarations of love: he now confronts the lady with the inescapable fact of hastening time and the shocking facts of inexorable death and the decay of the flesh. His honesty, thus, by implication and by his own shrewd strategy, makes the lady's reluctance to enjoy fully the pleasures of love in their allotted season seem rather foolish, completely illogical, and perhaps even perverse. His impatience with her foolish and unrealistic coyness is held in check by the outward politeness and understatement of lines 31–32, in which, like a schoolmaster lecturing a not-so-bright pupil, he says by way of summing up the logic of his argument:

> The grave's a fine and private place,
> But none, I think, do there embrace.

That the whole poem has been moving in the direction of tightly reasoned argument is suggested by the summing-up word "therefore" in the third and final section of the poem (the last fourteen lines). Having made the lady's conventional shrinking from surrender to an ardent lover seem grotesque and unnatural in the first twenty lines and having employed rather scathing irony at her expense in the second section, the speaker now turns to a conciliatory note of sweet reasonableness. In view of the relatively harsh realism of the second section (with its obsession with what worms do to the body in the grave), the speaker can now afford to assume and to ask the lady to admit tacitly that she is as eager for the experience as he is (her "willing soul transpires / At every pore with instant fires,"—that is, her inner and desiring self obviously, even physically, betrays what she cannot bring her face or her voice to agree to—that she is as strongly impelled toward sexual gratification as he is). Having refused to accept as a suitable substitute for love's consummation the idle and unsatisfactory composing of plaintive and complimentary love songs, he now discards all pretense and asks her to join with him in the violent, even animalistically physical, response to love:

> Now let us sport us while we may,
> And now, like amorous birds of prey,
> Rather at once our time devour
> Than languish in his slow-chapped power.

This insistence upon a frank recognition of the way in which love is realized upon the physical plane is carried forward by "Let us roll all our strength and all / Our sweetness up into one ball" and "tear our pleasures with rough strife / Thorough the iron gates of life."

But the poem is more than a witty and realistic attack upon the lady's conventional coyness. Intricately woven into the brisk argument is a kind of melancholy awareness of the brevity of youth and life, of mortality and mutability. The lover is ever mindful of life's hastening toward an inevitable end:

> But at my back I always hear
> Time's wingèd chariot hurrying near;
> And yonder all before us lie
> Deserts of vast eternity.

In this sense, much of what the speaker says takes on a new dimension: something more than mere gratification of the physical appetites is involved. For, as the poem moves along toward its end, it becomes plain that the speaker is stressing the importance of living fully each moment—in a kind of heroic defiance of Time's "slow-chapped power." And the apparently playful approach to love may be seen as a kind of witty or ironic defense in the face of human limitation. The savage destruction of the lady's attitude is not diminished, but the more pervasive theme of defiance of mortality operates within the poem like a second theme in a musical composition that is echoed even as the major theme soars.

Much of the foregoing has been prose paraphrase and prose interpretation of the core of meaning in the poem. What about the "artful arrangement of words"? In many poems, rhyme and meter work to reinforce the content. The four-stress lines (notice that a perfectly natural reading of the line tells us where to place the beat or accent: "Had' we but world' enough' and time'") suggest precision by a lecturing speaker—a precision in which key words, simple as they are in general, get the emphasis of stress. Often each thought unit or syntactical pattern is completed within the two lines of a rhyming couplet. Thus the succession of thoughts is kept basically simple and straightforward as the speaker concentrates on the simplicity and directness of his argument, an argument addressed to a foolish woman who has ignored logic and reality in her passion for coyness. The seeming flippancy of the speaker's approach and his accompanying seriousness are effectively merged in the final couplet, which brings the poem to a very sudden close:

Thus, though we cannot make our sun
Stand still, yet we will make him run.

The adverb "thus" emphasizes that this is to be a conclusion of the argument, and the whole burden of the previous steps in the argument—living fully and vitally in the face of man's inevitable end—is telescoped wittily into the figure of the busy lovers forcing the sun (the image of time) into a brisk trot; thus if they cannot really control time, they can at least, with *their* brisk pace, make it race by and seem to be controlled.

THE SHORT STORY AS FORMAL STRUCTURE: "YOUNG GOODMAN BROWN"

Although generally the New Critics themselves preferred to consider short lyric poems in displaying their close textual analysis, many of their followers have given much of their attention to fiction, especially the short story, which, even if it does not possess quite the same advantageous brevity as the lyric poem, can nevertheless be examined with comparably close scrutiny. One can look, as in the poem, for the telling word or phrase, the recurring or patterned imagery, the symbolic object, the hint or clue of meaning greater than that of the action alone (in the case of a story, the action is what we usually call *plot*). Since we can no more justify stopping with a mere summary of what outwardly happens in a story than we can with a mere prose paraphrase of the "content" of a lyric poem, we must look for the key to the form of a story in a balanced juxtaposition of plot or "content" with the theme or "larger implication" of the story. In short, we must arrive ultimately at a point where the structure of the story coincides with and illuminates its meaning. Again we must look at the various parts before we can tell what the whole is like.

As we have seen, the lyric poem generally describes a somewhat *dramatic* situation: a speaker (who need not be the poet at all, though often we can suppose it is) reacts to an experience, a feeling, an idea, or even a sensation of sight, touch, or smell. Only one voice is present in the lyric poem, but in other literary forms there usually is a group of characters. In the drama, the characters act and talk out their conflict and the resolution of the conflict; in fiction, a story is told by the author or by one of the characters in the story. The major difference between the short story and the novel—the important fictional types— is one of length and complexity of plot; the novel contains a larger number of characters, and its plot includes a number of situations. The short story characteristically is concerned with relatively few characters (sometimes really only one, as in Poe's "William Wilson" or "The Black Cat") and with only one major situation, which achieves its climax and solution and thus comes to an end. Like a news story, the short story is restricted in scope, but unlike the news story, the short story must possess that balance and design, that polish and finish, which we associate with the work of art. In short, like other imaginative literary works, it possesses *form*.

Hawthorne characteristically employs what is sometimes called an "allegorical" method; indeed, he often uses a "symbolic" method, which, of course, suggests more and richer meanings than are implicit in the allegory with its normal one-to-one relationship. The first paragraph of "Young Goodman Brown" suggests this allegorical bent, for the names of the two chief characters—Brown himself and his wife Faith—immediately suggest associations beyond those of an historical character or a Tom Smith or a Mary Jones. Although "Goodman" was a commonplace honorific for persons below the class of gentleman in both England and the Colonies, the use of "Young" with it and its constant repetition throughout the narrative suggest that Hawthorne intends to hint at more about the chief character— his youth, his innocence, his simple, unquestioned attachment to abstract faith. Yet his last name, Brown, points just as surely to a hint that the young man has affinities with the forest of gloom and darkness in which most of the story takes place, that strange world outside the settled, comfortable village of goodness and faith.

The urgency of the dark journey from home and trust and safety is emphasized by the conversation of Brown and Faith as he prepares to leave. Faith begs him to stay home and "put off" the journey "until sunrise." But Brown feels constrained to go, or wills to go in spite of her pleas. We also see that Brown himself is quite clear about the nature of the night's errand, for he says to Faith: "My journey, *as thou callest it,* forth and back again, must needs be done 'twixt now and sunrise" (our italics to emphasize his own certainty about what he is doing). Into a dark world, whose dimensions are only dimly suspected but whose attractions are irresistible, he will go; and the irony of his position is revealed in his asking his Faith: "What, my sweet, pretty wife, dost thou doubt me already, and we but three months married?" Ironic precisely because of his own superficial attachment to Faith and the deep doubts about the kind of reality he will encounter in the forest. This initial struggle between Brown and his Faith thus establishes formally and early the allegorical level of the journey and the issues involved in it. Not only is the willful voyager opposed to the innocent Faith, but all the simple values of the safe, light village are economically and immediately set against those equivocal and, as we shall see, unordered forces that lurk outside. It is an unequal contest, for Faith cannot summon any strong argument—only uneasy questions about the possible results of the voyage—to forestall Brown's departure.

And off he goes with only a passing pang of regret for his Faith. That he has some idea of what will take place is clearly suggested by his thought that perhaps Faith had some foreshadowing of "what work is to be done to-night" and that, moreover, " 'twould kill her to think it." Clearly Brown's object in the forest is inimical to Faith (or faith); he suspects the kind of risk he takes and accepts that risk although he promises himself that "after this one night" in darkness "I'll cling to her [that is, Faith's] skirts and follow her to heaven." Thus the allegorical functions of Faith and Brown, as well as the implications of the journey, are clearly set forth. The formal linking of Faith, the village, light, and unquestioned certainty, on the one hand, and Brown, the forest, darkness, and skepticism, on the other, has been established.

Although, as we have pointed out in Chapter 1, some knowledge of Puritan superstition and assurance about the Puritan role in the wilderness, the abode of Satan, may be helpful here, Hawthorne does give enough hints about the nature of the journey and the forest. The formal elements of place, time, atmosphere, and carefully contrived action tell us all we need to know. The journey begins at sundown, Brown hastens on "his present evil purpose," the road is "dreary, darkened by all the gloomiest trees of the forest," the solitude is complete, there is the discomfort of the traveler about fearful creatures that may lurk behind the trees, and Brown returns to the familiar world only at sunrise. A circular pattern of withdrawal and return provides a structure for the narrative in a generally Gothic context.

But the mystery is not to be of a conventional, melodramatic sort. For as Brown asks himself, "What if the devil himself should be at my very elbow!" that elderly figure instantly appears to chide Brown for being late. That the older man is no earthly being is suggested by his timetable; even in a pre-jet day he has made his way from Boston to the outskirts of Salem in fifteen minutes! And that Brown is neither surprised to see him nor ignorant of his powers is manifest from his explanation that "Faith kept me back a while." Of course, this explanation is true on two levels—both that of the young husband and that of the simple man of faith. On a formal level, the world of the forest is seemingly equated with that of the village. The characters who appear—including Brown himself, who aspires to inhabiting both worlds—seem to be basically like those of the village. Brown recognizes them by the names they bear in the village, and outwardly they seem to be going about their accustomed affairs. They wear the same clothes and exhibit the familiar mannerisms. The difference is, of course, that now they have taken on the values of the forest. As in Alice's journey into the world of the looking glass, the values of the village are completely reversed in the forest.

Hawthorne's comments upon the relationships between Satan and Brown bear some close reading, too. The older man resembles Brown and is "apparently in the same rank of life"; as if to reinforce the relationship, Hawthorne adds that "they might have been taken for father and son." And they *are* father and son: the younger man, as are all men, is the child of Satan, who, though he wears the clothes of Brown's class, "had an indescribable air of one who knew the world, and would not have felt abashed at the governor's dinner table or in King William's court." This is merely another way of saying that the principle of evil is at home everywhere or that wherever there is worldliness or uninhibited evil, there is Satan. But all this is communicated to us through the formal juxtaposition of the world Brown has left with the world he has now entered. If we are still in doubt about the supernatural associations of the older man, Hawthorne now allows us no doubt when he mentions the staff, which seems to "twist and wriggle itself like a live serpent." Obviously, this is the same traveler who came to Eden in the guise of a serpent and tempted Eve and Adam to forgo faith. Lest this seem too heavyhanded, Hawthorne seems to retreat a little when he says that the living movements of the snake-staff may have been caused by "an ocular deception, assisted by the uncertain light." But this way out for the reader has already been closed by the revelation that the older man and Brown had arranged a tryst in the forest and that the older man had traveled from Boston to Salem in something beyond record time. Nevertheless, in the forest the light *is* "uncertain," and "ocular deception" makes impossible the familiar categories of the village.

The traveler's identity and the nature of the tryst are further confirmed when Brown halfheartedly tries to back out of his commitment to the journey, using as a weak explanation that neither his ancestors nor the "good" people of New England in general have ventured on such a perilous trek. Again the "elder person" has a ready answer: not only has he been an intimate and active agent of Brown's father and grandfather, but he also has enjoyed "a very general acquaintance here in New England." The men of the Brown family have often ventured into the forests with the traveler of the crooked staff to carouse after midnight and to engage in forbidden rites. As Brown goes deeper into the forest with his guide, he encounters one by one all the sober church officials of Salem and the people who he had thought were completely incorruptible—Goody Cloyse, from whom he had learned his catechism, the minister, and Deacon Gookin. Each encounter is for Young Goodman Brown a step toward total disillusionment and a further breach between him and his faith. Moving further into darkness and density, Brown finds the topsy-turvy world of the forest irresistible. Yet after each encounter, he recalls his Faith and believes that he can still return to the safety and assurance of home.

But his commitment to the forces of darkness is sealed when from "a cloud of night" sweeping overhead he thinks he hears, mingled with the voices of his Salem neighbors, the sound of Faith's voice. The suspicion is confirmed when the pink ribbon, the only specific detail we have to associate with Faith, flutters down from above. In that moment, of course, Brown comes to *know* what he had all along suspected about the depravity of all mankind; this is an important point: if he had not *suspected* the truth of what he discovers, he would never have made the journey. Though the theological content comes from the world of the village, it is in the forest that he eloquently articulates it: "'My Faith is gone!' cried he, after one stupefied moment. 'There is no good on earth; and sin is but a name. Come, devil; for to thee is this world given.'" But such a recognition scene would seem superficially mechanical if it were not for the carefully established atmosphere of the forest (with its darkness and gloom) and the intrusion of the village into the forest.

Thus he rushes off, with the supersonic aid of the staff thoughtfully left him by Satan, toward a midnight rendezvous in the heart of the dark forest and the culmination of his knowledge of evil, diabolism, and depravity. The rendezvous, we discover, is the Puritan equivalent of a Black Mass—a solemn meeting at which hymns strangely like those of the choir of the Salem meetinghouse are sung and the form of a Puritan sermon is maintained. The congregation are clad in their usual drab garb and display their customary solemnity and gravity. Again, then, we see the careful juxtaposition of the forms and appearances of the village and meetinghouse with those of the forest and satanic orgy. The familiar world of fact and certainty has become one with the unknown world of fantasy and doubt. The people are the same, and the urgency of form and ritual has a similarity too obvious to miss. The only unusual elements are the roaring fire, the presence of the socially and politically prominent of the Colony, the easy mingling of the dissolute with the saintly, and "the Indian priests, or powwows, who had often scared their native forest with more hideous incantations than any known to English witchcraft." In detail after detail, the likeness of the meeting to the godly services Brown had known all his life is emphasized. But the meaning and purpose of ritual is reversed, for the object of the meeting is to admit converts to the communion of the damned; the converts are revealed to be Brown and Faith.

What Brown has learned is stated for him in the introduction to the confirmation service by Satan (who now "bore no slight similitude, both in garb and manner, to some grave divine of the New England churches"): all men are evil, all engage compulsively in evil, and all sanctity is merely appearance. At just the moment when the "mark of baptism" by blood is about to be placed on their heads by the "shape of evil," Brown cries out to save himself and Faith. In form the ritual of the forest preserves the sober decorum of the meetinghouse but adds to it the natural wildness which the village restricts to the inner heart of man.

Again Hawthorne engages in a deliberate withdrawal from a verdict on what happened. He tells the reader that Brown did not know whether Faith obeyed his anguished cry to "look up to heaven, and resist the wicked one." This retreat by the omniscient author from unequivocal statement is followed by the strangest equivocation of all: "Had Goodman Brown fallen asleep in the forest and only dreamed a wild dream of a witch-meeting?" Hawthorne then calmly says he will allow the reader to accept the possibility of dream if the reader wishes; but dream or fact, the effect is to change Brown's life forever—to change it so drastically that Brown is never able again to accept as valid the goodness of man. The result of the experience, whether fact or dream, is to take Brown beyond the point of no return. His innocence is lost forever, and with that loss of innocence comes virtually complete alienation from human kind. He has perceived the depths of evil to which all men and women are prone, and for the rest of his life he is never able to emerge from those depths. In the morning light he returns to the serene village, but he is a different man from the mildly skeptical young husband who departed the previous evening. In the intervening night he has added the perspective of the forest to that of the village. He has been exposed to the tragic view of the discrepancy between reality and appearance.

Hawthorne's strategy is important for perceiving the form and thus the meaning inherent in the form of his allegory. For, most important of all, in his concern with a young man's first confrontation with evil incarnate, he must get the dimensions of the story beyond those of *realism* and empirical fact. How to do this? The form of the tale is the answer: by somehow locating the narrative halfway between the relatively prosaic world of a young, newlywed man, beset by doubts about the world he has always known and taken at face value, and the shadowy world of dream and myth, the author can lend to his narrative an equivocal quality that straddles the borderline between factual experience and either dream or daydream. In short, Hawthorne refuses to identify either level as the province of real knowing: whichever carries the greatest impact for a man, therein lies the reality to which he commits the shaping of his life. Perhaps Young Goodman Brown did dream all the horrifying events of the journey within the forest, but he had deliberately set out for the journey against the pleas of Faith and even his own best judgment. It was a journey toward which his skeptical disposition had always been tending; whether it took place in a way that could be measured by distance traveled or only in ways that the heart and soul can traverse becomes finally irrelevant. By the ordering of the experience, equivocal as it may be, Hawthorne has delineated very sharply and clearly the important stages by which a young man with suspicions about the nature of mankind comes to a pessimistic or cynical conclusion. Another man might have arrived at a Rousseauesque commitment to the natural goodness of man; Brown, a child of the Puritans, arrived, not surprisingly, at a conviction of the innate depravity of man. When he died, his family and neighbors "carved no hopeful verse upon his tombstone, for his dying hour was gloom."

The formal stages by which Hawthorne managed the difficult problem of an allegorical exposure to the hard fact of evil in man might be likened to a dramatic situation (the adventures in the forest) which has both prologue (Brown's farewell to the village) and epilogue (his return). Full circle moves the narrative from sunset through nightmare to sunrise, but only in the careful, systematic juxtaposition of village and forest does Hawthorne find the formal mastery of the seemingly dual but actually inseparable worlds of good and evil.

FORM AND STRUCTURE IN THE NOVEL: *ADVENTURES OF HUCKLEBERRY FINN*

With the novel, the responsibilities of the reader beginning a serious study of literature become greater, not necessarily in kind but certainly in scope. He cannot keep constantly in view the full text of a novel as he can a relatively short lyrical poem; nor can he, as with a short story, work back and forth through a few pages of narrative, keeping whole passages clearly in mind. The novel customarily has many characters; the threads of the plot are extensive and perhaps complex. But there are certain touchstones a reader may use to examine the larger fictional work, to analyze its salient features, to find the key to form. Ultimately, if the novel is a good work of art, he should find the various perspectives from which he considered the sprawling narrative context beginning to merge as they illuminate each other. At these points of merger, the critical reader can make judgments about the form of the novel.

As we said earlier in this chapter, point of view, the position from which the story is told, is always to some degree important. Even the most common point of view—that of the omniscient and ever-present author, who tells the story in the third person—has its impact on the force of the narrative: we can look at the characters from the Olympian heights of their creator and judge, at least from what he explicitly says of them, what kind of people they are and what attitude we are to take toward their involvement in the circumstances of the plot. The author may interrupt his narrative to make moral judgments or to editorialize to his reader. In a completely unrestricted omniscient point of view, the author may jump back and forth from one group of widely separated characters to another; he can see into the minds and hearts of all characters equally well. The reader's judgments of character and responses to situations are utterly dependent on what the characters are allowed to say and do or on the editorial pronouncements the author may insert. The novels of James Fenimore Cooper and Jane Austen show the omniscient-author technique. Even more, the typical unsophisticated Western novel, with its formula, "meanwhile, back at the ranch," exhibits the omniscient author at his most obvious lack of pretense about point of view.

But in *Huckleberry Finn,* Twain devised a relatively sophisticated approach: he allows the central character to relate his "adventures" in his own way—a point of view called *first-person narrator.* This point of view requires the reader to view the narrative through the eyes of one of the characters; we are restricted to Huck's attitude toward other characters and to the events in which he and Jim are involved. T. S. Eliot refers to the difference in points of view as indicative of a major distinction between *Tom Sawyer* and *Huckleberry Finn:* Tom's story is told by an adult looking at a boy and his gang, whereas Huck's story is told by Huck himself. Granted that we can see beyond Huck's relatively simple narrative manner some dimensions of meaning not apparent to Huck, the point of view is so contrived (and controlled) that we are not expected to see meanings that are not at least latent or sometimes implicit in Huck's straightforward narration.

Several questions arise. What is the character of Huck like? How does his manner of telling his story control our responses to that story? Finally, how does this point of view assist us to perceive the emerging form of the novel?

To begin with, Huck is an objective narrator. He is objective about himself, even when that objectivity is apt to reflect discreditably upon himself; he is objective about the society he encounters, even when, as he often fears, that society possesses virtues and sanctions to which he must ever remain a stranger. He is an outcast, he knows that he is an outcast, and he does not blame the society that has made him an outcast; he always assumes in his characteristically modest way that he must be to blame for the estrangement. His deceptions, his evasions, and his lapses from conventional respectability are always motivated by the requirements of a given situation; he is probably the first thoroughgoing, honest pragmatist in American fiction. When he lies or steals, he assumes that society is right and that he is simply depraved. He does not make excuses for himself, and his conscience is the stern voice of a pietistic, hypocritical backwoods society asserting itself within a sensitive and wistful psyche. We know that he is neither depraved nor dishonest, because we can judge the society by the clues that emerge from the naive account of a boy about thirteen years old who has been forced to lie in order to get out of trouble, but who never lies about himself or to his reader. In part, his lack of subtlety is a measure of his reliability; he has mastered neither the genteel speech of "respectable" folk nor their deceit and penchant for pious platitudes. He is always refreshingly himself, even when he is telling a tall tale or engaging in one of his ambitious masquerades to get out of a jam.

Thus, the point of view Twain carefully establishes from the first words of the narrative offers a position from which the reader must consider the events of the narrative. That position never really deviates from the point of view of the truthful, clear-eyed gaze of the young hero. He becomes at once the medium of and the norm for the story that unfolds. By him (although he never overtly does it himself) we can measure the hypocrisy of Miss Watson, perceive the cumulative contrast between Huck and the incorrigible Tom Sawyer, and finally judge the society along the river.

Huck's characteristic mode of speech is ironic and self-effacing. Although he can at times be proud of the success of his tall tales and masquerades, in the things that matter he is given to understatement. Of his return to "civilized" life with the Widow Douglas, he comments simply, "Well, then, the old thing commenced again." Of the senseless horror with which the Grangerford-Shepherdson feud ends, Huck says with admirable restraint: "I ain't a-going to tell *all* that happened—it would make me sick again if I was to do that. I wished I hadn't ever come ashore that night to see such things. I ain't ever going to get shut of them—lots of times I dream about them." And in one of the most artfully conceived, understated but eloquent, endings in all fiction, Huck bids his reader and civilization good-bye simultaneously: "But I reckon I got to light out for the Territory ahead of the rest, because Aunt Sally she's going to adopt me and civilize me, and I can't stand it. I been there before."

The movement of the novel has its effect too on the total shape of the work. The apparently aimless plot with its straight-forward sequence—what happened, what happened next, and then what happened after that—is admirably suited to the personality of Huck as narrator. In the conventional romantic novel, of course, we expect to find a more or less complex central situation; in such a novel, two lovers come together by various stratagems of the novelist, they have their difficulties (they disagree about more or less crucial matters or they must contend with the obstacles of parents, a social milieu, the deprivations of war or cattle-rustlers or dozens of other possible impediments), their problems are resolved, and usually they are destined to live happily ever after. Even in such a classic novel as Jane Austen's *Pride and Prejudice,* the separate chapters and the pieces of the plot concern the manifestations, against the background of early-nineteenth-century English provincial life, of the many facets of Mr. Darcy's insuperable pride and Elizabeth Bennet's equally insuperable prejudice, but everything works toward the inevitable union of two very attractive young people.

In the case of *Huckleberry Finn,* however, there is no real center to the plot as such. Instead, we have a number of situa-tions or episodes loosely strung together by the presence of Huck and Jim as they make their way down the Mississippi from St. Petersburg, while the river itself flows through all, becoming really a vast highway across backwoods America. In the separate episodes, there are new characters who, after Huck's departure, usually do not reappear. There are new settings and always new situations. At the beginning, there are five chapters about the "adventures" of Huck and Tom and the gang in St. Petersburg; at the end, there are twelve chapters centering around the Phelps farm that chronicle the adventures of the boys in "freeing"

Jim; in between are twenty-six chapters in which Huck and Jim pursue freedom and in which Tom Sawyer does not appear. This large midsection of the book includes such revealing experiences as Jim and Huck's encounter with the "house of death" (chapter 9); the masquerade for the perceptive Mrs. Judith Loftus (chapter 11); the terror of being aboard the *Walter Scott* (chapters 12 and 13); Huck's life with the Grangerfords (chapters 17 and 18); the performance of the Duke and Dauphin at Parkville (chapter 20); the Arkansas premiere of Shakespeare and the shooting of Boggs by Colonel Sherburn (chapters 21 and 22); and, finally, the relatively lengthy involvement with the Wilks family (chapters 24–29).

Although the settings and the principal characters change, the episodes have a cumulative role: Huck learns bit by bit about the depravity hiding beneath respectability and even piety. He learns gradually and unwillingly that society or "civilization" is vicious and that the individual has small chance to remain himself against the onslaughts of the mass. Harmless as the sentimental tastes of the Grangerfords or their preference for the conventionally pretty may seem, we see through the pragmatic register of Huck that conventional piety masks depravity no more effectively than the high coloring of the chalk fruit compensates for the chips and the exposed chalk. Mrs. Judith Loftus, perhaps the best developed minor character in the entire novel, for all her sentimental response to the hackneyed story of a mistreated apprentice, sees the plight of the runaway slave merely in terms of the cash reward she and her husband may secure. Even the Wilks girls, as charming as they seem to the eyes of Huck, are easily taken in by the grossest sentimentality and pious clichés.

The framework of the plot is, then, a journey—a journey from north to south, and a journey from relative innocence to frightful knowledge. Huck tends to see people for what they are, but he does not suspect the depth and pervasiveness of evil and sheer meanness, of the inhumanity of man to man, until he has completed his journey. The relative harmlessness of Miss Watson's lack of compassion and her devotion to the letter rather than the spirit of the religious law or of Tom's incurable romanticism does not achieve its full perspective until Huck enters the basically good world of the Phelps farm, a world that is really the same as the good world of St. Petersburg and that is connected by the kinship of Aunt Sally and Aunt Polly. It is a world in which all the values of Tom Sawyer are again injected, but at the end Huck finds he has endured too much on his travels down the river to become Tom's foil again. Much has been written about the end of the novel; some critics, like Ernest Hemingway, have complained that the section about the Phelps farm is "cheating," that the novel should have ended with Huck and Jim floating down the river to an inevitable and tragic end. But precisely because in a sense Huck has come full circle, back into the world of St. Petersburg, the awful realization comes that "you must go home again." Huck sets off on another flight from an oppressive "civilization" into the temporary freedom of the Territory, but the Territory is no more immune from the encroachments of society than was the river; like the river, the Territory offers only a temporary respite. In the end, society will impose its inhuman values again, and Huck's life will be a series of retreats and temporary evasions—as was Leatherstocking's in Cooper's romances of the American frontier.

The characters, except for Jim and Huck, are stereotypes. The women, except perhaps for Mrs. Judith Loftus, are flat— either humor characters like the elderly women or incorrigibly pure, virginal females like Mary Jane Wilks or Sophia Grangerford. The men represent the frontier types Twain knew—the braggart, the superman like Colonel Sherburn, the vagrant actors like the Duke and the Dauphin, the lawyers, itinerant preachers, and backwoodsmen generally. But they suit his purpose well, for they permit the complex figures of Huck and Jim to show forth more admirably. This contrast enables Twain to imply over and over that human complexity comes through a genuine individualism and that the stereotype is the product of a rampant antiindividualism that characterizes the American society depicted in the novel.

One can imagine something like a descending scale of viciousness operating in the *dramatis personae* of the novel. The relatively harmless, "good" people like the Widow Douglas, the Wilks girls, and Aunt Sally and Uncle Silas rank near the top. Somewhere along the middle are the Grangerfords, whose basic kindness and devotion to what they suppose is an aristocratic tradition must be set against their overweening sentimentality, their canting theological commitments, and their single-minded devotion to a senseless and brutal blood feud whose causes have long dropped out of memory. Alongside the Grangerfords is Mrs. Judith Loftus, with her paradoxical combination of generosity to the homeless and mistreated white waif and unmitigated avarice and indifference to the miserable runaway slave. But the bottom of the scale is crowded with animalistic, predatory characters like the Duke and Dauphin, Pap Finn, and the mob that pursues Colonel Sherburn.

Looking thus at the characters, we can see something significant about the arrangement of the episodes. Huck's flight into freedom, although its origin lies in his need to escape both the "civilization" of Miss Watson and possible death at the hands of Pap, starts out really as a kind of lark—even a Tom Sawyer-type of adventure, with the simple objects of "getting away from it all" and at the same time helping Jim to escape into a free state. But the "adventures" become increasingly adventures in revelation for Huck; as he and Jim proceed down the river, the involvements with society take on a darker and darker cast. By the time he and Jim arrive at Pikesville and have been victimized by the Duke and Dauphin, they have seen every kind of depravity present in frontier society.

In a sense, the narrative moves in a circular pattern. Huck has left St. Petersburg in an attempt to escape from conventional gentility and decency. But he sees the same kind of conventional morality at the Phelps farm. Tom Sawyer returns to play more of his tricks, with Jim as victim this time. Thus, although Huck has gone home again (back to the world of St. Petersburg), he knows now that there is really no home for him. He was merely a social outcast before; now he is a moral outcast because he cannot accept conventional morality, which is after all part of "civilization." Thus at the end of the novel he is preparing to depart again—on another journey that time and history will bring full circle back to the state of "I been there before." Huck had been subjected to the same kind of cruel, senseless captivity at the hands of Pap that Jim must endure under Tom Sawyer at the Phelps farm. But for Huck, the final and tragic realization is that society is always arranging to "capture" the individual in one way or another—that members of society are themselves captives of an oppressive sameness.

For if the other characters in the novel exhibit their fraternity in a bleak sameness, addicted as they are to a gross brutality, a gross sentimentality, or a combination of the two, only Huck and Jim exhibit the capacity to pursue freedom. Another way to say this is to stress the contrast between the static, unchanging minor characters and the fluid, growing characters of Huck and Jim. Jim's social status markedly limits the possibilities for his liberation. Only Huck can pursue an elusive freedom, whose lineaments are hinted at by the great, flowing river, one aspect of the mighty force of nature that opposes the blighting force of the towns and farm communities.

Here is the major symbol in the novel; Twain points out this land-water contrast again and again. The villages and farms are the abode of those who knowingly or unknowingly oppose any sort of nonconformity with established social sanctions. The river, on the other hand, becomes the only place where one does not have to lie to himself or to others. In the lyrical passages in which Huck communicates, even with all his colloquial liabilities, his feelings about the river, its symbolic functions are made clear, as in the image-packed description (chapter 19) that follows the horrors of the Grangerford-Shepherdson carnage. In that memorable passage Huck pays tribute to the freedom and the contemplative attitude that the river offers the estranged fugitive. In contrast to the oppression of places on land, the raft offers release: "We said there warn't no home like a raft, after all. Other places do seem so cramped up and smothery, but a raft don't. You feel mighty free and easy and comfortable on a raft."

Like the river, Huck's narrative flows spontaneously and

ever onward. Around each bend lies a possible new adventure; in the eddies, a lyrical interlude. But always the river carries Huck and Jim out of each adventure toward another uncertain attempt to achieve freedom. That freedom is never really achieved is a major irony, but the book's structure remains linked to the river's flow within the circular frame suggested by the similarity of the Phelps farm to the beginning in St. Petersburg. The separate adventures become infinite variations on the attempt at freedom, but the final thwarting of freedom is achieved by the forces of St. Petersburg, particularly by the hypocritical gentility of the Phelpses with all its links to the values of the Widow Douglas and Miss Watson and by the cruel, inhumane romanticism of Tom Sawyer.

DIALECTIC AS FORM IN
HAMLET

The nature of drama gives it some relationship to every other literary genre. For example, like lyric poetry, its bent is always toward the direct presentation of the thoughts, feelings, yearnings, fears, and intentions of the speaker. But like the short story or the novel, drama has a narrative line. Thus a formalist rubric for analyzing a drama as a literary work (as opposed to the method a critic might follow in writing about an *acted* play) requires us to attend meticulously to the language of the text, to consider the thrust of every character's utterance, to weigh the rhetorical effects of every mode of address on the dramatic conflict and on the thematic structure of the play. In fiction, the writer can make many connections for the reader; as we have noted, the writer can even editorialize on the ideas implicit in the narrative. But with rare exceptions (for example, George Bernard Shaw), the playwright does not intervene directly; he has simply created a dramatic world. As one of Pirandello's characters in *Six Characters in Search of an Author* puts it, the characters of any finished work have "the fortune to find a fecundating matrix, a fantasy which could raise and nourish them: make them live for ever!" Moreover, there is a necessary connection between the kind of characters and the kind of conflict in which they are involved; again Pirandello's character, speaking as he does for all dramatic characters as opposed to actors, says: "The drama is in us, and we are the drama. We are impatient to play it. Our inner passion drives us on to this" (Act I). Such a necessary connection between the action of a play and the motivation of its characters—what they say and do—can be expected from any successful drama.

Of all Shakespeare's plays, *The Tragedy of Hamlet, Prince of Denmark,* has generated the greatest amount of commentary and criticism. No period since Shakespeare's day—and least of all our own—has been able to ignore the play. Fashions in criticism and scholarship come and go, but always this monument of Renaissance tragedy remains, like Keats's Grecian urn, to "tease us out of thought / As doth Eternity." But it has also teased many good critical minds *into* thought. As questions about stagecraft and the dramatic unities have come to seem less important, new questions about the poetic texture and the form of the work have arisen. For we now have ample testimony and example that the tragedy can be examined much as we would examine any long poetic work; and in the process of regarding the play as verbal structure, the patterns of which move together to produce interpretation, we lose nothing of its force as a play.

We can begin the task of "interpretation" by characterizing, as we must for any literary work, the *world* of the play. The setting, we know, is the castle of Elsinore in medieval Denmark. But what is this Denmark? It is, to be sure, largely a Denmark of Shakespeare's imagination—an imaginatively conceived state that has only tenuous relationships to the historical Denmark. But it is a world, peopled by Shakespeare's characters, that takes on meaning and definition from what happens and what is said in the play, and which in turn controls the kind of thing that can be done and said. We do not have to go further than the first scene of Act I to discover that it is a disturbed world and that a sense of mystery and anxiety preoccupies the soldiers of the watch. The

Ghost has appeared already and is expected to appear again. The guards instinctively assume that the apparition of the former king has more than passing import, and in their troubled questions to Horatio about the mysterious preparations for war, the guards show how closely they regard the connection between the unnatural appearance of the dead king and the welfare of the state. What we see emerging from this *world* of the play is that the guards have no ready answers for the uncertainty, the mystery, and their unshakable premonitions; this quandary is suggested by the abundance of their questions and the paucity of answers—a rhetorical phenomenon that recurs throughout the play, even in the soliloquies of Hamlet. That their special situation in Denmark is meant to have cosmic significance emerges incontrovertibly from the exchange between Hamlet and his friends, Rosencrantz and Guildenstern:

> HAMLET. Denmark's a prison.
> ROSENCRANTZ. Then is the world one.
> HAMLET. A goodly one; in which there are many confines, wards, and dungeons, Denmark being one o' th' worst. (II, ii)

These remarks recall the assertion of Marcellus as Hamlet and the Ghost go offstage: "Something is rotten in the state of Denmark" (I, iv, 90). Indeed Hamlet's obsession is both the product and the cure of the rottenness of Denmark, but the rottenness, he acknowledges, pervades the whole of nature: ". . . this goodly frame the earth seems to me a sterile promontory; this most excellent canopy, the air, look you, this brave o'erhanging firmament, this majestical roof fretted with golden fire—why, it appeareth nothing to me but a foul and pestilent congregation of vapors" (II, ii). Much earlier, before his encounter with the Ghost, Hamlet has expressed his extreme pessimism at man's having to endure earthly existence in the unwholesome realm of nature:

> How weary, stale, flat and unprofitable
> Seem to me all the uses of this world!
> Fie on't, ah, fie, 'tis an unweeded garden

> That grows to seed. Things rank and gross in nature
> Possess it merely. (I, ii)

As he speaks these lines, Hamlet apparently has no idea of the truth of his father's death but is much concerned about his mother's hasty marriage to the new king. He is, then, troubled excessively by a seeming paradox of existence: the fair, whether in the realm of nature or of man, becomes or falls irresistibly under the sway of the foul. In his inquiry into the nature and cause of the paradox, Hamlet centers his attention on Denmark as the model of nature and of human frailty. Therefore, we find a structural device in Hamlet's increasing concern with the relationships between Denmark and the cosmos, between man and nature. As question and answer, dialogue and soliloquy, succeed each other, the text of the play becomes a unified verbal design of repeated words and phrases—words and phrases that look forward to complete thematic assertion and backward to earlier associations.

As acts and scenes unfold, the play becomes a vast poem in which questions about "nature," man's "nature," the health of the state, and the destiny of mankind assume a dialectic intensity. Mystery, riddle, enigma, and metaphysical question become the focus of the dialogue. Particularly in his soliloquies does Hamlet ponder the questions that have disturbed and obsessed thoughtful men from Oedipus to Ahab. What begins with the soldiers of the watch in Act I as relatively simple questions is magnified throughout the course of the play. Increasingly complex and sophisticated explorations of the maddening gulf between reality and appearances become evident. Similarly, we see the contrast between what the simple man cheerfully accepts at face value and what the thoughtful man must probe for in seeking a possible cosmic significance that lurks beneath the apparently uncomplicated surface of utterance, act, or thing. In the world of *Hamlet,* we must consider the vast and critical distinction between "seem" and "be"—again, a structural key.

Another index to form appears in the distinction between the kind of statement we get from Hamlet and the kind we get from the other inhabitants of his strange world. Because Hamlet does not characteristically resort to conventional utterance or manners, the other major characters (except Horatio) assume that he is mad or at least temporarily deranged. Precisely because they *do* use the simple, relatively uncomplicated language of ordinary existence, he assumes that they are hiding or twisting the truth. No one who accepts "seeming" can be trusted by a man dedicated to the primacy of quest for "being." Even the Ghost's nature and origin (he may be a diabolical agent) are considered potentially questionable by Hamlet until he can test the validity of the Ghost's revelation by the "play within the play." Even Ophelia must be treated as the possible tool of the King and Polonius. The presence of Rosencrantz and Guildenstern is questioned immediately by Hamlet, and their mission on the journey to England is subjected to his suspicious scrutiny. Only Horatio (the simple man of faith and virtue) can be trusted, and even to him Hamlet cannot reveal the full dimensions of his unilateral conspiracy. Yet though Hamlet seems to speak in riddle and to act with evasion, the full force of his feeling and his increasing single-minded concentration upon his inevitable task are always contained in his utterances and his acts. The important qualification lies in his full knowledge that others do not comprehend his real meanings, nor are they vitally concerned with the apprehension of the truth about mankind, the state, or themselves.

But let us see how these contrasts are given formal expression. When the King demands some explanation for his extraordinary melancholy, Hamlet replies, "I am too much in the sun" (I, ii). The reply thus establishes, although the King does not perceive it, Hamlet's judgment of and opposition to the easy acceptance of "things as they are." And when the Queen tries to reconcile him to the inevitability of death in the natural scheme and asks, "Why seems it so particular with thee?" he enters upon a revealing contrast between the seeming evidences of mourning and real "woe"—almost unequivocally a condemnation of the Queen's apparently easy acceptance of his father's death and a vindication of his own resistance to viewing that death as merely an occasion for ceremonial "mourning duties."

To the joint entreaty of the King and Queen that he remain in Denmark, he replies only to his mother: "I shall in all my best obey you, madam" (I, ii). But in thus disdaining to answer the King, he has really promised nothing to his mother although she takes his reply for complete submission to the wishes of the royal couple. Again, we see that every statement of Hamlet tends to have a double meaning—a kind of countermeaning for the world of Denmark and a subtler meaning for Hamlet and the reader.

As we have mentioned, Hamlet's overriding concern, even before he knows about the Ghost's appearance, is the frustration of living in a world attuned to imperfection. He sees, wherever he looks, the pervasive blight in nature, especially human nature. Man, outwardly the crown of creation, is susceptible to "some vicious mole of nature," and no matter how virtuous he otherwise may be, "the dram of evil" or "the stamp of one defect" adulterates nobility (I, iv). He finds that "one may smile, and smile, and be a villain" (I, v). To the uncomprehending Guildenstern, Hamlet emphasizes his basic concern with the strange puzzle of corrupted and corruptible man: "What a piece of work is a man, how noble in reason, how infinite in faculties, in form and moving how express and admirable, in action how like an angel, in apprehension how like a god: the beauty of the world, the paragon of animals! And yet to me what is this quintessence of dust? Man delights not me—nor woman neither, though by your smiling you seem to say so" (II, ii). This preoccupation with the paradox of man, recurring as it does throughout the play, obviously takes precedence over the revenge ordered by the Ghost. From the beginning of Hamlet's inquiry about his world—whether he is considering his father's death, his mother's remarriage, the real or supposed defection of his friends, or the fallen state of man—we can see a developing pattern of meaning in which man's private world of marriage bed and drive for power becomes part and parcel of larger cosmic questions of identity and destiny.

Reams have been written about Hamlet's reasons for the delay in carrying out his revenge; for our purpose, however, the delay is not particularly important except as it emphasizes

Hamlet's preference for investigating the extent of the pervasive blight. Seemingly he accepts as more important a larger role as investigator and punitive agent of all mankind (for example, his bristling verbal attack upon the Queen, his accidental—but to his mind quite justifiable—murder of Polonius, his indignation about the state of the theater and his instructions to the players, his castigation of Ophelia, his apparent delight not only in foiling Rosencrantz and Guildenstern but also in arranging their destruction, his fight with Laertes over the grave of Ophelia). Hamlet, in living up to what he conceives to be a higher role than that of mere avenger, recurrently broods about his self-imposed mission, although he characteristically avoids naming it. In his warfare against bestiality, however, he asserts his allegiance to heaven-sent reason and its dictates:

> What is a man,
> If his chief good and market of his time
> Be but to sleep and feed? A beast, no more.
> Sure he that made us with such large discourse,
> Looking before and after, gave us not
> That capability and godlike reason
> To fust in us unused. Now, whether it be
> Bestial oblivion, or some craven scruple
> Of thinking too precisely on th'event—
> A thought which, quartered, hath but one part wisdom
> And ever three parts coward—I do not know
> Why yet I live to say, "This thing's to do,"
> Sith I have cause, and will, and strength, and means
> To do't.   (IV, iv)

With some envy he regards the active competence of Fortinbras as opposed to his own "craven scruple / Of thinking too precisely on th'event"—that is, his obligation to act to avenge his father's death. Although he promises himself to give priority to that obligation, he goes off instead to England on what he suspects to be a ruse, presumably because for the moment he prefers out-witting Rosencrantz and Guildenstern and the King. In short, almost from the first time he appears in the play, Hamlet obviously is convinced that to him is given a vast though somewhat general task:

> The time is out of joint. O cursèd spite
> That ever I was born to set it right!   (I, v)

The "time," like the place of Denmark, has been corrupted by men susceptible to natural flaws. And once again Hamlet's statement (this time in the philosophical, lyrical dimensions of *soliloquy*) offers formal establishment of the dialectic of the play —the opposition of two attitudes toward human experience that must achieve resolution or synthesis before the end of the play.

To the concept of setting things right, then, Hamlet gives his allegiance. And the order he supports is far beyond the precepts of expediency offered by Polonius, the apostle of practicality, or by Claudius, the devotee of power and sexuality. We see again and again his expression of devotion to an order so remote from the ken of most people that Hamlet appears at times to be inhuman—inhuman in the sense of his refusal to be touched by the ordinary scale of joy or sorrow. He will set straight the political and social order by ferreting out bestiality, corruption (of state, marriage bed, or theater), trickery, and deceit. He is obsessed throughout the play by the "dusty death" to which all must come, and his speeches abound in images of sickness and of death. But if he has finally gotten the King, along with his confederates, "Hoist with his own petard" (III, iv), Hamlet also brings himself through his own trickery, deceit, perhaps his own ambitions, to the fate of Yorick. Thus does the play turn upon itself. It is not a simple morality play. It begins in an atmosphere of mourning for the late king and apprehension about the appearance of the Ghost, and it ends with a scene littered with corpses. The noble prince, like his father before him, is, despite his intentions, sullied by the "foul crimes done in my days of nature" (I, v). All men apparently are, as Laertes says of himself, "as a woodcock to mine own springe" (V, ii), that is, like a fool caught in his own snare. And although all beauty and aspiration (a counterpoint theme) reduce ultimately to a "quintessence of dust," it is in Hamlet's striving, however imperfectly and destructively, to bend the order of nature to a higher law that we must see the play's tragic assertion in the midst of an otherwise pervasive and unrelieved pessimism.

The design of the work can be perceived in part by the elaborate play upon the words "see" and "know" and their cognates. Whereas the deity can be understood as "Looking before and after" (IV, iv), the player-king points out to his queen that there is a hiatus between what man intends and what he does: "Our thoughts are ours, their ends none of our own" (III, ii). Forced by Hamlet to consider the difference between her two husbands, Gertrude cries out in anguish against having to see into her own motivations:

> O Hamlet, speak no more.
> Thou turn'st mine eyes into my very soul,
> And there I see such black and grainèd spots
> As will not leave their tinct.   (III, iv)

But she does not see the Ghost of her former husband, nor can she see the metaphysical implications of Hamlet's reason in madness. The blind eye-sockets of Yorick's skull once "saw" their quota of experience, but most people in Denmark are content with surface appearances of life and refuse even to consider the ends to which mortality brings all men. The intricate weavings of images of sight thus become a kind of tragic algebra for the plight of a man who "seemed to find his way without his eyes" (II, i) and who found himself at last "placed to the view" of the "yet unknowing world" (V, ii). The traveling players had acted out the crime of Denmark on another stage, but their play seemed to most of the audience only a diversion in a pageant of images designed to keep men from really knowing themselves or their fellows as corrupted by nature and doomed at last to become "my Lady Worm's, chapless and knocked about the mazzard with a sexton's spade" (V, i). The contexts of these words provide a systematic enlargement of the play's tragic assertion about man's ignorance in the midst of appearances. Formally, the play progresses from the relatively simple speculations of the soldiers of the watch to the sophisticated complexity of meta-physical inquiry. There may not be final answers to the questions Hamlet probes, but the questions assume a formal order as their dimensions are structured by speech and action—in miniature, by the "play within the play," in extended form, by the tragedy itself.

Ophelia, in her madness, utters perhaps the key line of the play: "Lord, we know what we are, but we know not what we may be" (IV, v). Hamlet has said that if the King reacted as he expected to the play within the play, "I know my course" (II, ii). But he is never sure of his course, nor does he even know himself. In the prison of the world he can only pursue his destiny, which, as he realizes before the duel, inevitably leads to the grave. The contest between aspiring man and a natural order in which he is involved is all too unequal: idealism turns out to be a poor match for the prison walls of either Denmark or the grave.

CHAPTER

3

The psychological approach

Having discussed two of the basic approaches to literary understanding, the traditional and the formalistic, we will now examine a third interpretive perspective, the "psychological." Of all the critical approaches to literature, this is perhaps the most controversial, the most abused, and—for most readers—the least appreciated. Yet, for all the difficulties involved in its proper application to interpretive analysis, the psychological approach can be fascinating and rewarding. Our purpose in this chapter is threefold: (1) to account briefly for the misunderstanding of psychological criticism, (2) to outline the psychological theory most commonly used as an interpretive tool by modern critics, and (3) to show by examples how the reader may apply this mode of interpretation to enhance his understanding and appreciation of literature.

The idea of *enhancement* must be underscored as a preface to our discussion. It is axiomatic that no single approach can exhaust the manifold interpretive possibilities of a worthwhile literary work; each approach has its own peculiar limitations. As we have already discovered, the limitations of the traditional approach lie in its tendency to overlook the structural intricacies of the work. The formalistic approach, on the other hand, often neglects historical and biographical contexts that may provide important insights into the meaning of the work. In turn, the crucial limitation of the psychological approach is its aesthetic inadequacy: although psychological interpretation can afford many profound clues toward solving a work's thematic and symbolic mysteries, it can seldom account for the beautiful symmetry of a well-wrought poem or of a fictional masterpiece; though the psychological approach is an excellent tool for "reading between the lines," the interpretive craftsman must use other tools, such as the traditional and the formalistic, for a proper rendering of the lines themselves.

ABUSES AND MISUNDERSTANDINGS OF THE PSYCHOLOGICAL APPROACH

In the general sense of the word there is nothing new about the psychological approach. As early as the fourth century B.C., Aristotle used this approach in setting forth his classic definition of tragedy as combining the emotions of pity and terror to produce catharsis. The "compleat gentleman" of the English Renaissance, Sir Philip Sidney, with his statements about the moral effects of poetry—as well as such Romantic poets as Wordsworth and Coleridge, with their theories of the Imagination—was "psychologizing" literature. In this sense, then, virtually every literary critic has been concerned at some time with the psychology of writing or responding to literature.

During the twentieth century, however, psychological criticism has come to be associated with a particular school of thought: the psychoanalytic theories of Sigmund Freud and his followers. From this association have derived most of the abuses and misunderstandings of the modern psychological approach to literature. On the one hand, abuses of the approach have resulted from an excess of enthusiasm, which has been manifested in several ways. First, the practitioners of the Freudian approach often push their critical theses too hard, forcing literature into a Procrustean bed of psychoanalytic theory at the expense of other relevant considerations (for example, the work's total thematic and aesthetic context). Second, the literary criticism of the psychoanalytic extremists has at times degenerated into a special occultism with its own mystique and jargon exclusively for the "in-group." Third, many critics of the "psychological school" have been either literary scholars who have understood the principles of psychology imperfectly or professional psychologists who have had little feeling for literature as art: the former have abused Freudian insights through oversimplification and distortion; the latter have abused our literary sensibilities.

These abuses have given rise, on the other hand, to a widespread mistrust of the psychological approach as a tool for critical analysis. Conservative scholars and teachers of literature, often shocked by such terms as "anal eroticism," "phallic symbol," and "Oedipal complex" and confused by the clinical diagnoses of literary problems (for example, the interpretation of Hamlet's character as a "severe case of hysteria on a cyclothymic basis"), have rejected all psychological criticism, other than the common-sense type, as egregious nonsense. In some quarters this reaction goes so far as to brand the Freudian approach as not only "invalid" but even "indecent." By explaining a few of the principles of Freudian psychology that have been applied to literary interpretation and by providing some cautionary remarks, we hope to introduce the reader to a balanced critical perspective that avoids either of these extremist positions.

FREUD'S THEORIES

The core of Freud's contribution to modern psychology is his emphasis upon the unconscious aspects of the human psyche. Freud provided convincing evidence, through his many carefully recorded case studies, that most of our actions are motivated by psychic forces over which we have very limited control. He demonstrated that, like the iceberg, the human mind is structured so that its great weight and density lies beneath the surface (or the level of consciousness). In "The Anatomy of the Mental Personality, Lecture XXI," in *New Introductory Lectures on Psychoanalysis* (Norton, 1964), Freud discriminates between the levels of conscious and unconscious mental activity; he explains:

> The oldest and best meaning of the word "unconscious" is the descriptive one; we call "unconscious" any mental process the existence of which we are obligated to assume— because, for instance, we infer it in some way from its effects —but of which we are not directly aware. . . . If we want to be more accurate, we should modify the statement by saying that we call a process "unconscious" when we have to assume that it was active *at a certain time,* although *at that time* we knew nothing about it. (pp. 99–100)

Freud further emphasizes the importance of the unconscious by pointing out that even the "most conscious processes are conscious for only a short period; quite soon they become *latent,* though they can easily become conscious again" (p. 100). In view of this, Freud defines two kinds of unconscious:

> . . . one which is transformed into conscious material easily and under conditions which frequently arise, and another in the case of which such a transformation is difficult, can only come about with a considerable expenditure of energy, or may never occur at all. . . . We call the unconscious which is only latent, and so can easily become conscious,

the "preconscious," and keep the name "unconscious" for
the other.   (p. 101)

That most of the individual's mental processes are unconscious is thus Freud's first major premise. The second (which
has been rejected by a great many professional psychologists,
including some of Freud's own disciples, for example, Carl Jung
and Alfred Adler) is that all human behavior is motivated
ultimately by sexuality. Freud designates the prime psychic force
as *libido,* or sexual energy.

Starting from these two premises, we may examine several
corollaries of Freudian theory. Principal among these is Freud's
assignment of the mental processes to three psychic zones: the *Id,*
the *Ego,* and the *Super-Ego.* An explanation of these zones may
be illustrated with Freud's own diagram:

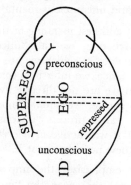

First, the diagram reveals immediately the vast portion of the
mental apparatus that is not conscious. Second, the drawing
helps to clarify the relationship between Ego, Id, and Super-Ego,
as well as their collective relationship to the conscious and the
unconscious. It should be noted that the Id is entirely unconscious and that only parts of the Ego and Super-Ego are conscious. With this diagram as a guide, we may define the nature
and functions of the three psychic zones.

The Id is the reservoir of libido, the primary source of all
psychic energy. It functions to fulfill the primordial life-principle,

which Freud considers to be the *pleasure principle*. Without consciousness or semblance of rational order, the Id is characterized by a tremendous and amorphous vitality. Speaking metaphorically, Freud explains this "obscure inaccessible part of our personality" as "a chaos, a cauldron of seething excitement [with] no organization and no unified will, only an impulsion to obtain satisfaction for the instinctual needs, in accordance with the pleasure principle" (pp. 103–104). He further stresses that the "laws of logic—above all, the law of contradiction—do not hold for processes of the id. Contradictory impulses exist side by side without neutralizing each other or drawing apart. . . . Naturally, the id knows no values, no good and evil, no morality" (pp. 104–105).

The Id is, in short, the source of all our aggressions and desires. It is lawless, asocial, and amoral. Its function is to gratify our instincts for pleasure without regard for social conventions, legal ethics, or moral restraint. Unchecked, it would lead us to any lengths—to destruction and even self-destruction—to satisfy its impulses for pleasure. Safety for the self and for others is not a concern of the Id; its concern is purely for instinctual gratification, heedless of consequence. For centuries before Freud, this force was recognized in human nature but often attributed to supernatural and external rather than natural and internal forces; the Id as defined by Freud is identical in many respects to the Devil as defined by theologians. Thus, the old saying that a rambunctious child (whose Id has not yet been brought under proper control by Ego and Super-Ego) is "full of the devil" has a certain psychological validity. We may also see in young children (and neurotic adults) the uncontrolled impulses toward pleasure that often lead to excessive self-indulgence and even to injury.

In view of the Id's dangerous potentialities, it is necessary that other psychic agencies function to protect the individual and society. The first of these regulating agencies, that which protects the individual, is the Ego. This is the rational governing agent of the psyche. Though the Ego lacks the strong vitality of the Id, it is needed to regulate the instinctual drives of the Id so that these energies may be released in nondestructive behavioral patterns. And though a portion of the Ego is unconscious, it is nevertheless what we ordinarily think of as the conscious mind. As Freud points out, "In popular language, we may say that the ego stands for reason and circumspection, while the id stands for the untamed passions." Whereas the Id is governed solely by the pleasure principle, the Ego is governed by the *reality principle*. In brief, the Ego serves as intermediary between the world within and the world without.

The other regulating agent, that which functions to protect society, is the Super-Ego. Largely unconscious, the Super-Ego is the moral censoring agency, the repository of conscience and pride. It is, as Freud says in "The Anatomy of the Mental Personality," "the representative of all moral restrictions, the advocate of the impulse toward perfection, in short it is as much as we have been able to apprehend psychologically of what people call the 'higher' things in human life" (p. 95). Acting either directly or through the Ego, the Super-Ego serves to *repress* or inhibit the drives of the Id, to block off and thrust back into the unconscious those impulses toward pleasure that society regards as unacceptable, such impulses as overt aggression, homosexuality, and the Oedipal instinct. Freud attributes the development of the Super-Ego to the parental influence that manifests itself in terms of punishment for what society considers to be "bad" behavior and reward for "good" behavior. An overactive Super-Ego creates an unconscious sense of guilt—hence, the familiar term "guilt complex" and the popular misconception that Freud advocated the relaxing of all moral inhibitions and social restraints. Where the Id is dominated by the pleasure principle and the Ego by the reality principle, the Super-Ego is dominated by the *morality principle*. In figurative terms, we might say that the Id would make us animals, the Super-Ego would have us behave as angels (or, worse, as creatures of social conformity), and that it remains for the Ego to keep us healthy human beings by maintaining a balance between these two opposing forces. It was this balance Freud advocated, rather than a complete removal of inhibiting factors.

One of the most instructive applications of this Freudian tripartition to literary criticism, which should be mentioned in passing, is the well-known essay "In Nomine Diaboli" by Dr. Henry A. Murray (*New England Quarterly*, XXIV, 435–452), a knowledgeable psychologist and a sensitive literary critic as well. In analyzing Herman Melville's masterpiece *Moby-Dick* with the tools provided by Freud, Murray explains the White Whale as a symbolic embodiment of the strict conscience of New England Puritanism—that is, as a projection of Melville's own Super-Ego. Captain Ahab, the monomaniac who leads the crew of the *Pequod* to destruction through his insane compulsion to pursue and strike back at the creature who has injured him, is interpreted as the symbol of a rapacious and uncontrollable Id. Starbuck, the sane Christian and first mate who struggles to mediate between the forces embodied in Moby-Dick and Ahab, symbolizes a balanced and sensible rationalism—that is, the Ego.

Though many scholars are reluctant to accept Freud's tripartition of the human psyche, they have not reacted against this aspect of psychoanalytic criticism so violently as against the application of his sexual theories to the interpretation of literature. Let us briefly examine the highlights of such theories. Perhaps the most controversial (and, to many persons, the most offensive) facet of psychoanalytic criticism is its tendency to interpret imagery in terms of sexuality. Following Freud's example in his interpretation of dreams, the psychoanalytic critic tends to see all concave images (ponds, flowers, cups or vases, caves, and hollows) as female or womb symbols, and all images whose length exceeds their diameter (towers, mountain peaks, snakes, knives, lances, and swords) as male or phallic symbols. Perhaps even more objectionable to some is the interpretation of such activities as dancing, riding, and flying as symbols of sexual pleasure. For example, in her Freudian study of Edgar Allan Poe's life and works, Princess Marie Bonaparte interprets the figure of Psyche in "Ulalume" as an ambivalent mother-figure, both the longed-for mother and the mother as Super-Ego who shields her son from his incestuous instincts, concluding with the following startling observation: "Psyche's drooping, trailing wings in this poem symbolise in concrete form Poe's physical impotence. We know that flying, to all races, unconsciously symbolises the sex act, and that antiquity often represented the penis erect and winged." For the skeptical reader Princess Bonaparte provides this explanation:

> Infinite are the symbols man has the capacity to create, as indeed, the dreams and religions of the savage and civilized well show. Every natural object may be utilised to this end yet, despite their multiple shapes, the objects and relations to which they attach are relatively few: these include the beings we loved first, such as mother, father, brothers or sisters and their bodies, but mainly our own bodies and genitals, and theirs. Almost all symbolism is sexual, in its widest sense, taking the word as the deeply-buried primal urge behind all expressions of love, from the cradle to the grave.   (p. 294)

Although such observations as these may have a sound psychoanalytic basis, their relevance to sound critical analysis has been questioned by many scholars. We may sympathize with this incredulousness when we encounter the Freudian essay that interprets even a seemingly innocent fairy tale like "Little Red Riding Hood" as an allegory of the age-old conflict between male and female in which the plucky young virgin (her red cap is a menstrual symbol) outwits the ruthless, sex-hungry "wolf."

Somewhat less controversial than Freudian dream symbolism are Freud's theories concerning child psychology. Contrary to traditional beliefs, Freud found infancy and childhood a period of intense sexual experience, sexual in a sense much broader than is commonly attached to the term. During the first five years of his life, the child passes through a series of phases in his erotic development, each phase being characterized by emphasis upon a particular *erogenous* zone, that is, a portion of the body in which sexual pleasure becomes localized. Freud indicated three such zones: the *oral,* the *anal,* and the *genital.* These zones are associated not only with pleasure in stimulation but also with the gratification of our vital needs: eating, elimination, and reproduction. If for some reason the individual is frustrated in gratifying these needs during childhood, his adult personality may be warped accordingly, that is, his development may be arrested or *fixated*. For example, adults who are compulsively fastidious may suffer, according to the psychoanalyst, from an anal-fixation traceable to overly strict toilet training during early childhood. Likewise, compulsive cigarette-smoking may be interpreted as a symptom of oral-fixation traceable to premature weaning. Even among "normal" adults, sublimated responses occur when the individual is vicariously stimulated by images associated with one of the major erogenous zones. In his *Fiction and the Unconscious,* for example, Simon O. Lesser suggests that the anal-erotic quality in *Robinson Crusoe* (manifested in the hero's scrupulous record-keeping and orderliness) accounts at least partially for the unconscious appeal of Defoe's masterpiece.

According to Freud, the child reaches the stage of "genital primacy" around the age of five years, at which time the Oedipus complex manifests itself. In simple terms, the Oedipus complex derives from the little boy's unconscious rivalry with his father for the love of his mother. Freud borrowed the term from the classic Sophoclean tragedy in which the hero unwittingly murders his father and marries his mother. In *The Ego and the Id* (W. W. Norton, 1962), Freud describes the complex as follows:

> . . . the boy deals with his father by identifying himself with him. For a time these two relationships [the child's devotion to his mother and identification with his father] proceed side by side, until the boy's sexual wishes in regard to his mother become more intense and his father is perceived as an obstacle to them; from this the Oedipus complex originates. His identification with his father then takes on a hostile colouring and changes into a wish to get rid of his father in order to take his place with his mother. Henceforward his relation to his father is ambivalent; it seems as if the ambivalence inherent in the identification from the beginning had become manifest. An ambivalent attitude to his father and an object-relation of a solely affectionate kind to his mother make up the content of the simple positive Oedipus complex in a boy.   (pp. 21–22)

Further ramifications of the Oedipus complex are a fear of castration and an identification of the father with strict authority in all forms; subsequent hostility to authority is therefore associated with the Oedipal ambivalence to which Freud refers. A story like Nathaniel Hawthorne's "My Kinsman, Major Molineux" has been interpreted by Professor Lesser as essentially a symbolic rebellion against the father-figure. And with this insight we may find meaning in the young hero's curious laughter as he watches the cruel tarring and feathering of his once-respected relative: the youth is expressing his unconscious joy in being released from parental authority—now he is free, as the friendly stranger suggests, to make his own way in the adult world without the help (and restraint) of his kinsman.

Probably the best known tour de force of Freudian criticism is the pioneering interpretation of *Hamlet* by Dr. Ernest Jones; we will now consider this famous essay.

APPLICATIONS OF THE PSYCHOLOGICAL APPROACH

Hamlet

Although Freud himself made some applications of his theories to art and literature, it remained for an English disciple, Dr. Ernest Jones, to provide us with the first full-scale psychoanalytic treatment of a major literary work. Dr. Jones's *Hamlet and Oedipus,* originally published as an essay in *The American Journal of Psychology* in 1910 and later revised and enlarged, is now conveniently available in a paperback edition (Doubleday Anchor Books, 1949); it remains a model of professional competence and scholarly thoroughness for the Freudian critic.

Dr. Jones bases his argument on the thesis that Hamlet's much-debated delay in killing his uncle, Claudius, is to be explained in terms of internal rather than external circumstances and that "the play is mainly concerned with a hero's unavailing fight against what can only be called a disordered mind." In his carefully documented essay Dr. Jones builds a highly persuasive case history of Hamlet as a psychoneurotic suffering from manic-depressive hysteria combined with an *abulia* (an inability to exercise will power and come to decisions)—all of which may be traced to the hero's severely repressed Oedipal feelings. Jones points out that no really satisfying argument has ever been substantiated for the idea that Hamlet avenges his father's murder as quickly as practicable. Shakespeare makes Claudius' guilt as well as Hamlet's duty perfectly clear from the outset—if we are to trust the words of the Ghost and the gloomy insights of the hero himself. The fact is, however, that Hamlet does not fulfill this duty until absolutely forced to do so by physical circumstances—and, even then, only after Gertrude, his mother, is dead. Jones also elucidates the strong misogyny that Hamlet displays throughout the play, especially as it is directed against Ophelia, and his almost physical revulsion from sex. All of this adds up to a classic example of the neurotically repressed Oedipus complex.

The ambivalence that typifies the child's attitude toward his father is dramatized in the characters of the Ghost (the good, lovable father with whom the boy identifies) and Claudius (the hated father as tyrant and rival), both of whom are dramatic projections of the hero's own conscious-unconscious ambivalence toward the father-figure. The Ghost represents the conscious ideal of fatherhood, the image that is socially acceptable:

> See, what a grace was seated on this brow:
> Hyperion's curls, the front of Jove himself,
> An eye like Mars, to threaten and command,
> A station like the herald Mercury
> New-lighted on a heaven-kissing hill,
> A combination and a form indeed,
> Where every god did seem to set his seal,
> To give the world assurance of a man:
> This was your husband.   (III, iv)

His view of Claudius, on the other hand, represents Hamlet's repressed hostility toward his father as a rival for his mother's affection. This new King-Father is the symbolic perpetrator of the very deeds toward which the son is impelled by his own unconscious motives: murder of his father and incest with his mother. Hamlet cannot bring himself to kill Claudius because, to do so, he must, in a psychological sense, kill himself. His delay and self-frustration in trying to fulfill the Ghost's demand for vengeance may therefore be explained by the fact that, as Dr. Jones puts it, "the thought of incest and parricide combined is too intolerable to be borne. One part of him tries to carry out the task, the other flinches inexorably from the thought of it" (pp. 78–79).

A corollary to the Oedipal problem in *Hamlet* is the pronounced misogyny and latent homosexuality in Hamlet's character. Because of his mother's abnormally sensual affection for her son, an affection that would have deeply marked Hamlet as a child with an Oedipal neurosis, he has in the course of his psychic development repressed his incestuous impulses so severely that this repression colors his attitude toward all women: "The total reaction culminates in the bitter misogyny of his outburst against Ophelia, who is devastated at having to bear a reaction so wholly out of proportion to her own offense and has no idea that in reviling her Hamlet is really expressing his bitter resentment against his mother" (p. 96). The famous "Get thee to a nunnery" speech has even more sinister overtones than are generally recognized, explains Jones, when we understand the pathological degree of Hamlet's condition and read "nunnery" as Elizabethan slang for "brothel."

> The underlying theme relates ultimately to the splitting of the mother image which the infantile unconscious effects into two opposite pictures: one of a virginal Madonna, an inaccessible saint towards whom all sensual approaches are unthinkable, and the other of a sensual creature accessible to everyone. . . . When sexual repression is highly pronounced, as with Hamlet, then both types of women are felt to be hostile: the pure one out of resentment at her repulses, the sensual one out of the temptation she offers to plunge into guiltiness. Misogyny, as in the play, is the inevitable result. (pp. 97–98)

Huckleberry Finn

Mark Twain's great novel has this in common with Shakespeare's masterpiece: both are concerned with the theme of rebellion—with a hostile treatment of the father-figure (it is interesting to note that in both works the father is finally slain and that knowledge of this death brings a curious sense of relief —and release—for the reader). As we have seen, from the psychoanalytic viewpoint all rebellion is in essence a rejection of parental, specifically paternal, authority. Sociologically speaking, Huck rebels against the unjust, inhumane restrictions of a society that condones slavery, hypocrisy, and cruelty; but Mark Twain showed a remarkable pre-Freudian insight when he dramatized this theme of rebellion in the portrayal of Huck's detestable father as the lowest common denominator of social authority. The main plot of the novel is launched with Huck's escape from pap (whose name, in keeping with the reductive treatment of the father-figure, is not capitalized), a flight that coincides with Jim's escape from Miss Watson.

Symbolically, Huck and Jim, in order to gain freedom and to regain prelapsarian bliss (the happiness enjoyed by Adam before the Fall), must escape whatever is represented by Miss Watson and pap (who reminds Huck of Adam all covered with mud, that is, Adam after the Fall). Despite their superficial and rather melodramatic differences, Miss Watson and pap have much in common. They represent extremes of authority: authority at its most respectable and at its most contemptible. What is more, they both represent social and legal morality, again in the extremes of the social spectrum. Notwithstanding his obvious worthlessness, pap is still Huck's sole guardian by law and holds the power of life and death, an authority condoned by society, over his son—just as Miss Watson has a similar power over Jim. In the light of such authority, Miss Watson and pap may be said to represent the Super-Ego (for example, when Huck goes against his conscience by refusing to turn Jim in to the authorities, it is the letter to Miss Watson that he tears up). In this sense, then, it is to escape the oppressive tyranny and cruel restraints of the Super-Ego that Huck and Jim take flight on the river.

Huckleberry Finn cannot by any means be read as a psychological allegory, and it would be foolish to set up a strict one-to-one ratio of characters and events to ideas, particularly since Mark Twain wrote the book with no notion of Freudian concepts. But like most great writers, Twain knew human nature; and, from the psychoanalytic perspective, a "linked analogy" can be seen between the structure of his novel and the Freudian structure of the human psyche. Water in any form is generally interpreted by the psychoanalysts as a female symbol, more specifically as a maternal symbol. From the super-egoistic milieu of society Huck and Jim flee to the river, where they find freedom. Except when invaded by men, the river is characterized by a strange, fluid, dreamlike peacefulness; Huck's most lyrical comments are those describing the beauty of the river:

> Two or three days and nights went by; I reckon I
> might say they swum by, they slid along so quiet and smooth
> and lovely. . . . Not a sound anywheres—perfectly still—
> just like the whole world was asleep. . . . [Then] the nice
> breeze springs up, and comes fanning you from over there,
> so cool and fresh and sweet to smell on account of the woods
> and flowers; but sometimes not that way, because they've
> left dead fish laying around, gars and such, and they do get
> pretty rank. . . . [And] we would watch the lonesomeness
> of the river, and kind of lazy along, and by and by lazy off
> to sleep. . . . It's lovely to live on a raft. We had the sky
> up there, all speckled with stars, and we used to lay on our
> backs and look up at them, and discuss about whether they
> was made or only just happened. . . . Jim said the moon
> could 'a' *laid* them; well, that looked kind of reasonable, so
> I didn't say nothing against it, because I've seen a frog lay
> most as many, so of course it could be done.   (chapter 19)

The foregoing passage is redolent with female-maternal imagery; it also suggests the dark, mysterious serenity associated with the prenatal state, as well as with death, in psychoanalytic interpretation. The tension between land and water may be seen as analogous to that between the conscious and the unconscious in Freudian theory. Lacking a real mother, Huck finds his symbolic mother in the river; in Freudian terms, he returns to the womb. From this matrix he undergoes a series of symbolic deaths and rebirths, punctuated structurally by the episodes on land. As James M. Cox (*Sewanee Review,* LXII, 389–405) has pointed out, Huck's fake murder in escaping from pap is crucial to our understanding the central informing pattern of death-and-rebirth: "Having killed himself, Huck is 'dead' throughout the entire journey down the river. He is indeed the man without identity who is reborn at almost every river bend, not because he desires a new role, but because he must re-create himself to elude the forces which close in on him from every side. The rebirth theme which began with Pap's reform becomes the driving idea behind the entire action." Enhancing this pattern is the hermaphroditic figure of Jim, Huck's adopted friend and parent, whose blackness coincides with the darkness associated with death, the unconscious, and the maternal (we are reminded of Whitman's celebration of death as the Dark Mother); Jim's qualities are more maternal than paternal—he possesses the gentleness, unquestioning loyalty, and loving kindness that we traditionally ascribe to the mother—in sharp contrast to the brutal authoritarianism of pap.

Viewed from a slightly different psychological angle, *Huckleberry Finn* is a story of the child as victim, embodying the betrayal-of-innocence theme that has become one of the chief motifs in American fiction. Philip Young, in his brilliant study, *Ernest Hemingway,* has detected similarities between Huck's plight and that of the Hemingway hero. Young sees Huck as the wounded child, permanently scarred by traumas of death and violence; he has counted thirteen separate corpses in the novel and observes that virtually every major episode in the book ends with violence or death. Young makes explicit the causal relationship between the traumatic experiences suffered by Huck (and later by Hemingway's protagonists) and the growing preoccupation with death that dominates much modern literature.

> [Huck] is a wounded and damaged boy. He will never get over the terror he has seen and been through, is guilt-ridden and can't sleep at night for his thoughts. When he is able to sleep he is tortured with bad dreams. . . . This is a boy who has undergone an unhappy process of growing up, and has grown clean out of his creator's grasp. . . . Precisely as Clemens could never solve his own complications, save in the unmitigated but sophomoric pessimism of his last books, so he could not solve them for Huck, who had got too hot to handle and was dropped. What the man never realized was that in his journey by water he had been hinting at a solution all along: an excessive exposure to violence and death produced first a compulsive fascination with dying, and finally an ideal symbol for it. (pp. 200–201)

This "ideal symbol" is the dark river itself, which is suggestive of the Freudian death-instinct, the unconscious instinct in all living things to return to the inorganic state and thereby achieve permanent surcease from the pain of living. Our recognition of these symbolic implications does not, by any means, exhaust the interpretive potential of Twain's novel; nor does it preclude insights gained from other critical approaches. Such recognition should *enhance* our appreciation of the greatness of *Huckleberry Finn* by revealing that Mark Twain produced a masterwork that, intentionally or not, has appealed in a profound psychological way to many generations of readers.

"YOUNG GOODMAN BROWN"

The theme of innocence betrayed is also central to Nathaniel Hawthorne's "Young Goodman Brown," the tale of the young bridegroom who leaves his wife Faith to spend a night with Satan in the forest. The events of that terrifying night are a classic "traumatic experience" for the youth. At the center of the dark wilderness he discovers a witches' Sabbath involving all the honored teachers, preachers, and friends of his village. The climax is reached when his own immaculate bride is brought forth to stand by his side and pledge eternal allegiance to the

Fiend of Hell. Following this climactic moment in which the hero resists the diabolical urge to join the fraternity of evil, he wakes to find himself in the deserted forest wondering if what has happened was dream or reality. Regardless of the answer, he is a changed man. He returns in the morning to the village and to his Faith, but he is never at peace with himself again. Henceforth he can never hear the singing of a holy hymn without also hearing echoes of the anthem of sin from that terrible night in the forest. He shrinks even from the side of Faith. His dying hour is gloom and no hopeful epitaph is engraved upon his tombstone.

Like most of Hawthorne's tales, "Young Goodman Brown" is built around a moral lesson. On one level the story is almost straight allegory, pertaining to the precarious state of man's Faith, signified by the bride's name. The hero's name, too, is allegorical: he is the Puritan version of Everyman; as the critics have pointed out, his is the story of the Fall—the transformation, through gaining a knowledge of sin, from Young Goodman Brown to Old Badman Brown.

Aside from the clearly intended allegory, however, we are interested in the story's underlying psychological meaning. We start with the assumption that, through symbolism and technique, "Young Goodman Brown" means more than it says. In this respect our task is one of extrapolation, an inferring of the unknown from the known. Our first premise is that Brown's journey is more than a physical one; it is a psychological one as well. To see what this journey means in psychological terms, we need to examine the setting, the time and place. The hero moves from the village of Salem into the forest. The village is a place of light and order, both social and spiritual order; Brown leaves Faith behind in the town at sunset and returns to Faith in the morning. The journey into the wilderness is taken in the night: "My journey . . . forth and back again," explains the young man to his wife, "must needs be done 'twixt now and sunrise." It is in the forest, a place of darkness and unknown terrors, that Brown meets the Devil. On one level, then, the village may be equated with consciousness, the forest with the dark well of the unconscious. But more accurately, the village, as a place of social and moral order (and inhibition) is analogous to Freud's Super-Ego, conscience and the morally inhibiting agent of the psyche; the forest, as a place of wild, untamed passions and terrors, has the attributes of the Freudian Id. As mediator between these opposing forces, Brown himself resembles the poor Ego, which tries to effect a healthy balance and is broken because it is unable to do so.

Why can't he reconcile these forces? Is his predicament that of all men, as is indicated by his name? If so, are all men destined to die in gloom? Certainly, Hawthorne implies, men cannot remain always in the village, outside the forest. And, sooner or later, all men must confront Satan. Let us examine this diabolical figure for a moment. When we first see him (after being prepared by Brown's expressed fear, "What if the devil himself should be at my very elbow!"), he is "seated at the foot of an old tree"—the "old tree" of forbidden fruit and the knowledge of sin. He is described as "bearing a considerable resemblance" to the hero himself; he is, in short, Brown's own alter ego, the dramatic projection of a part of Brown's psyche, just as Faith is the projection of another part of that psyche. The staff Satan is carrying and later gives to Brown is like "a great black snake, . . . a living serpent"—a standard Freudian symbol for the uncontrollable phallus. As he moves on through the forest, Brown encounters other figures, the most respected of his moral tutors: old Goody Cloyse, Deacon Gookin, his grandfather, and, at last, even Faith herself, her pink ribbon reflecting the ambiguity that Brown is unable to resolve (for *pink* is the mixture of *white* for purity and *red* for passion). Thoroughly unnerved, then maddened, by disillusionment, Brown capitulates to the wild evil of this heart of darkness and becomes "himself the chief horror of the scene, [shrinking] not from its other horrors." That the whole lurid scene may be interpreted as the projection of Brown's formerly repressed impulses is indicated in Hawthorne's description of the transformed protagonist:

> In truth, all through the haunted forest there could be nothing more frightful than the figure of Goodman Brown. On he flew among the black pines, brandishing his staff

with frenzied gestures, now giving vent to an inspiration of horrid blasphemy, and now shouting forth such laughter as set all the echoes of the forest laughing like demons around him. The fiend in his own shape is less hideous 'than when he rages in the breast of man.

Though Hawthorne implies that Brown's problem is that of Everyman, he does not suggest that all men share Brown's gloomy destiny. Like Freud, Hawthorne saw the dangers of an overactive suppression of libido and the consequent development of a tyrannous Super-Ego (though he thought of the problem in his own terms as an imbalance of head vs. heart). Goodman Brown is the tragic victim of a society that has shut its eyes to the inevitable "naturalness" of sex as a part of man's physical and mental constitution, a society whose moral system would suppress too many of man's natural instincts. Among the Puritans "nature" was virtually synonymous with "sin." In Hawthorne's *The Scarlet Letter,* little Pearl, illegitimate daughter of Hester Prynne and the Reverend Mr. Arthur Dimmesdale, is identified throughout as the "child of nature." In his speech to the General Court in 1645, Governor John Winthrop defined "natural liberty"—as distinguished from "civil liberty"—as "a liberty to do evil as well as good, . . . the exercise and maintaining of [which] makes men grow more evil, and in time to be worse than brute beasts. . . ." Hawthorne, himself a descendant of Puritan witch hunters and a member of the New England society whose moral standards had been strongly conditioned by its Puritan heritage, was obsessed with the nature of sin and with the psychological results of violating the taboos imposed by this system. Young Goodman Brown dramatizes the neurosis result-ing from such a violation. After his night in the forest he becomes a walking guilt complex, burdened with anxiety and doubt. Why? Because he has not been properly educated to confront the realities of the external world or of the inner world. Because from the cradle on he has been indoctrinated with admonitions against tasting the forbidden fruit—because sin and Satan have been inadvertently glamorized by prohibition—he has developed a morbid compulsion to taste thereof. He is not necessarily evil;

he is, like most young people, curious. But because of the severity
of Puritan taboos about "natural" impulses, his curiosity has
become an obsession. His dramatic reactions in the forest are
typical of what happens in actual cases of extreme repression.
Furthermore, the very nature of his wilderness fantasy sub-
stantiates Freud's theory that our repressed desires express themselves in our dreams, that dreams are symbolic forms of
wish-fulfillment. Hawthorne, writing more than a generation
before Freud, was a keen enough psychologist to be aware of
many of the same phenomena Freud was to systematize through
clinical evidence.

The Turn of the Screw

Perhaps the most famous story dealing with the theme of
sexual repression is Henry James's *The Turn of the Screw*. One
of the most celebrated ghost stories of our literature, this many-
faceted gem has been the focus of critical controversy since 1924,
when Edna Kenton published her Freudian analysis of the tale,
"Henry James to the Ruminant Reader: The Turn of the
Screw," *The Arts,* VI (1924), 245–255. This interpretation was
reinforced ten years later by the highly respected critic Edmund
Wilson in his "The Ambiguity of Henry James," *Hound and
Horn,* VII (1934), 385–406.

Briefly, *The Turn of the Screw* is the story of a young
English governess who takes a position as tutor and protectress
of two beautiful children living in a magnificent old country
mansion. The children's parents are dead, and their legal
guardian is a debonair bachelor uncle who lives in London and
does not want to be bothered with looking after his wards. He
hires the young governess-narrator with the provisions that she
is to be in complete charge at Bly, his country estate, and that
she will under no circumstances disturb him with appeals or
complaints about her problems there. Though she is only twenty
years old, she is to become governess of the estate as well as of
the children, and the uncle is to be left alone, disburdened of
worries about the welfare of his wards. The children, Miles and

Flora, are two perfectly well-mannered youngsters with whom the governess falls in love at first sight.

All seems to be well at Bly, except for the ugly mystery surrounding the relationship between the governess' predecessor, Miss Jessel, and the uncle's former valet, Peter Quint, both of whom are now dead. Also, there is the puzzling dismissal of little Miles from his school on the grounds that he "was an injury" to his fellow students. As best the governess can discover from rumor and from the scanty information given her by the housekeeper, Mrs. Grose, there had been "an affair" between Miss Jessel and Quint, carried on in the presence of the children, which had left some subtle mark of corruption on Miles and Flora. On several occasions after her arrival at Bly the governess sees the ghosts of Miss Jessel and Quint and deduces that they are somehow after the children, diabolically intent upon ensnaring their young souls. The actions of the children themselves, though superficially normal, suggest to the governess that her apprehensions are not without foundation. At the end of the narrative, little Flora turns against the governess and is taken off to the city by Mrs. Grose, as a means, presumably, of preserving her from further corruption by Miss Jessel. The governess stays at Bly with Miles and fights for his soul against the apparition of Peter Quint. In this final climactic struggle the governess seems to triumph in driving off the evil spirit, but the little boy dies from the terrible ordeal of being dispossessed.

No brief summary can do justice to the complexities and the exquisite horror of James's tale; our primary concern here is with its interpretive possibilities. In his Preface to *The Aspern Papers* James himself disavows all psychical implications in *The Turn of the Screw,* designating it as a pure and simple *amusette* intended "to catch those not easily caught (the 'fun' of the capture of the merely witless being ever but small), the jaded, the disillusioned, the fastidious"—in short, as a "perfectly independent and irresponsible little fiction"—a "Christmas-tide toy" designed "to rouse the dear old sacred terror."

Two questions may be asked about James's statements. Is he serious in disavowing a "clinical" intent? And, does it really matter whether or not he "intended" the story to be no more than a simple *amusette?* The first question is unanswerable: we cannot be sure about his stated purpose—perhaps it, too, is designed to "catch" the literal-minded reader. To the second question we must answer a qualified "no." In the strictest interpretive sense, James's conscious intentions are not directly relevant to our critical analysis of his story. Because the mind of the artist is structured essentially like other human minds and is therefore influenced by a welter of unconscious forces, the author may write more profoundly than he realizes. The important thing is not so much what the writer "intended" as what we as careful, intelligent readers find in his work. The fact is, a very strong case can be made for the "clinical" implications in the story.

In his essay on *The Turn of the Screw* (revised for *The Triple Thinkers,* John Lehmann, 1952), Edmund Wilson pointed out that no one except the governess ever admits to seeing the ghosts of Peter Quint and Miss Jessel. We assume that the children see them, as we infer this from their curious behavior, but in truth we have only the governess' word. Mrs. Grose, the simple, illiterate housekeeper whose name signifies her down-to-earthness, never apprehends either ghost, despite several opportunities to do so. She too relies only upon the word of the highly sensitive governess.

What, then, is the significance of the ghosts, and why does only the young governess see them? To the psychoanalytic observer, the answer is fairly obvious. The governess is suffering from hallucinations, the result of a severe case of sexual repression; the ghosts are dramatic projections of her own unconscious sexual desires. As James's narrator informs us at the beginning of the story, she has been reared as "the youngest of several daughters of a poor country parson." We may therefore infer that, in such a sheltered, feminine world, her normal libidinous instincts have been powerfully inhibited, like those of Goodman Brown, by her parents and by a Victorian middle-class society even more repressive than the Puritan. She is admittedly infatuated with the children's uncle—"a gentleman, a bachelor in the prime of life, such a figure as had never risen, save in a dream or an old novel, before a fluttered, anxious girl out of a Hampshire vicarage"—and it is dressed in the uncle's clothing that the red-headed Peter Quint first appears. Not only this, but Quint makes his first appearance on the tower, a phallic symbol, just as Miss Jessel first appears beside the lake, a female symbol. Wilson lends further support to his case by pointing out the pieces of wood with which little Flora is playing under the fascinated gaze of the governess at the time of Miss Jessel's initial appearance; the child is attempting to insert the mast of a toy ship (a concave vessel) into its appropriate hole. To sum up the Freudian case in Wilson's words:

> When we look back in the light of these hints, we are inclined to conclude from analogy that the story is primarily intended as a characterization of the governess: her somber and guilty visions and the way she behaves about them seem to present, from the moment we examine them from the obverse side of her narrative, an accurate and distressing picture of the poor country parson's daughter, with her English middle-class class-consciousness, her inability to admit to herself her natural sexual impulses and the relentless English "authority" which enables her to put over on inferiors even purposes which are totally deluded and not at all in the other people's best interests. . . . We find now that [this story] is a variation on one of [James's] familiar themes: the thwarted Anglo-Saxon spinster. . . .   (p. 95)

POE'S FICTION

Aside from Ernest Jones's *Hamlet and Oedipus* and Edmund Wilson's essay on *The Turn of the Screw,* probably the most famous—or infamous—psychoanalytic study of literature is Marie Bonaparte's *Life and Works of Edgar Allan Poe.* A pupil of Sigmund Freud, Princess Bonaparte is, like Dr. Jones, one of those rare critics who has combined a thorough professional knowledge of psychoanalysis with a comparable grasp of her literary subject. For the uninitiated her book is as fantastic as it is fascinating. Her main thesis is that Poe's life and works are informed throughout by the Oedipal complex: hatred of father and psychopathic love of mother. The rejection of authority forms the core of Poe's critical writings; the mother-fixation (the death-wish or longing to return to the womb, manifested for example in his obsession with premature burial) is the matrix for Poe's poetry and fiction. Even his fatal weakness for drink is explained as a form of escape that enabled him to remain faithful to his dead mother, through a rigidly enforced chastity which was further insured by alcoholic over-indulgence. As Princess Bonaparte writes,

> Ever since he was three, in fact, Poe had been doomed by fate to live in constant mourning. A fixation on a dead mother was to bar him forever from earthly love, and make him shun health and vitality in his loved ones. Forever faithful to the grave, his imagination had but two ways open before it: the heavens or the tomb according to whether he followed the "soul" or body of his lost one. . . .
>
> Thus, through his eternal fidelity to the dead mother, Poe, to all intents, became necrophilist. . . . Had [his necrophilia] been unrepressed, Poe would no doubt have been a criminal. (p. 83)

Using such psychoanalytic theories as her foundation, Princess Bonaparte proceeds to analyze work after work with a logical consistency that is as disturbing as it is monotonous. "The Cask of Amontillado" and "The Tell-Tale Heart," for example, are seen as tales of revenge against the father. The wine vault in the former story is a symbol of the "interior of the woman's body, . . . where the coveted, supreme intoxication dwells, [and] thus becomes the instrument of retribution. . . ." The victim in "The Tell-Tale Heart" is likewise interpreted as a symbol of Poe's hated foster-father, John Allan, and his horrible blind eye is a token of retributive castration. "The Fall of the House of Usher" is a psychoanalytic model of the Oedipal guilt-complex. Madeline Usher, the vault in which she is prematurely interred, the house itself, all are, according to Freudian symbology, mother-images. The weird tale of Ethelred, read to Roderick by the narrator and climaxed by the slaying of the dragon, is a reenaction of the slaying of the father to gain the mother-treasure.

BLAKE'S "THE SICK ROSE"

Though few writers lend themselves so readily as Poe to the psychoanalytic approach, a great deal of serious literature, if we accept Marie Bonaparte's premises, can be interpreted along those same basic lines established by Freud. Especially are the Romantic poets susceptible of Freudian interpretations since, as F. L. Lucas has asserted, Romanticism may be equated with the unconscious—as opposed to Classicism, which, with its emphasis upon restraint and order, is oriented toward the conscious, particularly the Ego and Super-Ego.

A richly symbolic poem like William Blake's "The Sick Rose" is exemplary:

O rose, thou art sick!
  The invisible worm,
That flies in the night,
  In the howling storm,

Has found out thy bed
  Of crimson joy;
And his dark secret love
  Does thy life destroy.

From the Freudian perspective, the sexual implications of Blake's imagery are fairly discernible. The rose is a classic symbol of feminine beauty. But this beauty is being despoiled by some agent of masculine sexuality: the worm, symbol of death, of decay, and also of the phallus (worm = serpent = sexual instinct). Again, as in Poe's "Ulalume," we encounter the metaphor of flying, Freudian symbol of sexual pleasure. Images of night, darkness, and howling storm suggest attributes of the unconscious or the Id, as in the forest of "Young Goodman Brown." The second stanza sets forth in rather explicit images the idea of sensual destruction. In short, Blake's poem is a vaguely disturbing parable of the death-instinct which psychoanalysts affirm is so closely conjoined with sexual passion. The sharp juxtaposition of "crimson joy" and "destroy" (coupled with "bed" and "his dark secret love") suggests that Eros, unmitigated by higher spiritual love, is the agent of evil as well as of mortality.

"To His Coy Mistress"

We see a similar juxtaposition in Andrew Marvell's "To His Coy Mistress," one of the most celebrated erotic poems in English literature. The speaker begins his proposition of love by stating an impossible condition: "Had we but world enough, and time, / This coyness, Lady, were no crime." Flattering his prospective mistress as "Lady" (a condition as improbable as those following, if we accept the cynical realism of the narrator), he proceeds to outline the "ideal" relationship of the two lovers:

> We would sit down and think which way
> To walk and pass our long love's day.
>
> . . .
>
> For, Lady, you deserve this state,
> Nor would I love at lower rate.

The speaker's argument in this first stanza achieves a fine sublimation: he has managed to refine his seductive motive of all its grossness yet, ever so subtly, has not swerved from his main purpose. His objective, despite the contradictory deceptiveness of "vegetable love" (a passion whose burning is so slow as to be imperceptible), is nevertheless the same: the woman must, ultimately at some distant time, capitulate to his desires. It is only a matter of time.

But this "only" makes all the difference in the world, as he demonstrates in his second stanza, shifting dramatically from the "soft sell" of the first stanza to the "hard sell":

> But at my back I always hear
> Time's wingèd chariot hurrying near;
> And yonder all before us lie
> Deserts of vast eternity.

The flying chariot of Time (again we find the subtle suggestion of sexual union in the image of flying) is juxtaposed against an eternity of oblivion, just as the slow but sure fecundity of a vegetable love growing to the vastness of empires is contrasted with the barren deserts of death. After setting forth this prospect, the speaker dares to reveal precisely what all this means in terms of love:

> Thy beauty shall no more be found,
> Nor, in thy marble vault, shall sound
> My echoing song; then worms shall try
> That long preserved virginity,
> And your quaint honor turn to dust,
> And into ashes all my lust.

This statement, in even sharper contrast with the gentle cajolery of the first stanza, is brutal—even coarse—in its explicitness. The "marble vault" is a thinly disguised vaginal metaphor suggesting, perhaps, both rigor mortis and the fleshless pelvis of the skeleton. "My echoing song" and the sensual meanings of the lines following are clear enough. From the eternal burning of a vegetable passion, in the face of reality, we see that all love must at last end in ashes—just as all chastity must end, the same as sexual profligacy, in dust. The speaker concludes his "hard sell" with a couplet unrivaled in our literature for mordant understatement:

> The grave's a fine and private place,
> But none, I think, do there embrace.

In the final stanza the speaker relaxes his harsh irony and appeals passionately to his reluctant sweetheart to seize the moment. Again, in contrast with both the vegetable metaphor of the first stanza and the frightening directness of the second stanza, he achieves a sublimation of sensual statement through the bold sincerity of his passion and through the brilliance of his imagery:

> Now therefore, while the youthful hue
> Sits on thy skin like morning dew,
> And while thy willing soul transpires

> At every pore with instant fires,
> Now let us sport us while we may,
> And now, like amorous birds of prey,
> Rather at once our time devour
> Than languish in his slow-chapped power.
> Let us roll all our strength and all
> Our sweetness up into one ball,
> And tear our pleasures with rough strife
> Thorough the iron gates of life:
> Thus, though we cannot make our sun
> Stand still, yet we will make him run.

Here, too, the sexual imagery is overt. The fire image, which smolders in stanza one and turns to ashes in stanza two, explodes into passion in this concluding stanza (Marie Bonaparte has pointed out that "Fire, in the unconscious, is the classic symbol of urethral eroticism"). Furthermore, in contrast to the tone of Blake's "Sick Rose," here love-as-destruction is set forth rapturously. The poet conveys, instead of sinister corruption, a sense of desperate ecstasy. The eating-biting metaphor (oral eroticism in its primal form) is fused with the flying symbol in "amorous birds of prey" and set with Metaphysical brilliance against the alternative of a slow cannibalistic dissolution within the horrible maw of Time. In his last four lines the lover drives his message home with an orgastic force through the use of harshly rhythmic spondees ("Thus, though" and "Stand still") and strongly suggestive puns ("make our sun" and "make him run").

To read Marvell's great poem as nothing more than a glorification of sexual activity is, of course, a gross oversimplification. "To His Coy Mistress" is much more than this, as we have indicated in the preceding chapters and will elaborate in the following chapters. We will agree with the formalistic critic that literature is autonomous, but we must also concur with critic Wayne Shumaker that it is "continuous with nonaesthetic life." As Simon Lesser has said, "Among stories whose artistic authenticity cannot be questioned we give the highest place precisely to those works which ignore no aspect of man's nature, which confront the most disagreeable aspects of life deliberately and unflinchingly. . . ." Great literature has always dealt not merely with those aspects of the human mind that are pleasant and conscious but with the total human psyche, many facets of which are both unpleasant and unconscious. The enduring appeal of Marvell's poem, like that of the other works we have examined, derives from this kind of artistic *and* honest confrontation.

This brings us to a final recapitulation, a word of caution as well as of defense, about the Freudian approach. First, in defense: incredibly farfetched as some psychoanalytic interpretations seem to many readers, such interpretations, handled by qualified critics, are not unsubstantiated in fact; they are based upon psychological insights often derived from and supported by actual case histories, and they are set forth in such works as those of Dr. Ernest Jones and Princess Marie Bonaparte with remarkable consistency. They are—if we accept the basic premises of psychoanalysis—very difficult to refute. Furthermore, regardless of their factual validity, such theories have had a tremendous impact upon modern writing (in the fiction of such novelists as James Joyce, Sherwood Anderson, Franz Kafka, and William Golding, to mention only a few) and upon modern literary criticism (for example, in the essays of such major critics as Edmund Wilson, Lionel Trilling, F. L. Lucas, and Frederick Hoffman). It is, therefore, important that the serious student of literature be acquainted with psychoanalytic theory.

The danger is that the serious student may become theory-ridden, forgetting that Freud's is not the only approach to literary analysis. To see a great work of fiction or a great poem primarily as a psychological case study is to miss its real significance and perhaps even its real meaning. A number of great works, despite the claims of the more zealous Freudians, do not lend themselves readily if at all to the psychoanalytic approach; and even those that do so cannot be studied exclusively from the psychological perspective. Literary interpretation and psychoanalysis are two distinct fields and, though they may be closely associated, they can in no sense be regarded as parts of one discipline. The literary critic who views the masterpiece solely through the lens of Freud sees art only through a glass darkly; on the other hand, the reader who rejects psychoanalysis as neurotic nonsense deprives himself of a valuable tool in understanding not only literature but human nature and himself as well.

CHAPTER

4

Mythological and archetypal approaches

In *The Masks of God: Primitive Mythology* (Viking, 1959), Joseph Campbell recounts a curious phenomenon of animal behavior. Newly hatched chickens, bits of eggshells still clinging to their tails, will dart for cover when a hawk flies overhead; yet they remain unaffected by other birds. Furthermore, a wooden model of a hawk, drawn forward along a wire above their coop, will send them scurrying (if the model is pulled backward, however, there is no response). "Whence," Professor Campbell asks, "this abrupt seizure by an image to which there is no counterpart in the chicken's world? Living gulls and ducks, herons and pigeons, leave it cold; but *the work of art strikes some very deep chord!"* (p. 31, our italics).

Professor Campbell's hinted analogy, though only roughly approximate, will serve nevertheless as an instructive introduction to the mythological approach. For it is with the relationship of literary art to "some very deep chord" in human nature that mythological criticism deals. The myth critic is concerned to seek out those mysterious artifacts built into certain literary "forms" which elicit, with almost uncanny force, dramatic and universal human reactions. He wishes to discover how it is that certain works of literature, usually those that have become, or promise to become, "classics," image a kind of reality to which readers give perennial response—while other works, seemingly as well constructed, and even some forms of reality, leave us cold. Speaking figuratively, the myth critic studies in depth the "wooden hawks" of great literature: the so-called "archetypes" or "archetypal patterns" which the writer has drawn forward along the tensed structural wires of his masterpiece and which vibrate in such a way that a sympathetic resonance is started deep within the reader.

An obviously close connection exists between mythological criticism and the psychological approach discussed in Chapter 3: both are concerned with the motives underlying human behavior. The differences between the two approaches are those of degree and of affinities. Psychology tends to be experimental and diagnostic; it is closely related to biological science. Mythology tends to be speculative and philosophic; its affinities are with religion, anthropology, and cultural history. Such generalizations, of course, risk oversimplification; for instance, a great psychologist like Sigmund Freud ranged far beyond experimental and clinical study into the realms of myth, and his distinguished protégé, Carl Jung, became one of the foremost mythologists of our time. Even so, the two approaches are distinct, and mythology is wider in its scope. For example, what psychoanalysis attempts to disclose about the individual personality, the study of myths reveals about the mind and character of a people. And just as dreams reflect the unconscious desires and anxieties of the individual, so myths are the symbolic projections of a people's hopes, values, fears, and aspirations.

According to the common misconception and misuse of the term, myths are merely primitive fictions, illusions, or opinions based upon false reasoning. Actually, mythology encompasses more than grade-school stories (in expensive illustrated editions) about the Greek and Roman deities or clever fables invented for the amusement of children (or for the harassment of students in college literature courses). It is true that myths do not meet our current standards of factual reality, but then neither does any great literature. Instead, they reflect a more profound reality. As Mark Schorer has said in *William Blake, The Politics of Vision* (Holt, 1946), "Myth is fundamental, the dramatic representation of our deepest instinctual life, of a primary awareness of man in the universe, capable of many configurations, upon which all particular opinions and attitudes depend" (p. 29). According to Alan W. Watts in *Myth and Ritual in Christianity* (Vanguard, 1954), "Myth is to be defined as a complex of stories—some no doubt fact, and some fantasy—which, for various reasons, human beings regard as demonstrations of the inner meaning of the universe and of human life" (p. 7). George Whalley asserts in *Poetic Process* (Routledge and Kegan Paul, 1953) that myth

> is a direct metaphysical statement beyond science. It embodies in an articulated structure of symbol or narrative a vision of reality. It is a condensed account of man's Being and attempts to represent reality with structural fidelity, to indicate at a single stroke the salient and fundamental relations which for a man constitute reality. . . . Myth is not an obscure, oblique, or elaborate way of expressing reality—it is the *only* way.

Myths are, by nature, collective and communal: they bind a tribe or a nation together in that people's common psychological and spiritual activities. In *The Language of Poetry,* edited by Allen Tate (Russell and Russell, 1960), Philip Wheelwright explains, "Myth is the expression of a profound sense of togetherness—a togetherness not merely upon the plane of the intellect . . . but a togetherness of feeling and of action and of wholeness of living" (p. 11). Moreover, like Melville's famous white whale (itself a mythic image), myth is ubiquitous in time as well as place: it is a dynamic factor everywhere in human society; it transcends time, uniting the past (traditional modes of belief) with the present (current values) and reaching toward the future (spiritual and cultural aspirations). In sum, to quote Professor Schorer again, "[Myth is] the essential substructure of all human activity" (p. 29).

Having established the significance of myth, we need to examine its relationship to archetypes and archetypal patterns. Although every people has its own distinctive mythology which may be reflected in legend, folklore, and ideology—although, in other words, myths take their specific shapes from the cultural environments in which they grow—myth is, in the general sense, universal. Furthermore, similar motifs or themes may be found among many different mythologies, and certain images that recur in the myths of peoples widely separated in time and place tend to have a common meaning or, more accurately, tend to elicit comparable psychological responses and to serve similar cultural functions. Such motifs and images are called "archetypes." Stated simply, archetypes are "universal symbols." As Professor Wheelwright explains in *Metaphor and Reality* (Indiana, 1962), such symbols are

> those which carry the same or very similar meanings for a large portion, if not all, of mankind. It is a discoverable fact that certain symbols, such as the sky father and earth mother, light, blood, up-down, the axis of a wheel, and others, recur again and again in cultures so remote from one another in space and time that there is no likelihood of any historical influence and causal connection among them. (p. 111)

Examples of these archetypes and the symbolic meanings with which they tend to be universally associated are listed below:

IMAGES

1. Water: the mystery of creation; birth-death-resurrection; purification and redemption; fertility and growth. According to

Carl Jung, water is also the commonest symbol for the unconscious.

a. The Sea: the Mother of all Life; spiritual mystery and infinity; death and rebirth; timelessness and eternity; the unconscious.

b. Rivers: also death and rebirth (baptism); the flowing of time into eternity; transitional phases of the life cycle; incarnations of deities.

2. Sun (fire and sky are closely related):   creative energy; law in nature; consciousness (thinking, enlightenment, wisdom, spiritual vision); father principle (moon and earth tend to be associated with female or mother principle); passage of time and life.

a. Rising Sun: birth; creation; enlightenment.

b. Setting Sun: death.

3. Colors:

a. Black (darkness):   chaos (mystery, the unknown); death; the unconscious; evil; melancholy.

b. Red: blood, sacrifice; violent passion; disorder.

c. Green: growth; sensation; hope.

4. Circle (sphere, egg):   wholeness; unity; God as Infinite; life in primordial form; union of consciousness and the unconscious— for example, the yang-yin of Chinese art and philosophy, which combines in the circle the yang (male) element (consciousness, life, light, and heat) with the yin (female) element (the unconscious, death, darkness, and cold).

5. The Archetypal Woman (including the Jungian *anima*):

    a. The Great Mother, Good Mother, Earth Mother: associated with birth, warmth, protection, fertility, growth, abundance; the unconscious.

    b. The Terrible Mother: the witch, sorceress, siren—associated with fear, danger, and death.

    c. The Soul-Mate: the princess or "beautiful lady"—incarnation of inspiration and spiritual fulfillment.

6. Wind (and breath): inspiration; conception; soul or spirit.

7. Ship: microcosm; mankind's voyage through space and time.

8. Garden: paradise; innocence; unspoiled beauty (especially feminine); fertility.

9. Desert: spiritual aridity; death; nihilism or hopelessness.

These examples are by no means exhaustive, but represent some of the more common archetypal images that the reader is likely to encounter in literature. He should also realize that the images we have listed do not necessarily function as archetypes every time they appear in a literary work; the discreet critic interprets them as such only if the total context of the work logically supports an archetypal reading.

ARCHETYPAL MOTIFS OR PATTERNS

1. Creation: this is perhaps the most fundamental of all archetypal motifs; virtually every mythology is built on some account of how the Cosmos, Nature, and Man were brought into existence by some supernatural Being or Beings.

2. Immortality: another fundamental archetype, generally taking one of two basic narrative forms:

    a. Escape from Time: the "Return to Paradise," the state of perfect, timeless bliss enjoyed by man before his tragic Fall into corruption and mortality.

    b. Mystical Submersion into Cyclical Time: the theme of endless death and regeneration—man achieves a kind of immortality by submitting to the vast, mysterious rhythm of Nature's eternal cycle, particularly the cycle of the seasons.

3. Hero Archetypes (archetypes of transformation and redemption):

a. The Quest: the Hero (Savior or Deliverer) undertakes some long journey during which he must perform impossible tasks, battle with monsters, solve unanswerable riddles, and overcome insurmountable obstacles in order to save the kingdom and perhaps marry the princess.

b. Initiation: the Hero undergoes a series of excruciating ordeals in passing from ignorance and immaturity to social and spiritual adulthood, that is, in achieving maturity and becoming a full-fledged member of his social group. The initiation most commonly consists of three stages or phases: (1) separation, (2) transformation, and (3) return. Like the Quest, this is a variation of the Death-and-Rebirth archetype.

c. The Sacrificial Scapegoat: the Hero, with whom the welfare of the tribe or nation is identified, must die in order to atone for the people's sins and restore the land to fruitfulness.

Finally, in addition to appearing as images and motifs, archetypes may be found in even more complex combinations as genres or types of literature which conform with the major phases of the seasonal cycle. In *Fables of Identity* (Harcourt, 1963), Northrop Frye provides the following table of archetypal phases with their correspondent literary types. (The reader may wish to consult Frye's *Anatomy of Criticism* for an extended explanation of these categories.)

1. The dawn, spring and birth phase. Myths of the birth of the hero, of revival and resurrection, of creation and (because the four phases are a cycle) of the defeat of the powers of darkness, winter and death. Subordinate characters: the father and the mother. The archetype of romance and of most dithyrambic and rhapsodic poetry.

2. The zenith, summer, and marriage or triumph phase. Myths of apotheosis, of the sacred marriage, and of entering into Paradise. Subordinate characters: the companion and the bride. The archetype of comedy, pastoral and idyll.

3. The sunset, autumn and death phase. Myths of fall, of the dying god, of violent death and sacrifice and of the isolation of the hero. Subordinate characters: the traitor and the siren. The archetype of tragedy and elegy.

4. The darkness, winter and dissolution phase. Myths of the triumph of these powers; myths of floods and the return of chaos, of the defeat of the hero. . . . Subordinate characters: the ogre and the witch. The archetype of satire. . . . (p. 16)

Professor Frye's contribution now takes us into the mythological approach to literary analysis. As our discussion of mythology has shown, the task of the myth critic is a special one. Unlike the traditional critic, who relies heavily on history and the biography of the writer, the myth critic is interested more in prehistory and the biographies of the gods. Unlike the formalistic critic, who concentrates upon the shape and symmetry of the work itself, the myth critic probes for the inner spirit which gives that form its vitality, its enduring appeal. And, unlike the Freudian critic, who is apt to see the hawk-chicken phenomenon cited in our introduction as symbolic of some form of sexual neurosis (perhaps the hawk is a father-image, and the coop a womb symbol), the myth critic assumes a broader perspective (he will seek to discover the prototypal hawk in whose image the model was carved and will look beyond our chicken to the primordial egg itself).

Yet, despite the special importance of the myth critic's contribution, this approach is, for several reasons, relatively new and poorly understood. In the first place, only during the present century have the proper interpretive tools become available through the development of such disciplines as anthropology, psychology, and cultural history. Second, many scholars and teachers of literature have remained skeptical of myth criticism because of its tendencies toward the cult and the occult. Finally, there has been a discouraging confusion over concepts and definitions among the myth "initiates" themselves, the sound and fury of which has caused many would-be myth critics to turn their energies to more clearly defined approaches such as the traditional or formalistic. In carefully picking our way through this maze, we can discover at least three separate though not necessarily exclusive disciplines, each of which has figured prominently in the development of myth criticism. We will examine these in roughly chronological order, noting how each may be applied to critical analysis.

ANTHROPOLOGY AND ITS USES

The rapid advancement of modern anthropology since the end of the nineteenth century has been the most important single influence on the growth of myth criticism. Shortly after the turn of the century this influence was revealed in a series of important studies published by the Cambridge Hellenists, a group of British scholars who applied recent anthropological discoveries to the understanding of Greek classics in terms of mythic and ritualistic origins. Noteworthy contributions by members of this group include *Anthropology and the Classics* (Oxford, 1908), a symposium edited by R. R. Marett; Jane Harrison's *Themis* (Cambridge, 1912); Gilbert Murray's *Euripides and His Age* (Holt, 1913); and F. M. Cornford's *Origin of Attic Comedy* (Arnold, 1914). But by far the most significant member of the British school was Sir James G. Frazer, whose monumental *The Golden Bough* has exerted an enormous influence upon twentieth-century literature, not merely on the critics but also on such creative writers as James Joyce, Thomas Mann, and T. S. Eliot. Frazer's work, a comparative study of the primitive origins of religion in magic, ritual, and myth, was first published in two volumes in 1890, later expanded to twelve volumes, and then published in a one-volume abridged edition in 1922. Frazer's main contribution was to demonstrate "The essential similarity of man's chief wants everywhere and at all times," particularly as these wants were reflected throughout ancient mythologies; he explains, for example, in the abridged edition (Macmillan, 1922), that

> Under the names of Osiris, Tammuz, Adonis, and Attis, the peoples of Egypt and Western Asia represented the yearly decay and revival of life, especially vegetable life, which they personified as a god who annually died and rose again from the dead. In name and detail the rites varied from place to place: in substance they were the same. (p. 325)

The central motif with which Frazer deals is the archetype of crucifixion and resurrection, specifically the myths describing "the Killing of the Divine King." Among many primitive peoples it was believed that the ruler was a divine or semidivine being whose life was identified with the life cycle in nature and in human existence. Because of this identification, the safety of the people and even of the world was felt to depend upon the life of the god-king. A vigorous, healthy ruler would insure natural and human productivity; on the other hand, a sick or maimed king would bring blight and disease to the land and its people. Frazer points out that if

> the course of nature is dependent on the man-god's life, what catastrophes may not be expected from the gradual enfeeblement of his powers and their final extinction in death? There is only one way of averting these dangers. The man-god must be killed as soon as he shows symptoms that his powers are beginning to fail, and his soul must be transferred to a vigorous successor before it has been seriously impaired by threatened decay. (p. 265)

Among some early peoples the kings were put to death at regular intervals to insure the welfare of the tribe; later, however, substitute figures were killed in place of the kings themselves, or the sacrifices became purely symbolic rather than literal.

Corollary to the rite of sacrifice was the "scapegoat" archetype. This motif centered in the belief that, by transferring the corruptions of the tribe to a sacred animal or man, then by killing (and in some instances eating) this scapegoat, the tribe could achieve the cleansing and atonement thought necessary for natural and spiritual rebirth. Pointing out that food and children are the primary needs for human survival, Frazer emphasizes that the rites of blood sacrifice and purification were considered by ancient peoples as a magical guarantee of rejuvenation, an insurance of life, both vegetable and human. If such customs strike us as incredibly primitive, we need only to recognize their vestiges in our own civilized world—for example, the irrational satisfaction that some people gain by the persecution of such minority groups as Negroes and Jews as scapegoats, or the more wholesome feelings of renewal derived from our New Year's festivities and resolutions, the homely tradition of spring-cleaning, our celebration of Easter, and even in the Eucharist. In this latter connection, it is perhaps unnecessary to point out that the central figure in the Christian religion played out the gruesome role of the god-king as scapegoat, so that man might achieve spiritual rebirth.

The insights given us by Frazer and the Cambridge Hellenists have been extremely helpful in myth criticism, especially in the mythological approach to drama. Many scholars theorize that tragedy originated from the primitive rites we have been describing. The tragedies of Sophocles and Aeschylus, for example, were written to be played during the Festival of Dionysos, annual vegetation ceremonies during which the ancient Greeks celebrated the deaths of the winter-kings and the rebirths of the gods of spring and renewed life.

Sophocles' *Oedipus* is an excellent example of the fusion of myth and literature. Sophocles produced a great play, but the plot of *Oedipus* was not his invention—it was a well-known myth long before he immortalized it as literature. Both the myth and the play contain a number of familiar archetypes, as a brief summary of the plot will indicate. The King and Queen of ancient Thebes, Laius and Jocasta, are told in a prophecy that their newborn son, after he has grown up, will murder his father and marry his mother. To prevent this catastrophe, the King orders one of his men to pierce the infant's heels and abandon him to die in the wilderness. But the child is saved by a shepherd and taken to Corinth, where he is reared as the son of King Polybus and Queen Merope, who lead the boy to believe that they are his real parents. After reaching maturity and hearing of the prophecy that he is destined to commit patricide and incest, Oedipus flees from Corinth to Thebes. On his journey he meets an old man and his servants, and quarrels with and kills them. Before entering Thebes he encounters the Sphinx, who holds the city under a spell, solves her riddle, and frees the city; his reward is the hand of the widowed Queen Jocasta. He then rules a prosperous Thebes for many years, fathering four children by Jocasta. At last, however, a blight falls upon his kingdom because Laius' slayer has gone unpunished. Oedipus starts an intensive investigation to find the culprit—only to discover that he himself is the guilty one, that the old man whom he had killed on his journey to Thebes was Laius, his real father. Overwhelmed by this revelation, Oedipus blinds himself with a brooch taken from his dead mother-wife, who has hanged herself, and goes into exile. Following his sacrificial punishment, Thebes is restored to health and abundance.

Even in this bare summary we may discern at least two archetypal motifs: (1) The Quest: Oedipus, as the Hero, undertakes a journey during which he encounters the Sphinx, a supernatural monster with the body of a lion and the head of a woman; by answering her riddle, he delivers the kingdom and marries the Queen; (2) The King as Sacrificial Scapegoat: the welfare of the state, both human and natural (Thebes is stricken by both plague and drought), is bound up with the personal fate of the ruler; only after Oedipus has offered himself up as a scapegoat is the land redeemed.

Considering that Sophocles wrote his tragedy expressly for a ritual occasion and for an audience whose religious beliefs were primitive by modern standards, we are hardly surprised that *Oedipus* reflects certain facets of the fertility myths described by Frazer. More remarkable, and more instructive for the student interested in myth criticism, is the revelation of similar facets in the great tragedy written by Shakespeare two thousand years later.

Hamlet

One of the first modern scholars to point out these similarities was Professor Gilbert Murray. In his "Hamlet and Orestes," delivered as a lecture in 1914 and subsequently published in *The Classical Tradition in Poetry* (Harvard, 1927), Murray indicated a number of significant parallels between the mythic elements of Shakespeare's play and those in *Oedipus* and the *Agamemnon* of Aeschylus. The heroes of all three works derive from the "Golden Bough Kings"; they are all haunted, sacrificial figures. Furthermore, as with the Greek tragedies, the story of Hamlet was not the playwright's invention but was drawn from myth. As literary historians tell us, the ancient Scandinavian legend of "Amlehtus" or "Amlet," Prince of Jutland, was recorded as early as the twelfth century by Saxo Grammaticus in his *History of the Danes* (Murray cites an even earlier passing reference to the prototypic Hamlet in a Scandinavian poem composed about 980). It is therefore apparent that the core of Shakespeare's play is mythic. In Professor Murray's words,

> The things that thrill and amaze us in Hamlet . . . are not any historical particulars about mediaeval Elsinore . . . but things belonging to the old stories and the old magic rites, which stirred and thrilled our forefathers five and six thousand years ago; set them dancing all night on the hills, tearing beasts and men in pieces, and giving up their own bodies to a ghastly death, in hope thereby to keep the green world from dying and to be the saviours of their own people. (p. 236)

By the time Sophocles and Aeschylus were producing their tragedies for Athenian audiences, such sacrifices were no longer performed literally but were acted out symbolically in the arena; yet their mythic significance was the same. Indeed, their significance was very similar in the case of Shakespeare's audiences. The Elizabethans were a myth-minded and symbol-receptive people. There was no need for Shakespeare to interpret for his audience: they *felt* the mythic content of his plays. And though myth may smolder only feebly in the present-day audience, we still respond, despite our intellectual sophistication, to the archetypes in *Hamlet*.

Such critics as Murray and, more recently, Francis Fergusson have provided us with clues to many of *Hamlet*'s archetypal mysteries. In *The Idea of a Theater* (Princeton, 1949), Fergusson discloses point by point how the scenes in Shakespeare's play follow the same ritual pattern as those in Greek tragedy, specifically in *Oedipus;* he perceives that

> in both plays a royal sufferer is associated with pollution, in its very sources, of an entire social order. Both plays open with an invocation for the well-being of the endangered body politic. In both, the destiny of the individual and of society are closely intertwined; and in both the suffering of the royal victim seems to be necessary before purgation and renewal can be achieved. (p. 118)

To appreciate how closely the moral norms in Shakespeare's play are related to those of ancient vegetation myths, we need only to note how often images of disease and corruption are used to symbolize the evil that has blighted Hamlet's Denmark. The following statement from Philip Wheelwright's *The Burning Fountain* (Indiana, 1954), explaining the organic source of good and evil, is directly relevant to the moral vision in *Hamlet*, particularly to the implications of Claudius' crime and its disastrous consequences. From the natural or organic standpoint,

> Good is life, vitality, propagation, health; evil is death, impotence, disease. Of these several terms *health* and *disease* are the most important and comprehensive. Death is but an interim evil; it occurs periodically, but there is the assurance of new life ever springing up to take its place. The normal cycle of life and death is a healthy cycle, and the purpose of the major seasonal festivals [for example, the Festival of Dionysos] was at least as much to celebrate joyfully the turning wheel of great creative Nature as to achieve magical effects. Disease and blight, however, interrupt the cycle; they are the real destroyers; and health is the good most highly to be prized. (p. 197)

Professor Wheelwright continues by pointing out that, because murder—not to be confused with ritual sacrifice—does violence to both the natural cycle of life and the social organism, the murderer is symbolically diseased. Furthermore, when the victim is a member of the murderer's own family (an even more compact organism than the tribe or the political state), the disease is especially virulent.

We should mention one other myth that relates closely to the meaning of *Hamlet:* the "Myth of Divine Appointment." This was the belief, strongly fostered by such Tudor monarchs as Henry VII, Henry VIII, and Elizabeth I, that not only had the Tudors been divinely appointed to bring order and happiness out of civil strife but also any attempt to break this divine ordinance (for example, by insurrection or assassination) would result in catastrophe—that is, social, political, and natural chaos. We see this myth reflected in several of Shakespeare's plays (for example, in *Richard III, Macbeth,* and *King Lear*) where interference with the order of divine succession or appointment results in both political and natural chaos, and where a deformed, corrupt, or weak monarch epitomizes a diseased political state. This national myth is, quite obviously, central in *Hamlet.*

The relevance of myth to *Hamlet* should now be apparent. The play's thematic heart is the ancient, archetypal mystery of the life cycle itself; its pulse is the same tragic rhythm that moved Sophocles' audience at the Festival of Dionysos and moves us today through forces which transcend our conscious processes. Thanks to the insights provided us by the anthropological scholars, however, we may perceive the essential archetypal pattern of Shakespeare's tragedy. Hamlet's Denmark is a diseased and rotten state because Claudius' "foul and most unnatural murder" of his King-brother has subverted the divinely ordained laws of nature and of kingly succession. The disruption is intensified by the blood kinship between victim and murderer. Claudius, whom the Ghost identifies as "The Serpent," bears the primal blood-curse of Cain. And, because the state is identified with its ruler, Denmark shares and suffers also from his blood-guilt. Its natural cycle interrupted, the nation is threatened by chaos: civil strife within and war without. As Hamlet exclaims, "The time is out of joint; O cursed spite, / That ever I was born to set it right!"

Hamlet's role in the drama is that of the Prince-Hero who, to deliver his nation from the blight that has fallen upon it, must not only avenge his father's murder but also offer himself up as a royal scapegoat. As a member of the royal family, Hamlet is infected with the regicidal virus even though he is personally innocent. We might say, using a pathological metaphor, that Claudius' murderous cancer has metastasized so that the royal court and even the nation itself is threatened with fatal deterioration. Hamlet's task is to seek out the source of this malady and to eliminate it. Only after a thorough purgation can Denmark be restored to a state of wholesome balance. Hamlet's reluctance to accept the role of cathartic agent is a principal reason for his procrastination in killing Claudius, an act which may well involve his own self-destruction. He is a reluctant but dutiful scapegoat, and he realizes ultimately that there can be no substitute victim in this sacrificial rite—hence his decision to accept Laertes' challenge to a dueling match that he suspects has been "fixed" by Claudius. The bloody climax of the tragedy is therefore not merely spectacular melodrama but an essential element in the archetypal pattern of sacrifice-atonement-catharsis. Not only must all those die who have been infected by the evil contagion (Claudius, Gertrude, Polonius, Rosencrantz and Guildenstern—even Ophelia and Laertes), but the Prince-Hero himself must suffer "crucifixion" before Denmark can be purged and reborn under the healthy new regime of Fortinbras.

Enhancing the motif of the Sacrificial Scapegoat is Hamlet's long and difficult spiritual journey—his initiation, as it were—from innocent, carefree youth (he has been a college student) through a series of painful ordeals to sadder, but wiser, maturity. His is a long night journey of the soul, and Shakespeare employs archetypal imagery to convey this thematic motif: *Hamlet* is an autumnal, nighttime play dominated by images of darkness and blood, and the hero appropriately wears black, the archetypal color of melancholy. The superficial object of his dark quest is to solve the riddle of his father's death. On a deeper level, his quest leads him down the labyrinthine ways of the human mystery, the mystery of man's life and destiny (observe how consistently his soliloquies turn toward the puzzles of life and of self). And, as with the riddle of the Sphinx, the enigmatic answer is "Man," the clue to which is given in Polonius' glib admonition, "To thine own self be true." In this sense, then, Hamlet's quest is the quest undertaken by all of us who would gain that rare and elusive philosopher's stone, self-knowledge.

Finally, if we wish to use the table of archetypal genres provided by Northrop Frye, we may see that in its dramatic progression *Hamlet* epitomizes the life cycle itself, containing elements of all the seasonal changes of nature. First, the summer phase is ironically travestied in the unsacred marriage and specious triumph of the new King, Claudius. Hamlet and his companions on the cold midnight watch are quick to perceive that the drunken revels of Claudius' court are but a sham and a mockery of the truly happy political state; Denmark is a fool's Paradise and, like Hamlet himself, is too much in the false sun of a counterfeit King-father. Second, the dominant seasonal phase is, of course, autumn (the archetype of tragedy itself). Here, as already seen, are the motifs of "the dying god, of violent death and sacrifice and of the isolation of the hero." We might note that such subordinate characters as Claudius, Polonius, Rosencrantz, and Guildenstern function in various ways as traitors—also, that the King and Polonius conspire to use Ophelia as an unwitting siren. We note, too, the elegiac tone of the play's conclusion, specifically in the speeches of Horatio and Fortinbras. Third, *Hamlet* is strongly imbued with the characteristics of the "darkness, winter, and dissolution phase," powers that threaten to overwhelm the land and plunge Denmark into chaos. The hero, haunted by the specter of defeat throughout the play, ultimately triumphs only in his death. As Gilbert Murray observes in *The Classical Tradition in Poetry* (Harvard, 1927), "Hamlet is no joyous and triumphant slayer. He is clad in black, he rages alone, he is the Bitter Fool who must slay the King" (p. 235)—in short, he is wrapped in the vestments of winter rather than summer. Though *Hamlet* is not a satire, it is rich in the elements of satire, particularly in the hero's own mordant irony (for example, his sarcastic remarks to Claudius and to the King's "stool pigeons," Polonius, Rosencrantz, and Guildenstern—also, the satiric jibes at the contemporary theater in his instructions to the players). Last, the conclusion of the tragedy is brightened by the promise of dawn, spring, and rebirth following Hamlet's defeat of the forces of darkness and winter by means of his sacrificial death.

From these examples we see that, archetypally speaking, *Hamlet* is one of the most richly orchestrated works in our literature. It is a veritable symphony of myth, and its music continues to haunt modern audiences because its central motifs elicit responses as old as mankind itself.

"To His Coy Mistress"—archetypes of time AND IMMORTALITY

Even though the mythological approach lends itself more readily to the interpretation of drama and the novel than to shorter literary forms such as the lyric poem, it is not uncommon to find elements of myth in these shorter works. In fact, mythopoeic poets like William Blake, William Butler Yeats, and T. S. Eliot carefully structured many of their works on myth. Even those poets who are not self-appointed myth-makers often employ images and motifs that, intentionally or not, function as archetypes. Andrew Marvell's "To His Coy Mistress" seems to fit into this latter category.

Because of its strongly suggestive (and suggested) sensuality and its apparently cynical theme, "To His Coy Mistress" is sometimes dismissed as an immature if not immoral love poem. But to see the poem as little more than a clever "proposition" is to miss its greatness. No literary classic survives because it is merely "clever," or merely well-written. It must partake somehow of the universal and, in doing so, may contain elements of the archetypal. Let us examine "To His Coy Mistress" with an eye to its archetypal content.

Superficially a love poem, "To His Coy Mistress" is, in a deeper sense, a poem about time. And, as such, it is concerned with immortality, a fundamental motif in myth. In the first two stanzas we encounter an inversion or rejection of traditional conceptions of human immortality. Stanza one is an ironic presentation of the "Escape from Time" to some paradisal state in which lovers may dally for an eternity. But such a state of perfect, eternal bliss is a foolish delusion, as the speaker suggests in his subjunctive "Had we . . ." and in his description of love as some kind of monstrous vegetable growing slowly to an infinite size in the archetypal garden. Stanza two presents, in dramatic contrast, the desert archetype in terms of another kind of time, naturalistic time. This is the time governed by the inexorable laws of nature (note the sun archetype imaged in "Time's wingèd chariot"), the laws of decay, death, and physical extinction. Stanza two is as extreme in its philosophical realism as the first stanza is in its impractical idealism.

The concluding stanza, radically altered in tone, presents a third kind of time—an Escape into Cyclical Time and thereby a chance for immortality. Again we encounter the sun archetype, but this is the sun of "soul" and of "instant fires"—images not of death but of life and creative energy, which are fused with the sphere ("Let us roll all our strength and all / Our sweetness up into one ball"), the archetype of primal wholeness and fulfillment. In *Myth and Reality* (Harper & Row, 1963), Mircea Eliade indicates that one of the most widespread motifs in immortality myths is the *regressus ad uterum* (a "return to the origin" of creation or to the symbolic womb of life)—also that this return is considered to be symbolically feasible by some philosophers (for example, the Chinese Taoists) through alchemical fire:

> During the fusion of metals the Taoist alchemist tries to bring about in his own body the union of the two cosmological principles, Heaven and Earth, in order to reproduce the primordial chaotic situation that existed before the Creation. This primordial situation . . . corresponds both to the egg [that is, the archetypal sphere] or the embryo

and to the paradisal and innocent state of the uncreated World. (pp. 83–84)

We are not suggesting that Marvell was familiar with Taoist philosophy or that he was consciously aware of immortality archetypes. What we wish to point out is that, in representing the age-old dilemma of time and immortality, Marvell employed a cluster of images charged with mythic significance. His poet-lover seems to offer the alchemy of love as a way of defeating the laws of naturalistic time; love is a means of participating in, even intensifying, the mysterious rhythms of Nature's eternal cycle. If life is to be judged, as some philosophers have suggested, not by duration but by intensity, then Marvell's lovers, at least during the act of love, will achieve a kind of immortality by "devouring" time or by transcending the laws of clock-time ("Time's wingèd chariot"). And if this alchemical transmutation requires a fire hot enough to melt them into one primordial ball, then it is perhaps also hot enough to melt the sun itself and "make him run." Thus we see that the overt sexuality of Marvell's poem is, in a mythic sense, suggestive of a profound metaphysical insight, an insight that continues to fascinate those philosophers and scientists who would penetrate the mysteries of Time and Eternity.

JUNGIAN PSYCHOLOGY AND ITS ARCHETYPAL INSIGHTS

The second major influence on mythological criticism is the work of Dr. Carl Jung, the great psychologist-philosopher and one-time student of Freud who broke with the master because of what he regarded as a too narrow approach to psychoanalysis. Jung believed *libido* (psychic energy) to be more than sexual; also, he considered Freudian theories too negative because of Freud's emphasis on the neurotic rather than the healthy aspects of the psyche.

Jung's primary contribution to myth criticism is his theory

of racial memory and archetypes. In developing this concept, Jung expanded Freud's theories of the personal unconscious, asserting that beneath this is a primeval, collective unconscious shared in the psychic inheritance of all members of the human family. Just as certain instincts are inherited by the lower animals (for example, the instinct of the baby chicken to run from a hawk's shadow), so are more complex psychic predispositions— that is, a "racial memory"—inherited by human beings. Jung believed, contrary to eighteenth-century Lockean psychology, that "Mind is not born as a *tabula rasa* [a clean slate]. Like the body, it has its pre-established individual definiteness; namely, forms of behaviour. They become manifest in the ever-recurring patterns of psychic functioning" (*Psyche and Symbol* [Doubleday Anchor, 1958], p. xv). Therefore, what Jung called "myth-forming" structural elements are ever-present in the unconscious psyche; he refers to the manifestations of these elements as "motifs," "primordial images," or "archetypes."

Jung was also careful to explain that archetypes are not inherited ideas or patterns of thought: "In reality they belong to the realm of activities of the instincts and in that sense they represent inherited forms of psychic behaviour" (p. xvi). In *Psychological Reflections* (Harper Torchbooks, 1961), he maintained that these psychic instincts "are older than historical man, . . . have been ingrained in him from earliest times, and, eternally living, outlasting all generations, still make up the groundwork of the human psyche. It is only possible to live the fullest life when we are in harmony with these symbols; wisdom is a return to them" (p. 42).

In stressing that archetypes are actually "inherited forms," Jung also went farther than most of the anthropologists, who tended to see these forms as social phenomena passed down from one generation to the next through various sacred rites rather than through the structure of the mind itself. Furthermore, in *The Archetypes and the Collective Unconscious* (Pantheon, 1959), he theorized that myths do not derive from external factors such as the seasonal or solar cycle but are, in truth, the projections of innate psychic phenomena.

> All the mythologized processes of nature, such as summer and winter, the phases of the moon, the rainy seasons, and so forth, are in no sense allegories of these objective occurrences; rather they are symbolic expressions of the inner, unconscious drama of the psyche which becomes accessible to man's consciousness by way of projection—that is, mirrored in the events of nature. (p. 6)

In other words, myths are the means by which archetypes, essentially unconscious forms, become manifest and articulate to the conscious mind. Jung indicated further that archetypes reveal themselves in the dreams of individuals, so that we might say that dreams are "personalized myths" and myths are "depersonalized dreams."

Jung detected an intimate relationship between dreams, myths, and art in that all three serve as media through which archetypes become accessible to consciousness. The great artist, as Jung observes in *Modern Man in Search of a Soul* (Harvest; first published in 1933), is the man who possesses "the primordial vision," a special sensitivity to archetypal patterns and a gift for speaking in primordial images, which enable him to transmit experiences of the "inner world" to the "outer world" through his art form. Considering the nature of his raw materials, it is only logical, suggests Jung, that the artist "will resort to mythology in order to give his experience its most fitting expression." This is not to say that the artist gets his materials second-hand: "The primordial experience is the source of his creativeness; it cannot be fathomed, and therefore requires mythological imagery to give it form" (p. 164). By asserting that the artist is "man" in a higher sense—"collective man"—and that "the work of the poet comes to meet the spiritual need of the society in which he lives" (p. 171), Dr. Jung restores him to the same exalted role to which Emerson, Whitman, and other romantic critics had assigned the poet in the nineteenth century.

While Dr. Jung himself wrote relatively little that could be called literary criticism, what he did write leaves no doubt that he believed literature, and art in general, to be a vital ingredient in human civilization. Most important, his theories have expanded the horizons of literary interpretation for those critics concerned to use the tools of the mythological approach and for psychological critics who have felt too tightly constricted by Freudian dogma.

SOME SPECIAL ARCHETYPES—*shadow, persona,* AND *anima*

In *The Archetypes and the Collective Unconscious* (Pantheon, 1959), Jung discusses at length many of the archetypal patterns that we have already examined, for example, water, colors, rebirth. In this way, though his emphasis is psychological rather than anthropological, a good deal of his work overlaps that of Frazer and the others. But, as we have already indicated, Jung is not merely a derivative or secondary figure; he is a major influence in the growth of myth criticism. For one thing, he provided some of the favorite terminology now current among myth critics; the term "archetype" itself, though not coined by Jung, enjoys its present widespread usage among the myth critics primarily because of his influence. Also, like Freud, he was a pioneer whose brilliant flashes of insight have helped to light our way in exploring the darker recesses of the human mind.

One major contribution is Jung's theory of *individuation* as related to those archetypes designated as the *shadow*, the *persona*, and the *anima*. Individuation is a psychological "growing up," the process of discovering those aspects of one's self that make one an individual different from other members of his species. It is essentially a process of recognition—that is, as he matures, the individual must consciously recognize the various aspects, unfavorable as well as favorable, of his total self. This self-recognition requires extraordinary courage and honesty but is absolutely essential if one is to become a well-balanced individual. Jung theorizes that neuroses are the results of the person's failure to confront and to accept some archetypal component of his unconscious. Instead of assimilating this unconscious element to his consciousness, the neurotic individual persists in projecting it upon some other person or object. In Jung's words, projection is "an unconscious, automatic process whereby a content that is unconscious to the subject transfers itself to an object, so that it seems to belong to that object. The projection ceases the moment it becomes conscious, that is to say when it is seen as belonging to the subject" (*Archetypes and the Collective Unconscious,* p. 60). In layman's terms, the habit of projection is reflected in the attitude that "Everybody is out of step but me" or "I'm the only honest person in the crowd." It is a commonplace that we can project our own unconscious faults and weaknesses on others much more easily than accept them as part of our own nature.

The *shadow, persona,* and *anima* are structural components of the psyche that man has inherited, just as the chicken has inherited his built-in response to the hawk. We encounter the symbolic projections of these archetypes throughout the myths and the literatures of mankind. In melodrama, such as the television or Hollywood Western, the persona, the anima, and shadow are projected respectively in the characters of the hero, the heroine, and the villain. The shadow is the darker side of our unconscious self, the inferior and less pleasing aspects of the personality which we wish to suppress. "Taking it in its deepest sense," writes Jung in *Psychological Reflections,* "the shadow is the invisible saurian [reptilian] tail that man still drags behind him" (p. 217). The most common variant of this archetype, when projected, is the Devil, who, in Jung's words in *Two Essays on Analytical Psychology* (Pantheon, 1953), represents "the dangerous aspect of the unrecognized dark half of the personality" (p. 94). In literature we see symbolic representations of this archetype in such figures as Shakespeare's Iago, Milton's Satan, Goethe's Mephistopheles, Conrad's Kurtz, and Golding's Lord of the Flies.

The anima is perhaps the most complex of Jung's archetypes. It is the "soul-image," the spirit of man's *élan vital,* his life force or vital energy. In the sense of "soul," says Jung, anima is "the living thing in man, that which lives of itself and causes life. . . . Were it not for the leaping and twinkling of the soul, man would rot away in his greatest passion, idleness" (*Archetypes and the Collective Unconscious,* pp. 26–27). Jung gives the anima a feminine designation in the male psyche, pointing out that "the anima-image is usually projected upon women" (in the female psyche this archetype is called the *animus*). In this sense, anima is the contrasexual part of man's psyche, the image of the opposite sex that he carries in both his personal and his collective unconscious. As an old German proverb puts it, "Every man has his own Eve within him"—in other words, the human psyche is bisexual, though the psychological characteristics of the opposite sex in each of us are generally unconscious, revealing themselves only in dreams or in projections on someone in our environment. The phenomenon of love, especially love at first sight, may be explained at least in part by Jung's theory of the anima: we tend to be attracted to members of the opposite sex who mirror the characteristics of our own inner selves. In literature, Jung regards such figures as Helen of Troy, Dante's Beatrice, Milton's Eve, and H. Rider Haggard's She as personifications of the anima. Following his theory, we might say that any female figure who is invested with unusual significance or power is likely to be a symbol of the anima. One other function of the anima is noteworthy here: the anima is a kind of mediator between the ego—the conscious will or thinking self—and the unconscious or inner world of the individual; this function will be somewhat clearer if we compare the anima with the persona.

The persona is the obverse of the anima in that it mediates between our ego and the external world. Speaking metaphorically, let us say that the ego is a coin: the image on one side is the anima; on the other side, the persona. The persona is the actor's mask that we show to the world—it is our social personality, a personality that is sometimes quite different from our true self. Jung, in discussing this social mask, explains that, to achieve psychological maturity, the individual must have a flexible, viable persona that can be brought into harmonious relation with the other components of his psychic make-up—also, that a persona that is too artificial or rigid results in such symptoms of neurotic disturbance as irritability and melancholy.

"YOUNG GOODMAN BROWN"

The literary relevance of Jung's theory of shadow, anima, and persona may be seen in our analysis of Hawthorne's story,

"Young Goodman Brown." In the first place, Brown's persona is both false and inflexible. It is the social mask of a God-fearing, prayerful, self-righteous Puritan—the persona of a "Good Man" with all the pietistic connotations. Brown considers himself both the good Christian and the good husband married to "a blessed angel on earth." In truth, however, he is much less the Good Man than the Bad Boy. His behavior from start to finish is that of the adolescent male. His desertion of his wife, for example, is motivated by his juvenile compulsion to have "one last fling with the boys" as a moral Peeping Tom (nowadays he would probably satisfy his urge with an excursion to the burlesque theater or a stag movie). His failure to recognize himself (and his own base motives) when he confronts Satan—his shadow— is merely another indication of his spiritual immaturity.

Just as his persona has proved inadequate in mediating between Brown's ego and the external world, so anima fails in relating to his inner world. It is only fitting that his "soul-image" or anima should be named Faith; his trouble is that he sees Faith not as a true wifely companion but as a mother (Jung points out that, during childhood, anima is usually projected upon the mother), as is revealed when he thinks that he will "cling to her skirts and follow her to heaven." In other words, if one's Faith has the qualities of "good old Mom," then one might expect to be occasionally indulged in one's juvenile escapades even if they are a little naughty (after all, boys will be boys!). But mature faith, like marriage, is a covenant which binds both parties mutually to uphold its sacred vows. If one party breaks this covenant, as Goodman Brown does, he must face the unpleasant consequences: at worst, separation and divorce; at best, suspicion (perhaps Faith herself has been unfaithful), loss of harmony, of trust, and of peace of mind. It is the latter consequences that Brown has to face. Even then, he still behaves like a child. Instead of admitting to his error and working maturely for a reconciliation, he sulks.

In clinical terms, young Goodman Brown suffers from a failure of personality integration. He has been stunted in his psychological growth (individuation) because he is unable to confront his shadow, recognize it as a part of his own psyche, and

assimilate it to his consciousness. He persists, instead, in projecting the shadow-image: first, in the form of the Devil; then upon
the members of his community (Goody Cloyse, Deacon Gookin,
and others); and finally, upon Faith herself (his anima), so that
ultimately, in his eyes, the whole world is one of shadow, or
gloom. As Jung explains in *Psyche and Symbol* (Doubleday
Anchor Books, 1958), the results of such projections are often
disastrous for the individual:

> The effect of projection is to isolate the subject from
> his environment, since instead of a real relation to it there is
> now only an illusory one. Projections change the world into
> the replica of one's own unknown face. . . . The resultant
> [malaise is in] turn explained by projection as the malevo-
> lence of the environment, and by means of this vicious circle
> the isolation is intensified. The more projections interpose
> themselves between the subject and the environment, the
> harder it becomes for the ego to see through its illusions.
> [Note Goodman Brown's inability to distinguish between
> reality and his illusory dream in the forest.]
>   It is often tragic to see how blatantly a man bungles his
> own life and the lives of others yet remains totally incapable
> of seeing how much the whole tragedy originates in himself,
> and how he continually feeds it and keeps it going. Not
> *consciously,* of course—for consciously he is engaged in be-
> wailing and cursing a *faithless* [our italics] world that re-
> cedes further and further into the distance. Rather, it is an
> unconscious factor which spins the illusions that veil his
> world. And what is being spun is a cocoon, which in the end
> will completely envelop him.   (p. 8)

Dr. Jung could hardly have diagnosed Goodman Brown's
malady more accurately had he been directing these comments
squarely at Hawthorne's story. That he was generalizing adds
impact to his theory as well as to Hawthorne's moral insight.

SYNTHESES OF JUNG AND ANTHROPOLOGY

As we can see from our interpretation of "Young Goodman
Brown," the application of Jungian theory to literary analysis is
likely to be closer to the psychological than to the mythological

approach. We should therefore realize that most of the myth critics who use Jung's insights also use the materials of anthropology. A classic example of this kind of mythological eclecticism is Maud Bodkin's *Archetypal Patterns in Poetry,* first published in 1934 and now recognized as the pioneer work of archetypal criticism. Miss Bodkin acknowledges her debt to Gilbert Murray and the anthropological scholars, as well as to Dr. Jung; she then proceeds to trace several major archetypal patterns through the great literature of Western Civilization, for example, Rebirth in Coleridge's *Rime of the Ancient Mariner;* Heaven-Hell in Coleridge's "Kubla Khan," Dante's *Divine Comedy,* and Milton's *Paradise Lost;* the Image of Woman as reflected in Homer's Thetis, Euripides' Phaedra, and Milton's Eve. The same kind of critical synthesis may be found in more recent mythological studies like Northrop Frye's brilliant *Anatomy of Criticism* (1957), in which literary criticism, with the support of insights provided by anthropology and Jungian psychology, promises to become a new "social science."

One of the best of recent myth studies is James Baird's *Ishmael: A Study of the Symbolic Mode in Primitivism.* Professor Baird's approach derives not only from Jung and the anthropologists but also from such philosophers as Susanne Langer and Mircea Eliade. Though he ranges far beyond the works of Herman Melville, Baird's primary objective is to find an archetypal key to the multilayered meanings of *Moby-Dick* (which, incidentally, Jung considered "the greatest American novel"). He finds this key in primitive mythology, specifically in the myths of Polynesia that young Melville had been exposed to during his two years of sea duty in the South Pacific (Melville's early success as a writer was largely due to his notoriety as the man who had lived for a month among the cannibals of Taipi). Melville's literary primitivism is authentic, unlike the sentimental primitivism of such writers as Rousseau, says Baird, because he had absorbed certain Oriental archetypes of "life symbols" and then transformed these creatively into "autotypes"—that is, individualized personal symbols.

The most instructive illustration of this creative fusion of archetype and autotype is Moby-Dick, Melville's infamous white whale. Baird points out that, throughout Oriental mythology, the "great fish" recurs as a symbol of divine creation and life; in Hinduism, for example, the whale is an avatar (divine incarnation) of Vishnu, "the Preserver contained in the all being of Brahma" (we might also note the designation of Christ as a "fisherman" in Christian doctrine). Furthermore, Baird explains that *whiteness* is the archetype of the all-encompassing, inscrutable deity, "the white sign of the God of all being who has borne such Oriental names as Bhagavat, Brahma—the God of endless contradiction." Melville combined these two archetypes, the great fish or whale and whiteness, in fashioning his own unique symbol (autotype), Moby-Dick. Baird's reading of this symbol is substantiated by Melville's remarks about the contrarieties of the color *white* (terror, mystery, purity) in his chapter on "The Whiteness of the Whale," as well as by the mysterious elusiveness and awesome power with which he invests Moby-Dick. Moby-Dick is therefore, in Baird's words, "a nonambiguous ambiguity." Ahab, the monster of intellect, destroys himself and his crew because he would "strike through the mask" in his insane compulsion to understand the eternal and unfathomable mystery of creation. Ishmael alone is saved because, through the wholesome influence of Queequeg, a Polynesian prince, he has acquired the primitive mode of accepting this divine mystery without question or hostility.

MYTH CRITICISM AND THE AMERICAN DREAM

In addition to anthropology and Jungian psychology, a third influence has been prominent in recent myth criticism, especially in the interpretation of American literature. This influence, deriving not only from those already mentioned but also from a new historical focus upon the informing myths of our culture, has shown itself in a growing interest in that cluster of indigenous myths called "The American Dream" and, subsequently, in an intensified effort by literary scholars to analyze those elements that constitute the peculiar "Americanness" of our literature. The results of such analysis indicate that the major works produced by American writers possess a certain uniqueness and that this uniqueness can largely be attributed to the influence, both positive and negative, of the American Dream.

The central facet of this myth-cluster is the Myth of Edenic Possibilities, which reflects the hope of creating a second Paradise, not in the next world and not outside time, but in the bright New World of the American continent. From the time of its first settlement America was seen from European eyes as a land of boundless opportunity, a place where man, after centuries of poverty, misery, and corruption, could have a second chance to fulfill, in reality, his mythic yearnings for a return to Paradise. As early as 1654 Captain Edward Johnson announced to the Old-World-weary people of England that America was The Place:

> All you the people of Christ that are here Oppressed, Imprisoned and scurrilously derided, gather yourselves together, your Wifes and little ones, and answer to your several Names as you shall be shipped for His service, in the Westerne World, and more especially for planting the united Colonies of new England. . . . Know this is the place where the Lord will create a new Heaven, and a new Earth in new Churches, and a new Commonwealth together.

Frederic I. Carpenter, in *American Literature and the Dream* (Philosophical Library, 1955), has pointed out that, although the Edenic Dream itself was "as old as the mind of man," the idea that "this is the place" was uniquely American:

> Earlier versions had placed it in Eden or in Heaven, in Atlantis or in Utopia; but always in some country of the imagination. Then the discovery of the new world gave substance to the old myth, and suggested the realization of it on actual earth. America became "the place" where the

religious prophecies of Isaiah and the Republican ideals of Plato [and even the mythic longings of primitive man, we might add] might be realized.   (p. 6)

The themes of moral regeneration and bright expectations, which derive from this Edenic myth, form a major thread in the fabric of American literature, from Crèvecoeur's *Letters from an American Farmer* through the works of Emerson, Thoreau, and Whitman to such modern writers as Hart Crane and Thomas Wolfe.

Closely related to the Myth of Edenic Possibilities is the concept of the American Adam, the mythic New World Hero. In *The American Adam* (Chicago, 1955), R. W. B. Lewis describes the type: "a radically new personality, the hero of the new adventure: an individual emancipated from history, happily bereft of ancestry, untouched and undefiled by the usual inheritances of family and race; an individual standing alone, self-reliant and self-propelling, ready to confront whatever awaited him with the aid of his own unique and inherent resources" (p. 5). One of the early literary characterizations of this Adamic hero is James Fenimore Cooper's Natty Bumppo, the central figure of the Leatherstocking Saga. With his moral purity and social innocence, Natty is an explicit version of Adam before the Fall. He is a child of the wilderness, forever in flight before the corrupting influences of civilization—and from the moral compromises of Eve (Cooper never allows his hero to marry). He is also, as we might guess, the literary great-grandfather of the Western hero: like Hopalong Cassidy and Matt Dillon, he is clean-living, straight-shooting, and celibate. (In his civilized version, the American Adam is the central figure of another corollary myth of the American Dream: the Dream of Success. The hero here is that popular figure epitomized in Horatio Alger's stories and subsequently treated in the novels of Howells, London, Dreiser and Fitzgerald: the Self-Made Man who, through luck, pluck, and all the Ben Franklin virtues, rises from rags to riches, or from log cabin to White House.)

More complex, and therefore more interesting, than this uncorrupted Adam is the American hero during and after the Fall. It is with this aspect of the Dream rather than with the adamant innocence of a Leatherstocking that our best writers have most often concerned themselves. The symbolic loss of Edenic innocence and the painful initiation into an awareness of evil constitutes a second major pattern in American literature from the works of Hawthorne and Melville through Mark Twain and Henry James to Hemingway and Faulkner. This is the darker thread in our literary fabric which, contrasting as it does with the myth of bright expectancy, lends depth and richness to the over-all design; it also reminds us of the disturbing proximity of Dream and Nightmare. From this standpoint, then, we may recall Hawthorne's Young Goodman Brown as a representative figure—the prototypal American hero haunted by that obsession with guilt and Original Sin which is a somber but essential part of America's Puritan heritage.

The English novelist D. H. Lawrence was first among the modern critics to perceive the "dark suspense" latent in the American Dream. As early as 1923 he pointed out the essential paradox of the American character in his *Studies in Classic American Literature* (Viking reissue, 1964), a book whose cantankerous brilliance has only lately come to be fully appreciated by literary scholars. "America has never been easy," he wrote, "and is not easy today. Americans have always been at a certain tension. Their liberty is a thing of sheer will, sheer tension: a liberty of THOU SHALT NOT. And it has been so from the first. The land of THOU SHALT NOT" (p. 5). Lawrence saw Americans as a people frantically determined to slough off the old skin of European tradition and evil, but constricted even more tightly by their New World heritage of Puritan conscience and inhibition. He pointed out the evidence of this "certain tension" in the writings of such classic American authors as Cooper, Poe, Hawthorne, and Melville. Though Lawrence is certainly not the only source of such insights, much of the recent myth criticism of American literature reflects some facet of his thesis.

HUCKLEBERRY FINN AS THE AMERICAN ADAM

Adventures of Huckleberry Finn is perhaps one of the half dozen most significant works in American literature. Many critics rank it among the masterpieces of world literature, and not a few consider it to be the Great American Novel. The reasons for this high esteem may be traced directly to the mythological implications of Twain's book: more than any other novel in our literature, *Huckleberry Finn* embodies myth that is both universal and national. The extent of its mythic content is such that we cannot hope to grasp it all in this chapter; we can, however, indicate a few of those elements that have helped to give the novel its enduring appeal.

First, *Huckleberry Finn* is informed by several archetypal patterns encountered throughout world literature:

1. *The Quest:* like Don Quixote, Huck is a wanderer, separated from his culture, idealistically in search of a reality more profound than that embraced by the materialistic society he has rejected.

2. *Water Symbolism:* the great Mississippi River, like the Nile and the Ganges, is invested with sacred attributes. As T. S. Eliot has written, the river is "a strong brown god"; it is an archetypal symbol of the mystery of life and creation—birth, the flowing of time into eternity, and rebirth (note, for example, Huck's several symbolic deaths, his various disguises and new identities as he returns to the shore from the river; also, the mystical lyricism with which he describes the river's majestic beauty). The river is also a kind of Paradise, the "Great Good Place" as opposed to the shore where Huck encounters hellish corruption and cruelty. It is, finally, an agent of purification and of divine justice.

3. *Shadow* and *Anima Archetypes:* pap, with his sinister repulsiveness, is a classic representation of the devil-figure. The anima-figure appears in several forms: the "Terrible Mother" (Miss Watson); the "Good Mother" (the Widow Douglas, Mrs.

Loftus, Aunt Sally Phelps; some critics have also included Nigger Jim in this category, but he is more accurately a hermaphroditic figure, embodying traits of both the archetypal Good Parents, in contrast to pap, the "Terrible Father"); the "Princess" or "Soul-Mate" (Sophia Grangerford and Mary Jane Wilks); and, with a little critical license, we might even grant Emmeline Grangerford the symbolic role of the "Dark Mother" (death).

4. *Initiation:*   Huck undergoes a series of painful experiences in passing from ignorance and innocence into spiritual maturity; he comes of age—is morally reborn—when he decides to go to hell rather than turn Jim in to the authorities.

In addition to these universal archetypes, *Huckleberry Finn* contains a mythology that is distinctively American. Huck himself is the symbolic American hero; he epitomizes conglomerate paradoxes that make up the American character. He has all the glibness and practical acuity that we admire in our businessmen and politicians; he is truly a self-made youth, free from the materialism and morality-by-formula of the Horatio Alger hero. He possesses the simple modesty, the quickness, the daring and the "guts," the stamina and the physical skill that we idolize in our athletes. He is both ingenious and ingenuous. He is mentally "sharp," but not intellectual. He also displays the ingratiating capacity for buffoonery that we so dearly love in our public entertainers. Yet, with all these extroverted virtues, Huck is also a sensitive, conscience-burdened "loner" troubled by man's inhumanity to man and by his own occasional callousness to Jim's feelings. Notwithstanding his generally realistic outlook and his practical bent, he is a moral idealist, far ahead of his age in his sense of human decency, and, at times, a mystic and a daydreamer—or, more accurately, a night-dreamer—who is uncommonly sensitive to the presence of a divine beauty in nature. He is, finally, the good Bad Boy whom Americans have always idolized in one form or another. And, though he is exposed to as much evil in human nature as young Goodman Brown had seen, Huck is saved from Brown's pessimistic gloom by his sense of humor and, what is more crucial, by his sense of humanity.

If we regard Huck as an archetypal American hero, then his story may be a parable of the nation's history. The "rite of passage" or initiation through which Huck suffers in moving toward spiritual maturity may symbolize the exciting but painful growth of a young, inexperienced, brightly hopeful nation from innocence into awareness—an awareness that, with all its promise of freedom and its Edenic possibilities, the New World was still haunted by the Old-World shadows of greed, hypocrisy, cruelty, injustice, and slavery. Despite its magnificent comedy and its vitality, *Huckleberry Finn* reflects those same nightmarish shadows that even in our own time threaten to obscure the American Dream. But, if at the core of Twain's book there is a certain dark suspense, there is also a promise of redemption. This promise glimmers in the hero's moral awakening and in his final rejection of a civilization committed to materialism, prejudice, and hypocrisy. Hopefully, if this parabolic analogy is valid, America is today in the process of rejecting those same specious values so that tomorrow we will be ready to "light out" for a new Territory where spiritual freedom can be found through moral enlightenment.

LIMITATIONS OF MYTH CRITICISM

It should be apparent from the foregoing illustrations that myth criticism offers some unusual opportunities for the enhancement of our literary appreciation and understanding. No other critical approach possesses quite the same combined breadth and depth. As we have seen, an application of myth criticism takes us far beyond the historical and aesthetic realms of literary study— back to the beginnings of mankind's oldest rituals and beliefs and deep into our own individual hearts of darkness. Considering the vastness and the complexity of mythology, a field of study whose mysteries the anthropologists and psychologists are still working to penetrate, our brief introduction can give the reader only a superficial and fragmentary overview. But we hope the interested student has received a glimpse of new vistas and that he will be encouraged to explore the dark continent of myth on his own.

We should point out some of the inherent limitations of the mythological approach. As with the psychological approach, the reader must take care that his enthusiasm for a new-found interpretive key does not tempt him to discard other valuable critical instruments or to try to open all literary doors with this single key. Just as the Freudian critic sometimes loses sight of a great work's aesthetic values in his passion for sexual symbolism, so the myth critic tends to forget that literature is more than a vehicle for archetypes and ritual patterns. In other words, he runs the risk of being distracted from the essential experience of the artifact itself; he forgets that literature is, above all else, art. As we have indicated before, the discreet critic will apply such extrinsic perspectives as the mythological and psychological only as far as they enhance the experience of the art form, and only as far as the structure and potential meaning of the work consistently support such approaches.

CHAPTER

5

The exponential approach

Regardless of which critical approach a reader may favor, he will always be concerned with the themes of a literary work and the ways in which he can follow those themes. Such thematic statements are frequently less explicit than implicit, if only because they are often made by the communicative and evocative power of symbols and images. One of the basic steps in the full appreciation of a work, then, is the recognition of such images and symbols. A related—and more important—step is to consider not only the isolated instances of these devices but more especially the artistic weaving of these instances into patterns. In this chapter we shall consider how to follow these patterns by learning to follow their exponents, that is, those people, objects, words that represent or symbolize the patterns.

These patterns are sometimes called motives or motifs; the latter spelling is preferred in this chapter to avoid confusion with motivations in characters, for there is no necessary relationship between motifs as the term is used here and motives for behavior. On the other hand, the literary use of motifs is similar to the use of subjects or themes (leitmotifs) in music. Also, what we are here calling the "exponential" approach or the tracing of motifs might be called the "symbolic" approach, and regularly in this chapter we will talk of symbols, especially when we speak of those images that are charged with meaning beyond their usual denotations. Sometimes these symbols are also archetypal images, as we have seen in the mythological approach; in this sense they are much the same as exponents of experience. However, rather than multiply terms and definitions, we shall emphasize the concept of the exponent because the term includes more than we sometimes mean by a specific image or symbol or archetype.

Whether we call this approach the exponential or the symbolic or coin a word like "motival" for it, we are doing what any close reader of literature does. We are recognizing patterns of images and symbols that lead us to a constantly deepening appreciation of the literature. Image leads to image, idea to idea, until ultimately we are led to experience the "meaning" of the work.

This pursuit of the image has provided literary scholarship with some outstanding contributions. Caroline Spurgeon, for example, catalogued Shakespeare's imagery in an effort to understand Shakespeare himself and his plays. Significantly for our present concern, her study was entitled *Shakespeare's Imagery and What It Tells Us*. Early in her book she says,

> The greater and richer the work the more valuable and suggestive become the images, so that in the case of Shakespeare I believe one can scarcely overrate the possibilities of what may be discovered through a systematic examination of them. It was my conviction of this which led me to as-

> semble and classify all his images, so as to have in orderly
> and easily accessible form the material upon which to base
> my deductions and conclusions.   (p. 5)

In this chapter we are not concerned with the biographical aspects that Miss Spurgeon sought in Shakespeare's imagery, but
we are concerned with seeing how consistent imagery can be
charged with meaning and symbolic force and hence can "tell
us" much.

Another classic of scholarship that traces motifs or patterns
of imagery is John Livingston Lowes's *The Road to Xanadu*.
Lowes found that the mind of Samuel Taylor Coleridge was a
"chaos" of stored information and images, a kind of "deep well"
within which these many details were in a constantly shifting
solution. Thus, when Coleridge thought of one "hooked atom,"
it quite likely suggested another, so that when he pulled the first
to the surface of his conscious mind it pulled a second, "hooks
and eyes" fashion. Together, the hooked atoms could be woven
into a "pattern" of intricate relationships, the "magical synthesis"
being provided by the "shaping spirit of the imagination."

Although the books of Kenneth Burke are more difficult for
the beginning student of literature, he too has shown us how to
follow patterns of imagery and symbols. (In *Counter-Statement*
[Hermes, 1953] he defines symbol as "the verbal parallel to a
pattern of experience" [p. 152].) Just as we are using the term
"exponent," he talks of "cues" and "clues" that lead us to
"clusters" of imagery and on to "symbolic meaning." As Stanley
Hyman points out, this technique is analogous to those of Miss
Spurgeon, Lowes, and Edward A. Armstrong, whose book
Shakespeare's Imagination (Drummond, 1946) extended Miss
Spurgeon's insights.

Such a tracing of thematic imagery is based on the premise
that significant literature does attempt to communicate, or at
least to embody, meaningful experience in an aesthetically ap-
pealing form. This is not to say that literature merely sugarcoats
a beneficial pill. But in the creation of any given work, a literary
artist has an idea or an actual experience or an imagined experience that he wishes to communicate. Consciously or other-

wise, he then chooses a means of embodying it. He must select, or his subconscious mind must present, specific devices, and he must arrange them so that he can embody or communicate the experience. Once the author has done this, we must recreate the experience, in part by carefully tracing the motifs used to communicate it. Bit by bit, as we notice instances of a motif, we work our way into the experience of the story, poem, or play. As we follow the hints of thematic statement, or recognize similar but new images, or identify related symbols, we gradually come to live the author's original experience. The evocative power of steadily repeated images and symbols makes the experience a part of our own consciousness and sensibility. Thus the image satisfies our senses, the pattern our instinctive desire for order, and the thematic statement our intellect and our moral sensibility.

This joy of fulfillment, almost of discovery, is at the heart of much artistic response. For example, in the fourteenth chapter of *Biographia Literaria,* Coleridge wrote of "the power of exciting the sympathy of the reader by a faithful adherence to the truth of nature, and the power of giving the interest of novelty by the modifying colors of imagination." Here Coleridge suggests the double principle of recognition and surprise, a principle often evident, for example, in his *Rime of the Ancient Mariner.* Extending this double principle to the study of motifs, we see that the recurrence of thematic statement, image, or symbol comes to be a pleasure whenever we find a new instance of a motif. Conversely, when we recognize the motif in a *different* manifestation, our pleasurable recognition is augmented by the pleasurable perception of difference. Nor is this all, for the perception of sameness and of difference is more than mere pleasurable stimulus, a play of the mind. It opens out to the richness and truth of a given experience by gradually revealing its essence to the reader. Coleridge himself, while stressing that the immediate purpose of poetry was pleasure, also said that its ultimate purpose was truth. Furthermore, the perception of sameness within difference is typical of the functioning of the mature mind, a mind capable of appreciating the complexities of reality.

The possibilities for varied appeals to the mind and to the

heart are limitless. In the first place, imagery itself can be as varied as the human senses—not just the appeals to the classic five, but to others and to variations and refinements of them. Miss Spurgeon, for example, would include as an image "any and every imaginative picture or other experience, drawn in every kind of way, which may have come to the poet, not only through any of his senses, but through his mind and emotions as well, and which he uses, in the forms of simile and metaphor in their widest sense, for purposes of analogy." Conventional enough are the consistent appeals to a dominant image, such as sound in Poe's "Bells," or sight, especially colors, in Poe's "Masque of the Red Death." Less conventional is Keats's "Eve of St. Agnes," which, for example, has not only classic appeals to the visual imagination but some effective thermal and gustatory images; he opposes heat and cold in "Full on this casement shone the wintry moon, / And threw warm gules on Madeline's fair breast," and he stresses taste when he describes

> . . . a heap
> Of candied apple, quince, and plum, and gourd;
> With jellies soother than the creamy curd,
> And lucent syrups, tinct with cinnamon.

Hemingway's "The Short, Happy Life of Francis Macomber" has a striking appeal to the kinesthetic sense when the speeding hunters pursue the buffalo. A notable use of the kinesthetic in the metrics of poetry is the sound of horses' hooves in Browning's "How They Brought the Good News from Ghent to Aix":

> I sprang to the stirrup, and Joris, and he;
> I galloped, Dirck galloped, we galloped all three.

Besides varying the sensuous appeals within a motif, the author can vary whole patterns. He can make one image pattern interact with another. He can let them run parallel, or on intersecting lines. He can complement or contrast one with another. He can intrigue, stimulate, or even startle us. In turn, we can discover one, only to be led gradually into another. We can see first the cracked exterior of Roderick Usher's home, and later watch the man's very mind cracking, and we can read with deeper understanding "The Haunted Palace" within the story. We can follow the brute animal imagery of "The Death of the Ball-Turret Gunner" and then realize that the same images also are images of maternal and familial love. We can follow thirteen lines of Sidney's "Come Sleep! O Sleep," only to find in the fourteenth that we have read a love sonnet, not a poem on sleep. We can sense the thermal images in "The Eve of St. Agnes" and then realize that we are reading, in part, about warm life and cold death. Regularly we can see that what we are discovering in the image pattern is the repeated but contrasting use of the same ideo-feeling.

Two of Shakespeare's sonnets are especially illustrative of these points. "That Time of Year" (Sonnet 73) employs three specific patterns in three successive quatrains. The first takes as its core the nearly bare tree in autumn, the second the nearly set sun as night approaches, the third the almost extinguished fire. Thus there are three separate images, or sets of images; but obviously they all share the quality of "almost," and not so obviously they are variations on the themes of heat and cold, death and decay. Each quatrain, though different from the other two, intensifies the other two by its similarities. Even more varied in its sameness is Shakespeare's "Like as the waves make towards the pebbled shore" (Sonnet 60). Again the three quatrains share a common theme—the effect of time—but the subject matter of each is at first glance unrelated to that of the other two. The first quatrain takes its pictures from the seashore, where each wave contends with the next in making its way towards the pebbled shore. The second uses more than imagery: it is also a synopsis of a person's growth, for "Nativity . . . / Crawls to maturity," only to be eclipsed when time later takes away what once it gave. The third quatrain takes its imagery from vegetation and farming ("flourish," "delves the parallels," "feeds on the rarities," "stands," "scythe," and "mow"). Seashore, growth, farming: three seemingly unrelated patterns, but all united in the central theme of time and its effects.

Variations within a pattern need not be limited to imagery,

as we have already seen in the growth synopsis of Shakespeare's sonnet. Thus the central theme of honor in *Henry IV, Part One,* is evident in explicit statements by a melodramatic Hotspur (I, iii; V, iv) and by a no-nonsense, pragmatic Falstaff (V, i; V, iii); in the regal demeanor and haughty tone of King Henry; and "the grinning honor [which] Sir Walter hath" as he lies dead. Some of this is imagistic (the dead Blunt, Hotspur's metaphorical language), but some of it is statement (as in III, ii). In addition, the theme of the play—the conflict between the wronged honor of one family and the wronged honor of another—is so pervasive that it is difficult to say where the motif does *not* appear. In *Moby-Dick* the mysteries of the universe are suggested repeatedly by the passages on the white whale himself, sometimes at length as in the chapter on the whiteness of the whale. But to these we must add the sea as an "image of the ungraspable phantom of life" (chapter 1); the puzzling painting of a ship in a storm (chapter 3); the several allusions to destiny or necessity, chance, and free will; the spirit spout (chapter 51); and the "monstrous" pictures of whales (chapter 55). There are many passages on mysteries and riddles, such as that about the mast-stander who is so lulled "by the blending cadence of waves with thoughts, that at last he loses his identity; takes the mystic ocean at his feet for the visible image of that deep, blue, bottomless soul, pervading mankind and nature . . ." (chapter 35).

In *The Return of the Native,* accidental occurrences follow so quickly upon one another that the theme of chance is developed largely from incidents in the plot sequence: an error in a marriage license; the timing of the return of the native; the coincidence as Mrs. Yeobright approaches her son's cottage, and Eustacia's failure to open for her; the snakebite; the consequent yet chance revelations of the circumstances of her death; the deaths of Eustacia and Damon. Thus motifs are not just matters of diversified image; they can be diverse actions or episodes, different personalities, or mixtures of pictures, meditations, and symbols. But always the disparate items blend; they fuse or synthesize. And our realization of the synthesis becomes the joy of discovering what we already have dimly perceived. We are stimulated, in Coleridge's phrase, to see a "unity, that blends, and (as it were) *fuses*, each into each, by that synthetic and magical power, to which we have exclusively appropriated the name of imagination."

Such, then, are the principles of the exponential approach and some of the critical, scholarly, and psychological background of this basic tool of the close reader. With these principles in mind, we may now look more closely at several literary works to see how the principles can be used to gain specific insights.

EXPONENTS IN "TO HIS COY MISTRESS": A SEMANTIC-PHILOSOPHIC USE

"Had we but world enough, and time" introduces the central motif of the poem: the space-time continuum. Rich in imagery, the motif is much more, for the structure of the poem depends on the subjunctive concept, the condition contrary to fact, which gives the whole poem its meaning. "Had we," the speaker says, knowing that they do not. From that point on, the hyperbole, the playfulness, the grim fear of annihilation are all based on the feeling of the speaker that he *is* bound by the dimensions of space and time. Clearly, this poem is a proposition made by the eternal male to the eternal female; just as clearly, and in a wholly different realm, the motif of space and time shows this poem to be a philosophical consideration of time, of eternity; of man's present pleasure (hedonism) and of salvation in an afterlife (traditional Christianity). In this way, Marvell includes in one short poem the range between man's lust and man's philosophy.

On the other hand, we find that the words used to suggest this range tend to be suggestive, to shift their meanings in such fashion as to demand that they be read at different levels at the same time. Let us begin with those exponents that represent the space motif. We have already seen how motifs can shift from one type of manifestation to another; in the same fashion, the space motif of the present poem appears not just in obvious but in veiled allusions. Instances of the space motif in the first section of the poem include "world," "sit down," "which way / To walk," the suggested distance between "Indian Ganges" and the Humber, the distance implicit in the allusions to the Flood and to the widespread Jews of the Diaspora, "vaster than empires," the sense of spatial movement as the speaker's eyes move over the girl's body, and the hint of spatial relationship in "lower rate." The word "long" (line 4) refers to time, but has spatial meaning too; several other words ("before," "till," "go," "last") also have overlapping qualities, but perhaps we strain too far to consider them.

Space and time are clearly related in the magnificent image of the opening lines of the second stanza: "But at my back I always hear / Time's wingèd chariot hurrying near." The next couplet provides "yonder," "before," "deserts," and, again, a phrase that combines both space and time: "vast eternity." In the third stanza the word "sits" echoes the earlier use of the word, and several words suggest movement or action in space: "transpires," "sport," "birds of prey," "devour," "languish in slow-chapped power," "roll," "tear . . . / Thorough." The space motif climaxes in an image that again incorporates the time motif, since the sun, by which man measures time, will not stand still in space but will be forced to run.

The time motif also appears in its own right, and not only by means of imagery. The word itself appears once in each stanza: near the beginning of stanzas one and two (lines 1, 22), and in the third as a central part of the lover's proposition (39). Clustering around this basic exponent are these phrases and allusions from the first stanza: the "long love's day" already mentioned, the specific time spans spent in adoring the girl's body and the vaster if less specific "before the Flood" and "Till the conversion of the Jews," the slow growth of "vegetable love" (one is reminded of the long-lived cedars of Lebanon), and the two uses of "age" (lines 17, 18). At the beginning of the second stanza the powerful image of Time's winged chariot as it moves across a desert includes the words "always" and "eternity." Other time words are "no more" and "long-preserved." There is also the sense of elapsed time in the allusions to the future decomposition of the lovers' bodies. The third stanza, although it delays the use of the word "time," has for its first syllable the forceful, imperative "now." The word appears twice more in the stanza (lines 37, 38). It is strengthened by "instant," "at once," and "languish in [Time's] slow-chapped power." The phrase "thorough the iron gates of life," though it has more important meanings, also may suggest the passing from temporal life into the not so certain eternity mentioned earlier. The concluding couplet of the poem, as already shown, combines space and time. Further, it may extend time backwards to suggest Old Testament days and classic mythology: Joshua stopped the sun so that the Israelites could win a battle, and, even more pertinently, Zeus lengthened the night he spent with Amphitryon's wife.

For the poem is also a love poem, both in its traditional context of the courtly love complaint and in the simple fact of its subject matter: fearing that the after-life may be a vast space without time, the speaker looks for a means of enjoying whatever he can. This *carpe diem* theme is not uncommon, nor is the theme of seduction. What gives the poem unusual power, however, is the overbearing sense of a cold, calculated drive to use the pleasures of sex to counterbalance the threats of empty eternity. Thus a second major motif used to present the theme, after the space-time relationship, is the sexual. Now let us see what exponents help us to follow this theme.

The title itself immediately sets up the situation. In the second line, the word "coyness" leads us into the poem itself; even the word "crime" suggests the unconventional (though crime and conventional morality are reversed in the context of the lover's address). The motif gradually emerges, romantically at first, but more frankly, even brutally, as the speaker continues. In the first stanza, the distant Ganges and the redness of rubies are romantic enough; the word "complain," in the sense of the courtly lover's song, echoes the whole courtly tradition. The word "love" appears twice before the courtly catalogue of the lady's beautiful body. The catalogue in turn builds to a climax with the increasing time spans and the veiled suggestiveness of "rest" and "part."

The second stanza, though it continues to be somewhat veiled, is less romantic, and it becomes gruesome even while insisting upon sexual love. The lady's beauty will disappear in the marble vault, we are told, and we may associate the word "marble" with the marbled texture and loveliness of the living girl's skin. Now, however, the lover stresses the time when that loveliness will be transferred to stone. In the same type of transference, the lover's song, which finds no echoes in that vault, is a veiled image of unrealized sexual union in life. Worms will corrupt the girl in a way that the lover could not. "Quaint honor" probably is an ironic play on words to suggest the pudendum. The fires of lust will become ashes (with an implicit comparison to the coldness of marble), and the stanza closes with puns on "private" and "embrace."

The third stanza resumes the romantic imagery of the first ("youthful hue," "morning dew"), but it continues the bolder imagery of the second section. "Pore" is a somewhat unromantic allusion to the girl's body, and "instant fires" reminds of the lust and ashes of the preceding stanza. "Sport" takes still a different tack, though it reminds us of the playfulness of the first stanza. After this line, the grimness of the second stanza is even more in evidence. The amorous birds are not turtledoves, but birds of prey, devouring time—and each other. Although the romantic and the brutal combine in the speaker's suggestion that they "roll all our strength and all / Our sweetness up into one ball," the emphasis on the rough and violent continues in the paradoxical "tear our pleasures with rough strife." Once the coy lady's virginity is torn away, the lover will have passed not through the pearly gates of eternity, but through the iron gates of life. Thus the lover's affirmation of life, compounded of despair and defiance, is made by his suggestion that the birth canal of life and procreation is preferable to the empty vault and to the deserts of vast eternity. On the one hand, the exponents of the sexual motif point to a degeneration from romantic convention in the first section to scarcely veiled explicitness in the last. But on the other hand, the speaker has proceeded from a question about the nature of eternity and the meaning of the space-time relationship in this world to an affirmation of what he suspects is the only reality left him. The very concreteness, the physicality of the sexual motif, provides an answer to the philosophic speculation about space, time, and eternity. Obviously different, the motifs just as obviously fuse to embody the theme of the poem.

There are other, lesser motifs that we could trace if space permitted, such as wings and birds, roundness, and minerals and other things of earth (rubies, marble, iron, ashes, and dust). Each of these serves as an exponent for greater insights into the poem.

A completely different type of motif, much less dependent on specific imagery, is the interplay of sardonic humor and hyperbole on the one hand, with the brutal and gruesome on the other. Much of this has already been suggested insofar as these contrasting tones relate to the romantic love-sexual love contrast. The present point is that tones as such can also run through a literary work. Here the pleasant exaggerations of the first section are answered in ironic echo by the sardonic understatement of "The grave's a fine and private place, / But none, I think, do there embrace." Both tones contrast the matter-of-fact tones of the second and third stanzas. The apparently factual last couplet of the first stanza is actually the most hyperbolical of all. Also, the apparent flatness of the final couplet of the poem masks a boldly impossible statement at the literal level (though it is metaphorically possible). Even the verbs of the poem can serve as exponents for this interplay. The subjunctive nature of the first stanza is evident in "had we," "were," "shouldst," the four uses of "would," and the four uses of "should"—a total of eleven times in twenty lines. This mood changes to the simple expectancy of the indicatives in the second stanza. In turn, these two stanzas lead into the imperatives of the third, where the two uses of "let us" are the key verbs of that section, excepting only the matter-of-fact indicative of the final couplet. Thus, tone, as well as images and symbols, functions as a motif in literature and can manifest itself even in the grammar of verbs.

EXPONENTS IN "YOUNG GOODMAN BROWN": A THEOLOGICAL USE

Perhaps the most obviously recurrent symbol in "Young Goodman Brown" is the pink ribbons worn by Goodman Brown's wife, Faith. They are mentioned three times in the first page or so of the story. Near the center of the story, a pink ribbon falls, or seems to fall, from a cloud that Goodman Brown sees, or thinks he sees, overhead. At the end of the story, when Faith eagerly greets her returning husband, she still wears her ribbons. Clearly Hawthorne meant them to be suggestive, an exponent of one or of several of the themes of his tale. But of what? Are they emblematic of love, of innocence, of good? Conversely, do they suggest evil or hypocrisy or the ambiguous and puzzling blend of good and evil? Are they symbolic of sex and femininity or of Christian faith? Should we even attempt to limit the meaning to one possibility? Would we be wise—or slovenly—to let the ribbons mean more than one thing during the story? Of one thing we can be sure: to follow the motif as it guides us to related symbols is to probe the complex interweaving of ideas within the story. Specifically, we shall see that the mystery of the pink ribbons is—at least among other things—an exponent of the mysteries of theology.

Since the Puritan setting of "Young Goodman Brown" is basic to the story, we can expect that some of its thematic patterns derive from traditional Christian concepts. For example, readers generally assume that Goodman Brown loses his faith, either in Christ or in human beings, or in both. Thomas E. Connolly (*American Literature*, XXVIII, 370–375) has argued, on the other hand, that the story is an attack on Calvinism, and that Faith (that is, faith) is not lost in the story; on the contrary, he says, Goodman Brown is confirmed in his faith, made aware of "its full and terrible significance." Either way—loss of faith or still firmer belief—we see the story in a theological context.

While we do not have to accept either of these views, we do not have to deny them either. Instead, let us accept this theological context. As a matter of fact, let us extend this theological view by following the exponents of faith, hope, and charity (love), and their opposed vices. We shall find them in a two-fold context: first, Christian revelation and tradition; and, second, a demonic liturgy raised up as a defiant travesty of traditional Christianity.

We can assume that Hawthorne was familiar with some of the numerous passages from the Bible that bear upon the present interpretation. Twice in the first epistle to the Thessalonians, St. Paul mentions the need for faith, hope, and charity (1:3 and 5:8). In I Corinthians 13, after extolling charity as the most abiding of the virtues, Paul concludes his eloquent description with this statement: "So there abide faith, hope and charity, these three; but the greatest of these is charity." St. Peter wrote in his first epistle, "But above all things have a constant mutual charity among yourselves; for charity covers a multitude of sins" (4:8). To these may be added the telling passages on love of God and love of neighbor (Matthew 22:36–40, Romans 13:9–10) and related passages on charity (such as Colossians 3:14 and I Timothy 1:5). Faith, hope, and charity, we should note, have traditionally been called the theological virtues because they have God (*theos*) for their immediate object.

Quite possibly Hawthorne had some of these passages in mind, for it appears that he wove into the cloth of "Young Goodman Brown" a pattern of steady attention to these virtues. Surely he provided a clue for us when he chose a name for Goodman Brown's wife. By naming her Faith, he gave faith first place in the story, not necessarily because faith is the story's dominant theme (contrary to what many critics believe, love may well be the dominant theme), but because faith is traditionally listed as the first of these three virtues. Thus, allusions to faith could be made explicit in so many passages in the story and implicit in so many others that they would provide an exponent to suggest clearly the other two virtues. Further, Faith's name is appropriate enough in a Puritan setting (as is Goodman's, which may be read as a proper name as well as an epithet) ; as a symbol her name would not be farfetched and would permit many passages to grow directly from it.

An analysis of these passages, for example, shows not only explicit mentions of faith but also implicit allusions to faith (and doubt), to hope (despair), and to love (hate). The first scene includes these: "And Faith, as the wife was aptly named . . ."; "My love and my Faith"; ". . . dost thou doubt me already . . . ?"; ". . . he looked back and saw the head of Faith still peeping after him with a melancholy air . . ."; "Poor little Faith!"; and ". . . I'll cling to her skirts and follow her to heaven." Both Goodman Brown and the man he meets in the forest make similar allusions in the second scene, where we read: "Faith kept me back a while"; "We have been a race of honest men and good Christians"; "We are a people of prayer, and good works to boot . . ." (a hint of the theological debate on faith and good works); "Well, then, to end the matter at once, there is my wife, Faith"; "that Faith should come to any harm"; and ". . . why I should quit my dear Faith and go after [Goody Cloyse]." In the episode after the older man leaves Goodman Brown, we have these passages: "so purely and sweetly now, in the arms of Faith!"; "He looked up to the sky, doubting whether there really was a heaven above him"; "With heaven above and Faith below, I will yet stand firm against the devil!"; "a cloud," "confused and doubtful sound of voices," "he doubted"; " 'Faith!' shouted Goodman Brown, in a voice of agony and desperation"; and "My Faith is gone! . . . Come, devil . . . And, maddened with despair. . . ." The last scenes, the forest conclave and young Goodman Brown's return home, offer these: " 'But where is Faith?' thought Goodman Brown; and, as hope came . . ."; "the wretched man beheld his Faith . . . before that unhallowed altar"; " 'Faith! Faith!' cried the husband, 'look up to heaven . . .' "; "the head of Faith . . . gazing anxiously"; "a distrustful, if not a desperate man"; ". . . he shrank from the bosom of Faith . . . and turned away"; and "no hopeful verse . . . , for his dying hour was gloom."

With these passages in mind, let us pause to recall that there

may be both symbolical and allegorical uses of the word "faith."
Such an ambivalent use can complicate a reading of the story. If
the tale is allegorical, for example, it may be that Goodman
gained his faith—that is, the belief that he is one of the elect—
only three months before the action of the story, since he and
Faith have been married three months. The fall of the pink
ribbon may be a sin or a fall, just as Adam's fall was the original
sin, a lapse from grace. The allegory may further suggest that
Goodman shortly loses his new faith, for "he shrank from the
bosom of Faith." But allegory is difficult to maintain, often requiring a rigid one-to-one equivalence between the surface meaning and a "higher" meaning. Thus, if Faith is faith, and Goodman loses the latter, how do we explain the fact that Faith remains with him and even outlives him? Strict allegory would
require that she disappear, perhaps vanish in that dark cloud
which the story associates with her. On the other hand, a pattern
of symbolism centering around Faith is easier to handle, and may
even be more rewarding by offering us more pervasive, more
subtly interweaving ideas which, through their very ambiguity,
suggest the difficulties of the theological questions in the story.
Such a symbolic view also frees the story from a strict adherence
to the Calvinistic concept of election and conviction in the faith,
so that the story becomes more universally concerned with
Goodman as Everyman.

Whether we emphasize symbol or allegory, however, Goodman must remain a character in his own right, one who pro-
gressively loses faith in his ultimate salvation, in his forebears
as members of the elect or at least as "good" people, and in his
wife and fellow townspeople as holy Christians. At a literal level,
he does not lose Faith, for she greets him when he returns from
the forest, she still wears her pink ribbons, she follows his corpse
to the grave; furthermore, she keeps her pledge to Goodman,
for it is *he* who shrinks from her. In other words, Goodman has
not completely lost Faith; rather he has lost faith, a theological
key to heaven.

But even when faith is lost, not all is lost, though it may
very nearly be. That total loss comes later and gradually as

Goodman commits other sins. We can follow this emerging pattern when we recall that the loss of faith is closely allied to the loss of hope; we find that in the story despair, the vice opposed to hope, can be easily associated with doubt, the vice opposed to faith. For example, the two vices are nearly allied when Goodman recognizes the pink ribbon: " 'My Faith is gone!' cried he, after one stupefied moment. 'There is no good on earth; and sin is but a name. Come, devil; for to thee is this world given.' And, maddened with despair, so that he laughed loud and long, did Goodman Brown grasp his staff and set forth again. . . ."

Doubt, while surely opposed to belief, here leads to despair as much as to infidelity. Many of the passages that point to faith thus also point to hope. When Goodman says, "I'll follow her to heaven," he expresses hope as well as belief. When he says, "With heaven above and Faith below," he hopes to "stand firm against the devil." When he cries, "Faith, look up to heaven," he utters what may be his last hope for salvation. Once again we see how motifs function: it is easy to touch the web at any one point and make it vibrate elsewhere.

Thus we must emphasize that Goodman's hope is eroded by increasing doubt; we recall that the passages already quoted include the words "desperate," "despair," and "no hopeful verse." When Goodman reenters the town, he has gone far toward a complete failure to trust in God. His thoughts and his actions when he sees the child talking to Goody Cloyse border on the desperate, both in the sense of despair and in the sense of frenzy. Later, we know that he has fully despaired, for his dying hour is gloom.

"But the greatest of these is charity," and "charity covers a multitude of sins," the Scriptures insist. Goodman sins against this virtue too, and as we follow these exponents we may well conclude that Hawthorne considered this sin the greatest sin in Goodman's life. Sins against love of neighbor are important in other Hawthorne stories. It is a sin against charity that Ethan Brand and Roger Chillingworth commit. It is a sin against charity that Rappaccini's daughter accuses Guasconti of: "Farewell, Giovanni! Thy words of hatred are like lead within my heart; but they, too, will fall away as I ascend. Oh, was there not, from the first, more poison in thy nature than in mine?" In *The House of the Seven Gables,* it is love that finally overcomes the hate-engendered curse of seven generations.

In "Young Goodman Brown," perhaps the motif is first suggested in the opening scene, when Goodman refuses his wife's request that he remain: "My love and my Faith," replied young Goodman Brown, "of all nights in the year, this one night must I tarry away from thee. . . . What, my sweet, pretty wife, dost thou doubt me already, and we but three months married?" Significantly, the words "love" and "Faith" are used almost as synonyms, and the pink ribbons are mentioned in the next sentence. Later, Goodman's love of others is diminished when he learns that he is of a family that has hated enough to lash "the Quaker woman so smartly through the streets of Salem" and "to set fire to an Indian village." Instead of being concerned for his own neighbor, he turns against Goody Cloyse, resigning her to the powers of darkness: "What if a wretched old woman do choose to go to the devil . . . ?" He turns against Faith and against God Himself when, after the pink ribbon has fallen from the cloud, he says, "Come, devil; for to thee is this world given." To be sure, he still loves Faith enough at the forest conclave to call upon her yet to look to heaven; but next morning when she almost kisses her husband in front of the whole village, "Good-man Brown looked sternly and sadly into her face, and passed on without a greeting." By this time he is becoming guilty of the specific sin called rash judgment. Rashly does he make successive judgments on his neighbors: he shrinks from the blessing of "the good old minister," he disparages the prayers of old Deacon Gookin, he snatches a child away from the catechizing of "Goody Cloyse, that excellent old Christian." Stubbornly does he thenceforth isolate himself from his fellow men and from his own wife: on the Sabbath day he questions their hymns and their sermons, at midnight he shrinks from his wife, at morning or eventide he scowls at family prayers. Having given his allegiance to the devil, he cannot fulfill the injunction of the second great commandment any more than he can fulfill that of the first. Unable to love himself, he is unable to love his neighbor.

"Faith, hope, and charity: these three" he has lost, replacing them with their opposed vices, and Hawthorne has provided us with exponents for them all. Now we can explore further, for the two counterrunning patterns exist in a context of additional motifs—the symbolic patterns associated with the Garden of Eden and with the Mass, communion, and baptism. Thus, apart from the motif of virtues and their opposing vices, we have motifs both from Old Testament tradition and from New Testament liturgy. Let us look first at the echoes of the Old Testament. The forest into which Goodman ventures, dark and forbidding as it is, equates generally with temptation and sin. Clearly Goodman is uneasy about venturing upon this temptation, about leaving Faith behind him. But as any sinner might think, he seems to say, "Just this once, and then. . . ." Specifically, however, the forest equates with the Garden of Eden, where grew the Tree of Knowledge of Good and Evil. Thus it is not surprising that Goodman meets there the Puritan dark man, just as Eve had done long before. To be sure, this time the man is "in grave and decent attire" and he has "an indescribable air of one who knew the world and who would not have felt abashed at the governor's table or in King William's court. . . ." But in the story he is soon identified with specific evil actions in the past, and when Goody Cloyse meets him, she screams, "The devil!" Though he appears as a man this time, not as the serpent of Genesis, he carries a staff that writhes like a snake; and we recall not only the snake of the Garden of Eden, but Aaron's staff which, when thrown down before Pharaoh, turned into a snake (Exodus 7:9–12). Should we miss the motif in its early instance, Hawthorne soon draws the explicit comparison of the staff to "the rods which its owner had formerly lent to the Egyptian Magi." When Goodman approaches the central temptation in the forest congregation of devotees, he, like Adam, is initiated into the knowledge of his race; at the same time, we may recall a maxim in *The New England Primer*: "In Adam's fall, we sinned all."

Still following these echoes of the Old Testament story, we can now associate the Calvinist setting of early New England. Hawthorne and Goodman Brown, we must note here, are not necessarily thinking in identical ways. Instead, Hawthorne permits Goodman's speeches and those of the dark man to carry forward the theological implications of man's depraved nature. It is Goodman Brown who sees evil in all he sees, including himself and Faith. As he and Faith, like Adam and Eve before them, stand at the place of temptation (where not two but four trees mark the place of sin), it is the dark man who insists upon their identity with their race, upon their knowledge of evil:

> Welcome, my children, to the communion of your race. Ye have found thus young your nature and your destiny.
>
> . . .
>
> Yet here are they all in my worshipping assembly.
>
> . . .
>
> By the sympathy of your human hearts for sin . . .
>
> . . .
>
> It shall be yours to penetrate, in every bosom, the deep mystery of sin . . .
>
> . . .
>
> Evil is the nature of mankind. Evil must be your only happiness. Welcome again, my children, to the communion of your race.

Thus, when Goodman calls upon Faith to look up to Heaven, he cannot forget that the pink ribbon has already fallen from heaven. For the Calvinist Goodman, original sin is a reality; his cry to Faith is quite literally postlapsarian, and the fall cannot be wished away.

But whether Hawthorne or his reader is Calvinist or not, whether the fall is dream or not, the damage is done to Goodman. On this Hawthorne and the reader can agree, for faith, hope, and love come near to vanishing along with the forest conclave when it dissolves into ambiguous shadow. In this way, Hawthorne need not commit himself to Calvinism or, conversely, to an attack upon it. As with the dream, "be it so if you will." The effect on Goodman remains: whether because of his own fault or because of the depraved nature that is a consequence of Adam's fall, Goodman has lost faith, and hope, and charity; he has lost them in a context derived from the Old Testament story of original sin.

The perversion of these three virtues, especially the travesty of the cardinal injunction to love God and neighbor, has a counterpart in still another pattern of images and symbols. If we perceive the exponents of the story of Genesis—garden, trees, devil, snake and staff—we must be aware too of New Testament motifs, based in part on the same objective items. For example, the forest ritual is a perversion of the Mass; instead of being a demonstration of God's love for man, it is the devil's mass or the witches' Sabbath described by Cotton Mather in his "Hortatory and Necessary Address," a section of his *Wonders of the Invisible World:* "These Witches . . . have met in Hellish Rendezvouzes, wherein the Confessors do say, they have had their diabolical Sacraments, imitating the *Baptism* and the *Supper* of our Lord." Just as the orthodox Mass is a ritual involving congregation and priest, the forest conclave has a congregation presided over by a kind of minister. "Converts" or "proselytes" await admission to the group. Before the group rises "a rock, bearing some rude, natural resemblance either to an altar or a pulpit, and surrounded by four blazing pines, their tops aflame, their stems untouched, like candles. . . ." In the rock is something akin to a baptismal font, "A basin . . . hollowed, naturally, in the rock." It may contain water, "reddened by the lurid light," or liquid flame, "or was it blood?" If it is the latter, it incorporates not only baptismal imagery but also hints of the Holy Grail, the vessel which, according to widespread legend, contained the blood of Christ at the Last Supper and after his sacrificial crucifixion. There are several allusions to communion, once during the forest walk, when the dark man says that he has drunk the communion wine with many deacons, and twice in his address to the conclave. During that conclave both the idea and the word are stressed. Although the vision vanishes before Goodman and Faith partake of the sacramental sign of baptism, which through the hint of blood is both baptism and communion, the "sable form" twice urges upon them "the communion of your race" and develops the concept of their bond, their "sympathy" (thus, communion) with other evil persons. Finally, if Goodman is the equivalent of the Old Testament Adam, he is the ironic contrast to the New Testament Adam, a travesty of the loving Christ, whose sacrificial blood—if it is in the font—is there only for desecration at a devil's mass.

In orthodox Christianity, the principles of theology are presented both explicitly and implicitly in the Scriptures; in turn, Christian liturgy is derived from those Scriptures. In "Young Goodman Brown" the motifs of faith, hope, and charity blend each into each in a context which derives from both the Old and New Testaments, and which is informed by a parody of Christian liturgy. If the blend sometimes confuses us, like the alternating light and dark of the forest conclave, and more particularly like the mystery of the pink ribbons, it is perhaps no less than Hawthorne intended when he used motifs to suggest Goodman's knowledge of good and evil, a knowledge that rapidly becomes confusion. For Goodman Brown, it is a knowledge by which he seems to turn the very names of Goodman, Goody, and Gookin into variant spellings of "evil," just as he transmutes faith, hope, and charity into their opposed vices.

EXPONENTS IN *ADVENTURES OF HUCKLEBERRY FINN:* A SOCIO-POLITICAL USE

As we turn our attention to the novel, we find that the use of motifs is not different from the use made in the genres we have already considered. But there is an amplitude in the novel that goes beyond that of the poem and the short story. Hence the novel may more easily develop or suggest many things at many levels. *Adventures of Huckleberry Finn* unquestionably does so. What we can observe in this chapter is how one pattern can suggest a means of entry into the rich stores of the novel; we do not exhaust the book.

As a matter of fact, the motifs that run through *Huckle-*

berry Finn are so numerous and so diverse that only recently (some would say since 1948) have critics begun to probe the depths of the book, showing in study after study how the threads of many themes run through the novel. Among these themes are the questions of religion, of conscience, and of good and evil; the nature of aristocracy, of kingship; the criticism of slavery, of caste, of "civilization"; Huck's maturation and his initiation into adult life; the search for a father; the prevalence of cruelty and violence; escape, the death wish, and the womb image; humor, in an abundance of forms; and the river, as a god and as a means of rebirth.

But this fullness need not frighten the reader from tracing these themes for himself, for each of them has its exponents. Each provides clues that enable the reader to delve deeper and deeper into a given theme and to see the relationship between one theme and another. No matter how widely any one of these themes may range, it is an idea that must be founded on the facts of what Twain wrote, on the words that present this idea. For example, one of the most encompassing ideas in the novel is that of civilization. Thus, it is not only interesting but important for the full appreciation of the book that we note Huck's attitude toward civilization. In chapter 1 he says, "The Widow Douglas she took me for her son, and allowed she would civilize me . . ."; with this we may compare the last two sentences of the novel: "But I reckon I got to light out for the territory ahead of the rest, because Aunt Sally she's going to adopt me and civilize me, and I can't stand it. I been there before." Huck also says in the sixth chapter: "This [possible return to the Widow] shook me up considerable, because I didn't want to go back to the widow's any more and be so cramped up and civilized, as they called it." Of course the questions of what civilization is and who is civilized appear in many forms throughout the novel. The point here is that at beginning and end Twain uses the very word to remind us of the idea; he uses an exponent to represent the pattern.

Keeping in mind this emphasis on specific words on one side and wide dimensions on the other, let us now look at just one aspect of civilization, the novel's direct references to kings and related matters. On the one side, we find that the words "king," "duke," "dauphin," and "royalty" and the names of kings occur so often that they etch themselves into our minds. On the other side, these words and allusions are exponents for the entire complex of aristocracy, feudal lordship, serfdom, and slavery. From this complex we may easily move still deeper into an appreciation of Twain's sociological criticism, his views on political and religious tyranny, and his attack on the romanticism that causes Americans to this day to respond to the trappings associated with royalty—ranging from the New Orleans Mardi Gras to national beauty queens and some television programs. The sociological and political pattern—so large in itself—is closely entwined, then, with the equally large theme of romanticism. But by restricting ourselves to the motif of kingship we can deal specifically with one approach to a theme about which full-length books and numerous articles have been written. Let us see now how such a study might begin.

With the exception of Tom's passing reference to an "emperor's daughter" near the end of chapter 3, the first mention of kings is in chapter 14, "Was Solomon Wise?" Significantly for Twain's treatment of monarchy, the common-sense answer that Jim offers is that Solomon's proverbial wisdom amounted only to "de dad-fetchedes' ways I ever see." After Jim fairly well establishes the foolishness of Solomon, Huck goes on to talk about other kings:

> So I went to talking about other kings, and let Solomon slide. I told about Louis Sixteenth that got his head cut off in France long time ago; and about his little boy the dolphin, that would 'a' been a king, but they took and shut him up in jail, and some say he died there.
>
> "Po' little chap."
>
> "But some says he got out and got away, and come to America."
>
> "Dat's good! But he'll be pooty lonesome—dey ain' no kings here, is dey, Huck?"
>
> "No."
>
> "Den he cain't git no situation. What he gwyne to do?"

The chapter containing this passage is not the only one that alludes to kings in its title. Others are "The Duke and the Dauphin Come Aboard," "What Royalty Did to Parkville," "The Orneriness of Kings," "The King Turns Parson," "I Steal the King's Plunder," and "The Pitiful Ending of Royalty." In short, seven of the forty-three chapter titles allude to royalty in an American frontier setting—incongruous in one way, but consistent with the folly of Solomon's "wisdom."

These last six chapter titles result from Huck's having aided two renegades, the younger of whom soon announces, "By rights, I am a duke!" Of course it is not long before the older one counters with a claim to be "the late Dauphin," the very person about whom Huck has told Jim. From this time forth, references to "the duke" and "the king" and epithets like "Your Grace" and "Your Majesty" sprinkle the pages. The two scoundrels even invent some new titles for each other, as when the duke says, "But the histrionic muse is the darling. Have you ever trod the boards, Royalty?" The king answers no, and then the duke says, "You shall, then, before you're three days older, Fallen Grandeur." But perhaps the king already has gotten the better of the duke with his mispronunciation of the duke's assumed name of Bridgewater as Bilgewater. At any rate, the duke and the king appear under their titles on almost every page of the middle third of the novel: royalty now floats on the Mississippi.

In addition, the presence of the two "frauds"—one of Huck's favorite words for them—is the effective means of introducing a number of allusions to kings, especially those who appear in drama—a form of make-believe. For example, the duke tries to teach the king a garbled soliloquy from *Hamlet*, a play about kings and a prince, and he confusedly echoes *Macbeth*, another play about kings. There are allusions to plays about Richard III and King Lear. But not only do the frauds echo the pseudoreality of drama: they themselves produce a "drama." In at least six separate instances—chapters 22, 24, 28, 31 (twice), and 33—we are reminded of the very name of their spectacle, "The Royal Nonesuch"; by it Twain seems to suggest that just as there are nonreal kings on the Mississippi who talk of make-believe dramas, there are "no such" things as royalty—anywhere—for any claim to royalty is a fraud. The "orneriness" of kings is demonstrated in a different way by Huck's confused but hilarious lecture to Jim on the villainous royalty he knows of from history. In the brilliant catalogue he includes Henry VIII, Charles II, Louis XIV, Louis XV, James II, Edward II, Richard III, "them Saxon heptarchies," and "forty more." Then he sums up: "All I say is, kings is kings, and you got to make allowances. Take them all around, they're a mighty ornery lot. It's the way they're raised." One more king is mentioned at length before Huck is rid of his royal parasites. This time Huck has less disparaging—if somewhat manufactured and irrelevant—things to say about William IV, whom Huck claims to have seen regularly at church. When he is caught in the lie by one of the Wilks girls, he simply creates one more incongruous picture, that of King William taking sea baths in an inland city.

Even after royalty meets its pitiful end in tar and feathers, Huck is still not free from kings and their baleful influence, for now Tom Sawyer reenters the story, bringing with him his highly romantic—and therefore equally fraudulent—concept of kings, ladies of the courts, and coats of arms. Tom's lecture on royal, or at least aristocratic, escapes compares with Huck's on the orneriness of kings; like Huck he catalogues aristocrats, mentioning specifically Baron Trenck, Casanova, Benvenuto Cellini, and Henri IV, and alludes to the romantic old areas of Languedoc and Navarre. Later, after Huck makes one more ludicrous error about royalty (he has William the Conqueror on the *Mayflower*), Tom adds another list: "Look at Lady Jane Gray," he says; "look at Gilford Dudley; look at old Northumberland. . . . Jim's *got* to do his inscription and coat of arms. They all do." Tom then describes the projected coat of arms, mixing some traditional terms and colors of heraldry with his own interpretations and symbolisms. Having criticized kings, Twain now seems to say that the heraldic emblem is just as fraudulent—or as legitimate—as any coat of arms ever was. Near the end of the book we find still more allusions, two to Louis XIV and two to Louis XVI; Twain's choice of these seems consistent with the idea of fraud and its reward: Louis XIV was known as the Sun King; Louis XVI was beheaded during the Reign of Terror.

Such are the kings and dukes and aristocratic ladies and gentlemen who people Huck's world and Tom's reading. They are "nonesuch" and pitiful rascals; they are unwise and ornery; they are imprisoned and executed. They are frauds all, whether Huck and Jim know them to be such or Tom unwittingly shows them to be so.

Such, too, is the pattern of kingship. Where does it lead? To be sure, it is an indictment of royalty and aristocracy in ages past and in distant lands. But it is more than that. It is an indictment of the American counterpart on the frontier and in the South. In other words, the pattern is an exponent of one of America's sorriest chapters in history—the preservation of the feudal concept of overlords and vassals in the American system of planters and slaves. Let us look again at Tom's suggested coat of arms: "On the scutcheon we'll have a bend *or* in the dexter base, a saltire *murrey* in the fess, with a dog, couchant, for common charge, and under his foot a chain embattled, for slavery . . . ; crest, a runaway nigger, *sable,* with his bundle over his shoulder on a bar sinister. . . ." Of course Tom is naively unaware of the moral significance of slavery and of the cruelty he inflicts upon the compliant Jim (Tom, we must remember, has not had the instructive experiences Huck has had). Even so, Tom unwittingly brings in the indictment: his coat of arms includes the imagery of the dog and the chain and the theme of domination suggested by the reclining dog; he himself uses the word "slavery," and there are possible puns in the words "common charge" and "bar sinister." Above these details stands the whole ironic paradox of a coat of arms for "a runaway nigger, *sable."* Just as Twain has already asked who is royal and who is fraud, he now asks who is noble and who is slave.

The coat of arms is a clear and specific exponent of the motif of kingship. But earlier in the novel we have met a less clear variation of the pattern, one that is more pervasive but no less real—the variation in the chapters in which the Grangerfords and the Shepherdsons appear. As with many episodes in the novel, there are several motifs: we can immediately recognize the antiromanticism seen elsewhere in the book; the attack on pseudoculture, bad poetry, and tasteless interior decoration; and possibly even the conflicts between grange (farm) workers and shepherds (with further echoes of Cain and Abel, Romeo and Juliet). But we are here concerned specifically with how the two families fit the pattern of royalty and aristocracy. If we remember that the word "gentleman" was once reserved only to the aristocracy, we can see the significance of Huck's description of Colonel Grangerford: "Colonel Grangerford was a gentleman, you see. He was a gentleman all over; and so was his family. He was well born, as the saying is, and that's worth as much in a man as it is in a horse, so the Widow Douglas said, and nobody ever denied that she was of the first aristocracy in our town. . . ." Shortly after this passage Huck describes the ritualistic toast the Grangerford children drink to their parents: there is ceremonious bowing, and the children stand until the elders are seated.

Such are the pseudoroyalty on the banks of the Mississippi. And they are not alone, for the Shepherdsons are "another clan of aristocracy around there." By now, however, the point is obvious, and we know what will soon happen to them all. In spite of their veneer of culture, their decorous formality within the family, these people are no better than Huck's Henry VIII, who "used to marry a new wife every day, and chop off her head next morning." Their feud is no better—and no worse—than the butchery of Richard III or Henry VIII or the French Revolution, nor any more or less sensible in its result than the tarring and feathering of another set of aristocratic personages in this novel. One can only oppose to it the un-Solomon-like wisdom of Sophia Grangerford (her first name means "wisdom"), who runs away from the entire foolishness.

A novel has ample space for many themes and for exponents to guide the reader to them, and it can develop these themes at many levels at once. Certainly this is true of *Huckleberry Finn.* We have traced just one of these themes, that of kingship as it recurs in words and in the names of kings and aristocratic persons. But the theme also raises questions about what kingship is, where it can be found, what types of tyranny and foolishness it thrives on, what effects it has, what slavery it imposes. It impinges on the themes of morality and romanticism. Finally, it raises these questions in the context of some of the richest humor in American literature, humor that stands both as indictment of and cure for human folly.

To paraphrase Huck, this is what comes of handling words.

EXPONENTS IN *HAMLET*:
A HISTORICAL-PSYCHOLOGICAL USE

Like Twain's *Huckleberry Finn*, Shakespeare's *The Tragedy of Hamlet, Prince of Denmark,* is a highly complex masterpiece; the play, like the novel, has so many levels that scholars continue to find great rewards in studying it. Again, however, we need not panic as we approach a work that challenges experts. The tools we have used are still available. In considering *Huckleberry Finn* we used exponents as guides to just one aspect, kingship, of a much larger theme, civilization. Now we will be bolder: we will start with one specific symbol, but we will go much farther into what it suggests. First, that specific symbol.

Several times in the play, but in different ways, we find allusions to traps. Polonius injudiciously uses the image to warn Ophelia away from Hamlet's "holy vows of heaven," vows which, he says, are "springes to catch woodcocks" (I, iii). More significant is Hamlet's deliberate misnaming of "The Murder of Gonzago"; he calls it "The Mousetrap" (III, ii), because it is, as he says elsewhere, "the thing / Wherein I'll catch the conscience of the King" (II, ii). Claudius feels that he is trapped: "O limèd soul, that, struggling to be free, / Art more engag'd" (III, iii). Hamlet, in the hands of plotters, finds himself "thus be-netted round with villainies" (V, ii). The dying Laertes echoes his father's image when he tells Osric that he is "as a woodcock to mine own springe" (V, ii). Thus we begin with traps—springes, lime, nets, and mousetraps. Now these are normally for animals, and surely animals are here—the woodcocks, the mice. But we are talking of human beings, persons who are trapped like animals. Perhaps they are animals. Perhaps their dilemmas are traps. With these larger questions now raised, we can proceed.

Of several major motifs orchestrated in the play, we will consider four at length: the various kinds of love; the relationship of reason, madness, and brutishness; the conflict between thought and action; and the influence of religion and culture. Revenge is of course at the heart of this tragedy of blood, and much has been said of it; we shall confine ourselves to a consideration of revenge only as it appears within the contexts of the four motifs mentioned. As we have seen in other works considered earlier in this chapter, we shall see again that interlocking patterns, comparisons, and contrasts abound. For example, we could begin with love and move from that to madness (as Polonius thinks Hamlet has done) and thus see irrational man as an animal; then we could come full circle to the motif of love in the crude sensualism of Gertrude and Claudius. Similarly, we could note repeated allusions to fate and to memory and the patterns of symbolism that involve not only animals and traps but also rottenness and decay and gardens, for these exponents also lead us into the themes of the play.

Let us first consider love. This basic theme ranges in the play from the purest form of friendship through varieties of familial and romantic love down to lust (remembered by Polonius and realized between Gertrude and Claudius) and even incest (as seen by the Ghost and Hamlet in Gertrude's new marriage).

Immediately we see how one motif absorbs another. As we know from historical criticism, this revenge tragedy is like a number of lesser plays written in the same era. The obvious and conventional motivation of the drama is Hamlet's desire for revenge against his murderous uncle. But Shakespeare takes this traditional theme and fuses it with the larger pattern of love; in this way he greatly complicates Hamlet's dilemma. First, Hamlet's hatred of his uncle is paradoxically motivated by his love of his father. Second, his disappointment with his mother ("Frailty, thy name is woman") derives partly from his disillusionment with her for her forsaking the memory of "Hyperion" for a "satyr," partly from the jolt given to his youthful concepts of romantic love, partly from his reaction to a marriage he considers incestuous. But perhaps the greatest element in this disappointment, at least for many modern interpreters of the play, is the emotional turmoil brought on by the Oedipus complex: Hamlet's feelings for his mother are not only those of a cast-off son, but those of a rejected and jealous lover. Third, Hamlet's notions of romantic love, which his mother helps to shatter, are centered in Ophelia. This romantic love steadily complicates Hamlet's own turmoil—and further orchestrates the entire theme. Polonius, without Hamlet's knowledge, forbids Ophelia to see the Prince; the Ghost's demand for revenge makes it impractical for Hamlet to think of courtship; reasons of state may necessitate his marrying elsewhere (I, iii); Ophelia's lie about her father's whereabouts convinces Hamlet of her disaffection and duplicity (III, i). The combination of these elements prompts Hamlet's violent reaction against Ophelia—and against "woman," including his mother: ". . . if thou wilt needs marry, marry a fool; for wise men know well enough what monsters you make of them" (III, i).

Though less important than the emotions centering on romantic love, Hamlet's friendship for Horatio deserves special mention as what is possibly the purest form of love in the play. Certainly for Elizabethan audiences, friendship was one of the highest virtues. Friendship between man and man was looked upon not through modern eyes that tend to see homosexual implications but through Elizabethan eyes that saw Platonic idealism. Thus Hamlet is able to say to Horatio:

> Nay, do not think I flatter
> For what advancement may I hope from thee
> That no revenue hast but thy good spirits
> To feed and clothe thee? . . .

And he adds:

> Since my dear soul was mistress of my choice

> And could of men distinguish, her election
> Hath seal'd thee for herself. . . .
> > > > Give me that man
> That is not passion's slave, and I will wear him
> In my heart's core, ay, in my heart of heart,
> As I do thee.   (III, ii)

Hamlet's varied emotional attachments have counterparts in the Polonius family at two levels: (1) there is a series of individual foil relationships; (2) the lesser family is a group symbolic of the royal family. Realizing this, we must broaden the orchestration—almost double the instruments. It is well to remember at this point that minor characters frequently are used to help us understand the protagonists (the foil relationship), and that a minor plot may be used to balance and clarify the main action. Of the first sort we have Hamlet-Laertes, the Ghost-Polonius, and Gertrude-Ophelia; of the second, we find that the minor plot reaches its catastrophe (the deaths of Polonius and Ophelia) earlier than the fifth act and that it has themes similar to those of the main action. The familial pattern is obvious early in the play when Laertes bids farewell to his father and his sister. His sense of filial duty, even to a doddering old man, and Ophelia's simple, obedient "I shall obey, my lord," are shortly echoed in Hamlet's cry to the Ghost,

> Remember thee!
> Ay, thou poor ghost, while memory holds a seat
> In this distracted globe.   (I, v)

Ophelia's love for her father appears poignantly—and echoes Hamlet's cry—when, after her beloved has slain her father, she sings her songs in the mad scene of Act IV and says, "There's rosemary, that's for remembrance. Pray you, love, remember. . . ." (IV, v). The two familial patterns interlock in Acts IV and V, when Laertes works for revenge for Polonius' death at Hamlet's hands and struggles with Hamlet over Ophelia's body. Thus, in the Polonius family, the entire pattern of active duty and filial obedience, combined with sincere love, contrasts

with Hamlet's own dormant obligation to achieve revenge—
although he loves sincerely. Nor is the similarity lost on Hamlet,
who says of Laertes: "For by the image of my cause, I see / The
portraiture of his" (V, ii).

Hamlet's love of his parents and Ophelia, his friendship for
Horatio, the affections within the Polonius family—all are either
noble or conventionally acceptable. Other exponents suggest,
however, the lust between Gertrude and Claudius, a brutish love
to which even they at least implicitly admit. Although their
marriage is apparently legal (Henry VIII had a dispensation for
a similar marriage), Hamlet and the Ghost both call it incestuous,
and its lustful, animal nature is a motif projected through images
and symbols throughout the play. For example, the Ghost calls
Claudius "that incestuous, that adulterate beast" who lies in "a
couch for luxury and damned incest" (I, v). With similar
imagery Claudius admits that he murdered to win the Queen as
well as the crown; his fratricide is "rank, it smells to heaven;
. . ." (III, iii). When the Queen admits her guilt to Hamlet, she
looks into her soul and sees there "such black and grainèd
spots / As will not leave their tinct." Hamlet remonstrates with
her for living

> In the rank sweat of an enseamed bed,
> Stew'd in corruption, honeying and making love
> Over the nasty sty! . . .   (III, iv)

When Hamlet kills Claudius he says, "Here, thou incestuous, murderous, damned Dane" (V, ii). In short, their love
is much like the lust defined in Shakespeare's Sonnet 129: "lust
in action [is] the expense of spirit in a waste of shame." Even if
we grant that there is something nobler than lust in Gertrude's
love for Claudius (witness her behavior when Laertes confronts
them in Act IV), the Gertrude-Claudius attraction contrasts
with the purer loves among the other characters.

The animal imagery of the play (and of Sonnet 129) leads
us to explore further the contrast between man's brutish and
man's higher natures, for the contrast is not merely a matter of

lust and ideal love. Hamlet makes the contrast for us in a passage filled with words that serve us as exponents:

> What is a man,
> If his chief good and market of his time
> Be but to sleep and feed? A beast, no more.
> Sure, He that made us with such large discourse,
> Looking before and after, gave us not
> That capability and god-like reason
> To fust in us unus'd. Now, whether it be
> Bestial oblivion, or some craven scruple
> Of thinking too precisely on th' event,—
> A thought which, quarter'd, hath but one part wisdom
> And ever three parts coward,—I do not know
> Why yet I live to say, "This thing's to do, . . ."   (IV, iv)

Claudius later talks of the loss of judgment, "Without the which we are pictures, or mere beasts" (IV, v). And yet it is this same Claudius whose irrational lusts detract from his humanity and whose drinking spurs Hamlet's thoughts on men and their vices (I, iv). Irrationality in the form of mental illness, when the "god-like reason" ceases to function, appears in three different ways in the play. Ophelia is completely insane in Act IV: having lost both father and lover, she is reduced to singing plaintive, even bawdy songs. Polonius, though not insane, is surely senile; ironically, it is he who tries to find the cause of Hamlet's lunacy, and the degeneration he traces is comparable to the toll the years have taken on him. Hamlet is, of course, not insane: his own explanations attest to his sanity and his pretended insanity (I, v; III, ii; III, iv). But his pretense and his emotional intensity are further indices of the themes of sanity and insanity, reason and unreason, the human and the animal. Ophelia's lament about him shows this interplay:

> O, what a noble mind is here o'erthrown!
> The courtier's, soldier's, scholar's, eye, tongue, sword;
> The expectancy and rose of the fair state,
> The glass of fashion and the mould of form,
> The observ'd of all observers, quite quite down!

> And I, of ladies most deject and wretched,
> That suck'd the honey of his music vows,
> Now see that noble and most sovereign reason,
> Like sweet bells jangled, out of tune and harsh;
> That unmatch'd form and feature of blown youth
> Blasted with ecstasy.   (III, i)

It is a lovely but only partially accurate description; it gains its full relevance in the next act, when Ophelia herself is "blasted with ecstasy."

These three levels of mental aberration—true insanity, pretended insanity, and utter senility—are in a sense negative exponents of the question, "What is man?" It is to the higher aspects of man's nature that Hamlet addresses himself when he exclaims: "What a piece of work is a man!" The motifs that we have just followed, the very ones Ophelia thinks of, are here too: "What a piece of work is a man! How noble in reason! How infinite in faculty! In form and moving how express and admirable! In action how like an angel! In apprehension how like a god! The beauty of the world! The paragon of animals! And yet, to me, what is this quintessence of dust?" (II, ii). Implicit here is that man is an animal endowed with a deep ability to love ("infinite in faculty"); hence we recall the motif of the kinds of love. Explicit here is that man is also noble in reason; hence we recall the contrast between reason and insanity. Furthermore, man can "move" and "act" and "apprehend," and this combination becomes our next major concern.

Here is another motif that stretches through the whole play. We might call it the tension between thought and action, since Hamlet is a man of both. It is evident in the most famous speech of all, the "To be or not to be" soliloquy, when Hamlet says,

> Thus conscience [reflection] does make cowards of us all;
> And thus the native hue of resolution
> Is sicklied o'er with the pale cast of thought,
> And enterprises of great pith and moment
> With this regard their currents turn awry,
> And lose the name of action.   (III, i)

In two other soliloquies Hamlet is concerned with the relationship between thought and his own failure to act: "Now I am alone" (II, ii) and "How all occasions" (IV, iv). Late in the play he reminds Laertes of his (Hamlet's) mixture of action and inaction: ". . . though I am not splenitive and rash, / Yet have I something in me dangerous . . ." (V, i). Another clear statement of this motif is that by Claudius (who regularly deserves careful comparison with Hamlet):

> That we would do,
> We should do when we would; for this "would" changes,
> And hath abatements and delays as many
> As there are tongues, are hands, are accidents; . . . (IV, vii)

However much he is aware of his internal struggle between reflection and action, Hamlet does act. He keeps the secret of the Ghost; he arranges for the play within the play; he kills Polonius (taking him for Claudius); he foils the emissaries escorting him to England and later deals with the pirates; he bests Laertes and kills Claudius, and though he acts impetuously, he finds good in impetuosity:

> Rashly,—
> And prais'd be rashness for it: let us know
> Our indiscretion sometime serves us well
> When our deep plots do pall; . . . (V, ii)

On other occasions, however, he is the thinker: his five soliloquies, his talks with Horatio and with Rosencrantz and Guildenstern, his fears that the Ghost might be a devil, his decision not to kill Claudius in Act III. This contrast between Hamlet the man of thought and Hamlet the man of action keeps both character and play in constant tension. Sometimes like Horatio, the man of thought, sometimes like Laertes and Fortinbras, the men of action, Hamlet veers toward one side, then the other, and does not carry out his will until he is about to die. Having killed Claudius, he dies in the arms of the scholar Horatio, but his eulogy is pronounced by the soldier Fortinbras.

Much of this tension in Hamlet is the result of two conflicting ethics. The vengeance desired by both Hamlet and the Ghost derives generally from the tradition of the blood feud, perhaps from the ancient culture of the Danes. Conceivably, the spirit of the *comitatus*—the loyalty between chieftain and followers—is still present: the King has been killed, the blood feud requires that he be avenged, filial duty demands that Hamlet perform the rite. Possibly the Germanic concept of Wyrd (Fate) is also reflected in Hamlet's several allusions to Fate (I, iv; V, i; V, ii). But Hamlet's Germanic culture notwithstanding, the Everlasting has fixed his canon against suicide (I, ii) and against murder and revenge. For Hamlet is not only Teutonic, he is Christian. The highest ethic of the Christian is to love. To murder is to violate this principle, as even Claudius well knows; his offense "hath the primal eldest curse upon 't, / A brother's murder." Surely Claudius' thoughts about Cain and Abel find an echo in Hamlet's hesitancy to murder his uncle. Even the Ghost, while urging revenge, says that the "best" of murders is "most foul." Hamlet's knowledge of Christianity serves him ironically well at the turning point of the play when he deliberately postpones murdering Claudius. He realizes that possibly Claudius has achieved perfect contrition; if such is the case, then Claudius will go to the Christian's heaven, and the pagan's revenge will be incomplete. Thus Hamlet must wait for a time when Claudius' soul is in greater jeopardy: when he mistakes Polonius for Claudius, he kills the old man in the Queen's bedchamber, where Claudius' lust may have damned his soul anew; when he kills Claudius, it is after Claudius has plotted murder. So does the Christian injunction to love one's enemies clash with the ancient injunction to avenge one's king and father. So do thought and action resolve themselves.

Besides the four motifs we have followed, other threads of thematic imagery and statement have their place in the tapestry of the art that is *Hamlet,* each thread working out its pattern to present the richness of the experience. But we have done enough. We now know that the full experience of Shakespeare's most famous play can begin with a perception of the exponents of the finely wrought motifs of the drama.

What we have seen in *Hamlet* is what we have seen throughout this chapter. Like the threads of a tapestry, like the notes and chords and melodies of music, the images, the statements, the themes of literature rise and fall, meet and join or clash. Any one of these can be an exponent of the entire pattern, a clue to the full experience. Once we understand how these exponents help us, we gain much insight into the nature of literary art and communication. As in life, we may not at first perceive all the relationships inherent in a situation, but as we gradually become aware of them they project to us the richness and complexity of the art object; we enjoy and we profit from the discovery of the unknown and the recognition of the dimly perceived.

CHAPTER

6

Some other methods

"How do you learn to *read* this way? *Where* do you learn this? Do you take a course in *symbols* or something?"

With a rising, plaintive pitch to her voice, with puzzled eyes and shaking head, a college student once asked those questions after her class had participated in a lively discussion of the multiple levels in Henry James's *The Turn of the Screw*. As with most students when they are first introduced to a serious study of literature, members of this group were delighted, amazed— and dismayed—as they themselves helped to unfold the rich layers of the work, to see it from perspectives of form and of psychology, to correlate it with the author's biography and its cultural and historical context.

But that particular student, who was both fascinated and dismayed by the "symbols," had not yet taken a crucial step in the learning process: she had not perceived that the practice of close reading, the bringing to bear of all kinds of knowledge, and the use of several approaches are in themselves the course in "symbols or something." What we have traced in this volume is not a course in the occult; it is not something that can be indulged in only by those who have access to the inner sanctum. For, after all, as Wordsworth wrote in 1800 in his Preface to the *Lyrical Ballads,* the poet "is a man speaking to men." As we said earlier, a poet or a dramatist embodies an experience in a poem or a play, embodies it—usually—for *us,* his readers; and we respond simply by reliving that experience as fully as possible.

To be sure, not all of us may want to respond in this fashion. There was, for example, the secondary-school teacher who listened to a fairly long and detailed explication of a five-line poem, "The Death of the Ball-Turret Gunner" by Randall Jarrell; later she took the lecturer aside and said with something more than asperity, "I'd *never* make my class try to see all of *that* in a poem." Perhaps not. But is the class better or worse off because of this attitude?

Clearly, the authors of this book believe that we readers are the losers when we fail to see in a work of literature all that may be legitimately there. We have presented a selection of approaches to literary criticism, fully aware that many have been left out and that much has been generalized. But we have suggested here some of the tools that enable a reader to "criticize," that is, to judge and to discern so that he may better be able to see the truth of a literary work, to relate it to the continuum of human experience, to appreciate its form and style—in short, to perceive the art that gives vitality to the work.

Of course one should not be too enthusiastic: judgment and discernment imply reason and caution, and too often even seasoned critics, forgetting the etymology of "critic," become personal and subjective or even preoccupied with tangential

concerns. Classes of students, their minds suddenly open to psychoanalytic criticism, run gaily through a pastoral poem and
joyously find Freudian symbols in every rounded hill and stately
tree. Some read a simple poem like William Carlos Williams'
"The Red Wheelbarrow" and, unwilling to see simplicity and
compression as virtues enough—and as much more than mere
"simpleness"—they stray from the poem into their individual
mazes. They forget that any interpretation must be supported
logically and fully from the evidence within the literary work
and that the ultimate test of the validity of an interpretation
must be its self-consistency. Conversely, sometimes they establish
a fairly legitimate pattern of interpretation for a work, only to
find something that seems to be at odds with it; then, fascinated
or startled by the new element, they forget that this new element
is not valid unless it proves to be integral when viewed from a
vantage point that permits a unified picture of both the original
pattern and the new element. In short, a given object of literary
art has its unique aesthetic experience; the reader is no more at
liberty to mar it with careless extensions than the author is free
to do so with infelicitous inclusions.

We must also remember to be eclectic in our choices of
critical approaches to a given literary work. Our choices are
determined by the same discretion that controls what we ex-
clude, by our concern for the unique experience and nature of a
piece of literature. Just as not all approaches are useful in all
cases, a given work demands its own combination of approaches.
Perhaps we would not be too far wrong to suggest that there
are as many approaches to literary works as there are literary
works; all we can do is to draw from the many approaches the
combination that best fits a particular literary creation. As David
Daiches said at the end of his book *Critical Approaches to
Literature,* "Every effective literary critic sees some facet of
literary art and develops our awareness with respect to it; but
the total vision, or something approximating it, comes only to
those who learn how to blend the insights yielded by many
critical approaches" (p. 393).

That is why we have chosen to present a selection of approaches and why some of the chapters have even blended several methods. And this blending is as it should be: it is not easy, and it would be fallacious to try, to keep the work always separate from the life of the author and a view of his times; to divide the study of form from the study of basic imageries; to segregate basic imageries from archetypes or from other exponents of the experience of the work. There has of necessity even been some amount of repetition from chapter to chapter, for the chapters exist as emphases rather than as mutually exclusive entities.

We have given some suggestions based on fairly common procedures of literary criticism. We have not exhausted the possibilities. To paraphrase Hamlet, there is more in art and literature than is dealt with in this handbook, bold reader. With this in mind, we will call attention to some of these other possibilities.

SOCIOLOGICAL

For example, one of the methods more frequently mentioned in histories of criticism, although currently less in favor than it once was, is the sociological approach. During the 1930s, when a number of our writers were interested in social reform, there was considerable stress on the uses of literature in the proletarian revolt and on seeing literature as a projection of the movement of social history. It was even suggested that dialectical materialism could provide a sufficiently large frame of reference, a foundation, to include the varieties of knowledge that might be brought to bear on literary interpretation; but, as Stanley Hyman points out in *The Armed Vision,* "Marxism in practice has hardly made good its claim as an all-embracing integrative system" (p. 389). Furthermore, in recent years the effects of war and the awakening to the crises of democracy have eroded this approach to literature, at least in the free world. Nevertheless, it remains a valid means of measuring and interpreting the themes and techniques of much worthy literature. Social, but non-

Marxist, criticism has of course had a traditional place in the interpretation of imaginative writing, and thus was mentioned in Chapter 1. That it remains a productive approach is evident from the work of the Southern Agrarians, the works of Faulkner and their interpretation, and studies of the American Midwest and frontier.

LINGUISTIC

Another means of interpretation that could have received much greater stress, though it too has been touched on in this book, is what might be called the linguistic approach, a term that can include a variety of techniques. A thorough knowledge of words and their ways is clearly needed for reading literature, but such knowledge is only a beginning. With the advance of modern linguistics we are becoming increasingly concerned with semantics, with meaning, with the very "meaning of meaning"; much modern interpretation of literature, for example, derives from William Empson's stress on the ambiguities inherent in words and languages, as in *Seven Types of Ambiguity* (Chatto and Windus, 1930). On a somewhat different tack, we are also asking about the nature of language as symbol, even as a type of symbolic action. Is a literary work "about" something, or is it a something itself? What does Archibald MacLeish mean in "Ars Poetica" when he writes, "A poem must not mean / But be"?

APPRECIATIVE

One of the most popular ways for a beginning reader to approach literature is also one of the most risky. It is always tempting for the immature reader to see the literary work exclusively in terms of himself, and, even worse, in terms of an overly simple response, "I liked it" or "I didn't like it." To be sure, personal preferences have a valid place in the judging of a work: one may feel fairly confident that a given work is aesthetically effective or psychologically accurate—yet not respond to it. But we must always be aware of the need for standards and for sensible attitudes with defensible premises as means of judging. Such an approach may be called the impressionistic or, better, the appreciative approach to literature, since impressionism has sometimes had specialized meanings not only in literature but also in other arts, such as painting. Some of the best of literary criticism has been done in what might be called an appreciative way. One prerequisite is that the person forming such opinions must have a far-ranging taste, a wide reading background, a sense of judgment and discernment that is as much a mark of his personality as it is of his literary perceptiveness. Such were John Dryden, Samuel Johnson, and Matthew Arnold. For example, Dr. Johnson's excellent observation about *Paradise Lost* in his *Life of Milton* tells us something about the greatness and the fault of the poem, but perhaps more about Johnson himself:

> *Paradise Lost* is one of the books which the reader admires and lays down and forgets to take up again. None ever wished it longer than it is. Its perusal is a duty rather than a pleasure. We read Milton for instruction, retire harassed and overburdened, and look elsewhere for recreation; we desert our master and seek for companions.

Matthew Arnold also depended greatly on personal response (though he might have argued otherwise) when he offered the "touchstone" theory of criticism. He suggested that specific passages that come from admittedly great works or writers and which recommend themselves for certain reasons can be compared with the work or passage in hand. Such a comparison with the "touchstones," then, facilitates a value judgment. This type of criticism, open to suspicion on intrinsic grounds alone, is even more open to suspicion if the critic has not the already great knowledge and power of judgment of a Dryden, a Johnson, an Arnold. Nonetheless, judgment in terms of the impression made on the reader has been effective in the hands of these writers and others like the Romantics Lamb, Hazlitt, and De Quincey. The beginning reader will of course have similar responses; they will be valid partly to the extent that he informs himself and tests his responses by comparing them with those of intelligent, cultivated guides.

ARISTOTELIAN

Similarly demanding and presumptive of a knowledge of literary analysis tradition is the use of a set of principles such as Aristotle's. This is not to say that a beginning reader cannot immediately profit from a knowledge of a work like the *Poetics*. In the *Poetics,* Aristotle reviewed the literature of his culture, and from his knowledge of works such as Homer's and Sophocles' and his insights into human beings he developed or induced principles for the analysis and evaluation of literature. Those principles can be used from the outset as a means of entering a work of art, but they can and should be studied repeatedly for true understanding. The beginning reader should realize that the Aristotelian approach can be quite complex—and fascinating— when used by those who have sufficient training and experience in literature, philosophy, and psychology. In contemporary criticism some writers may be called neo-Aristotelian in the sense that they "scrupulously [induce] from poetic practice," as Hyman puts it (p. 387). Or, in a somewhat different sense, one may be neo-Aristotelian by emphasizing literature as an *imitation* (Aristotle's *mimesis*) of human experience. Some critics in this century, such as the "Chicago School" (Ronald Crane, Elder Olson, Norman MacLean, Richard MacKeon), have been particularly associated with neo-Aristotelianism. Even T. E. Hulme and T. S. Eliot can be mentioned here, although neither was in the Chicago Group, and they in turn have an antecedent in Matthew Arnold, whose 1853 Preface to his poems was notably Aristotelian. Among some of these writers a special stress is laid on the significance of plot and to a lesser extent on character development; Aristotle stressed those aspects as two of the six "formative elements" in the drama. Francis Fergusson, who may be called a myth critic, also has stressed an Aristotelian objectivity (imitation) in his attempts to penetrate to the nature of drama.

GENERIC

The brief mentions made of genres in Chapter 1 have been predicated on the long-held distinctions in literature that arise from the large and fairly clear divisions such as fiction, drama, and poetry and subdivisions of these—for example, novel and short story, tragedy and comedy, lyric and epic. Still greater stress may be laid on genres, or the generic approach, and the focus changed somewhat, if one approaches literature from the point of view of Northrop Frye, who in his *Anatomy of Criticism* addresses himself to such conventional terms as drama, epic, and lyric, and points out that "the central principle of genre is simple enough. The basis of generic distinctions in literature appears to be the radical of presentation. Words may be acted in front of a spectator; they may be spoken in front of a listener; they may be sung or chanted; or they may be written for a reader" (pp. 246–247). Later he says, "The purpose of criticism by genres is not so much to classify as to clarify such traditions and affinities, thereby bringing out a large number of literary relationships that would not be noticed as long as there were no context established for them" (pp. 247–248). But what follows in Frye's essay is a far-ranging treatment of the distinguishing characteristics of literary types. He discusses not only Aristotelian distinctions but anthropology, psychology, religion, distinctions of verbal music, and the like.

The relevance of such difficult matters for the beginning reader is that once again he is led to realize the constantly deepening significance that literature may hold for him. Why has man evolved these variants of literary expression? What is achieved by each of them? Can we not better understand a given work once we understand its properties?

GENETIC

Still another approach to a work of literature is that which studies the growth and development, or genesis, of the work. This genetic approach is another of those methods of study that are not so readily available to the beginning reader as some are. But it helps even the beginning reader to know that we can more fully understand a work if we have, for example, manuscript copies showing its stages of development, or if we know the sources from which the author was drawing in developing his own work. A manuscript copy of Frost's "Stopping by Woods on a Snowy Evening" shows how he worked out his words and rhyme scheme, crossing out words not conducive to the experience of the poem. At the same time, his own (separate) comments on the writing of the poem help us to interpret what the marks in the manuscript suggest. Milton's notes over a long period of time show us how he gradually came to write *Paradise Lost* and something of his conception of what he was working toward. The sources of Sir Thomas Malory's *Le Morte Darthur* help us greatly in evaluating the art of his romance and the establishment of his purposes, even to knowing whether he intended to write one book (the commonly accepted view) or a compendium of eight stories, a theory that has been argued.

Critical study of this type presupposes that the reader has access to notebooks, diaries, manuscripts, and the like, and clearly is not within the range of most readers. Nevertheless, the knowledge that an advanced reader learns much from such an approach to a work of literature can forcibly remind the beginning reader that a work of art does not just happen and does not exist simply as pages in an anthology. The beginning reader can then with greater confidence ask what the author intended in his composition, what choices he made, what effect he was striving for, or by what principle the work took on its final shape. Genetic studies remind us of the validity of these questions.

Generic and genetic approaches to interpretation, as well as some of the other methods touched on, are admittedly demanding, at least in their farther reaches. We have not, of course, been able to cover them adequately here. What we do suggest to the reader who is entering upon a mature study of literature is that, as with all of the approaches considered in this volume, these latter means of interpreting literature may take him more fully into a work.

• • •

This book has not pretended to be definitive; it has tried to be suggestive. There is a kind of openness about it: at one end, we have assumed much about the rationale of literary expression, and we have not tried to defend it before a court of accusers; at the other end, we have not tried to lead the reader to a full understanding of matters that even great critics have not always been able to resolve. Rather, let us look out to this very openness, knowing that the values of literature are there for our joy and benefit, inviting us to try our hand, too.

For literature is a part of the richness of human experience. It at once thrives on it, feeds it, and constitutes a significant part of it. When we realize this, we never again can be satisfied with the simple notions that a story is something only for the idler or the impractical dreamer, that a poem is merely a "pretty" combination of sounds and sights, that a significant drama is equivalent to an escapist motion picture or a television melodrama. Browning's Fra Lippo Lippi says,

> This world 's no blot for us,
> Nor blank; it means intensely, and means good:
> To find its meaning is my meat and drink.

To find that meaning Fra Lippo Lippi studies the world—and then projects his findings into his paintings. In the same fashion, Browning embodies *his* findings about art and life in the poem "Fra Lippo Lippi." So it is with any worthy piece of literature. As something that draws from life, nourishes and enriches it, and is of the essence of its fullness, significant literature deserves a variety of critical approaches.

When we use intelligently such tools as have been described in this book, we should be capable of a more mature response to literature—and, hopefully, to life.

BIBLIOGRAPHY

The following list of books is kept short deliberately, and tends to focus on those that are generally available—many in paperback—and that are suggestive of the principles demonstrated in this book. Many of them are simple but rewarding reading; some are more demanding. As with this book of critical approaches, this list is intended to be suggestive rather than exhaustive.

Works of General Interest and Surveys of Critical History

Daiches, David. *Critical Approaches to Literature.* Englewood Cliffs, N.J.: Prentice-Hall, 1956 (available in Norton paperback).

Hyman, Stanley Edgar. *The Armed Vision: A Study in the Methods of Literary Criticism,* rev. and abridged ed. New York: Vintage Books (paperback), 1955.

Thrall, William Flint, and Addison Hibbard. *A Handbook to Literature,* rev. and enlarged by C. Hugh Holman. New York: Odyssey Press, 1962 (available in Odyssey paperback).

Wimsatt, William K., Jr., and Cleanth Brooks. *Literary Criticism: A Short History.* New York: Alfred A. Knopf, 1957.

Works That Are Helpful for the Particular Approaches (Italic numbers indicate the chapters for which the books have special relevance)

Aristotle. *Poetics* (available in several paperback editions, e.g., Hill and Wang, Gateway, University of North Carolina).   *1, 6*

Baird, James. *Ishmael: A Study of the Symbolic Mode in Primitivism.*
    New York: Harper Torchbooks (paperback), 1960.   *4*

Bodkin, Maud. *Archetypal Patterns in Poetry: Psychological Studies of
    Imagination.* New York: Oxford University Press, 1948 (available
    in Oxford paperback).   *4*

Bonaparte, Marie. *The Life and Works of Edgar Allan Poe: A Psycho-
    Analytic Interpretation,* trans. by John Rodker. London: Imago
    Publishing Company, 1949.   *3*

Booth, Wayne C. *The Rhetoric of Fiction.* University of Chicago Press,
    1961 (available in paperback in Phoenix Books).   *2*

Bradley, A. C. *Shakespearean Tragedy,* 2nd ed. London: Macmillan
    and Company, 1914 (available in paperback in Meridian
    Books).   *1*

Brooks, Cleanth, and Robert B. Heilman. *Understanding Drama:
    Twelve Plays.* New York: Holt, Rinehart, and Winston,
    1948.   *2*

Brooks, Van Wyck. *The Ordeal of Mark Twain.* New York: Meridian
    Books (paperback), 1955.   *1, 3*

Burke, Kenneth. *Counter-Statement,* 2nd rev. ed. Los Altos, California:
    Hermes Publications, 1953.   *5*

Drew, Elizabeth. *Poetry: A Modern Guide to Its Understanding and
    Enjoyment.* New York: Dell Publishing Company (paperback),
    1959.   *2*

Fraiberg, Louis. *Psychoanalysis and American Literary Criticism.*
    Detroit: Wayne State University Press, 1960.   *3*

Freud, Sigmund. *New Introductory Lectures on Psychoanalysis,* trans.
    and ed. by James Strachey. New York: W. W. Norton and Com-
    pany, 1964 (available in Norton paperback).   *3*

Fromm, Erich. *The Forgotten Language.* New York: Grove Press, 1957
    (available in Evergreen paperback).   *3, 4*

Frye, Northrop. *Anatomy of Criticism: Four Essays.* Princeton Uni-
    versity Press, 1957.   *2, 4, 5, 6*

Frye, Northrop. *Fables of Identity.* New York: Harcourt, Brace and
    World, 1963 (available in paperback in Harbinger Books).   *4*

Gordon, Caroline, and Allen Tate. *The House of Fiction,* 2nd ed. New
    York: Charles Scribner's Sons (paperback), 1960.   *2*

Hoffman, Frederick J. *Freudianism and the Literary Mind.* 2nd ed.
    Baton Rouge: Louisiana State University Press, 1957 (available
    in paperback in Evergreen Books).   *3*

Jacobi, Jolande. *The Psychology of C. G. Jung.* Yale University Press, 1962 (available in Yale paperback).   *4*

Johnson, Samuel. *Lives of the English Poets.* New York: E. P. Dutton and Company, 1925, 2 vols. (Everyman edition).   *1, 6*

Jung, C. G. *Psychological Reflections,* ed. by Jolande Jacobi. New York: Harper Torchbooks (paperback), 1961.   *4*

Kenner, Hugh. *The Art of Poetry.* New York: Holt, Rinehart, and Winston, 1959.   *2*

Lesser, Simon O. *Fiction and the Unconscious.* Boston: Beacon Press, 1957 (available in paperback in Vintage Books).   *3*

Lowes, John Livingston. *The Road to Xanadu: A Study in the Ways of the Imagination.* Boston: Houghton Mifflin Company, 1927 (available in paperback in Sentry Editions).   *1, 5, 6*

Mordell, Albert. *The Erotic Motive in Literature,* rev. ed. New York: Collier Books (paperback), 1962.   *3*

Shumaker, Wayne. *Literature and the Irrational: A Study in Anthropological Backgrounds.* Englewood Cliffs, N.J.: Prentice-Hall, 1960.   *3, 4*

Sidney, Sir Philip. *The Defense of Poesy* (available in collections of Sidney's work and in anthologies).   *1, 6*

Spurgeon, Caroline. *Shakespeare's Imagery and What It Tells Us.* Cambridge University Press, 1935.   *5*

Wilson, J. Dover. *What Happens in "Hamlet."* Cambridge University Press, 1935 (available in Cambridge paperback).   *1*

Young, Philip. *Ernest Hemingway.* New York: Holt, Rinehart and Winston, 1952.   *1, 3, 4, 5*

ANDREW MARVELL

To his coy
mistress

Had we but world enough, and time,
This coyness, Lady, were no crime.
We would sit down and think which way
To walk and pass our long love's day.
Thou by the Indian Ganges' side   5
Shouldst rubies find; I by the tide
Of Humber would complain. I would
Love you ten years before the Flood,
And you should, if you please, refuse
Till the conversion of the Jews.   10
My vegetable love should grow

Vaster than empires, and more slow;
An hundred years should go to praise
Thine eyes and on thy forehead gaze;
Two hundred to adore each breast,   15
But thirty thousand to the rest;
An age at least to every part,
And the last age should show your heart.
For, Lady, you deserve this state,
Nor would I love at lower rate.   20

But at my back I always hear
Time's wingèd chariot hurrying near;
And yonder all before us lie
Deserts of vast eternity.
Thy beauty shall no more be found,   25
Nor, in thy marble vault, shall sound
My echoing song; then worms shall try
That long preserved virginity,
And your quaint honor turn to dust,
And into ashes all my lust: 30
The grave's a fine and private place,
But none, I think, do there embrace.

Now therefore, while the youthful hue
Sits on thy skin like morning dew,
And while thy willing soul transpires   35
At every pore with instant fires,
Now let us sport us while we may,
And now, like amorous birds of prey,
Rather at once our time devour
Than languish in his slow-chapped power.   40
Let us roll all our strength and all
Our sweetness up into one ball,
And tear our pleasures with rough strife
Thorough† the iron gates of life:
Thus, though we cannot make our sun   45
Stand still, yet we will make him run.

† **thorough:** through

NATHANIEL

HAWTHORNE

Young Goodman Brown

Young Goodman Brown came forth at sunset into the street at Salem village; but put his head back, after crossing the threshold, to exchange a parting kiss with his young wife. And Faith, as the wife was aptly named, thrust her own pretty head into the street, letting the wind play with the pink ribbons of her cap while she called to Goodman Brown.

"Dearest heart," whispered she, softly and rather sadly, when her lips were close to his ear, "prithee put off your journey until sunrise and sleep in your own bed to-night. A lone woman is troubled with such dreams and such thoughts that she's afeard of herself sometimes. Pray tarry with me this night, dear husband, of all nights in the year."

"My love and my Faith," replied young Goodman Brown, "of all nights in the year, this one night must I tarry away from thee. My journey, as thou callest it, forth and back again, must needs be done 'twixt now and sunrise. What, my sweet, pretty wife, dost thou doubt me already, and we but three months married?"

"Then God bless you!" said Faith, with the pink ribbons; "and may you find all well when you come back."

"Amen!" cried Goodman Brown. "Say thy prayers, dear Faith, and go to bed at dusk, and no harm will come to thee."

So they parted; and the young man pursued his way until, being about to turn the corner by the meeting-house, he looked back and saw the head of Faith still peeping after him with a melancholy air, in spite of her pink ribbons.

"Poor little Faith!" thought he, for his heart smote him. "What a wretch am I to leave her on such an errand! She talks of dreams, too. Methought as she spoke there was trouble in her face, as if a dream had warned her what work is to be done to-night. But no, no; 'twould kill her to think it. Well, she's a blessed angel on earth; and after this one night I'll cling to her skirts and follow her to heaven."

With this excellent resolve for the future, Goodman Brown felt himself justified in making more haste on his present evil purpose. He had taken a dreary road, darkened by all the gloomiest trees of the forest, which barely stood aside to let the narrow path creep through, and closed immediately behind. It was all as lonely as could be; and there is this peculiarity in such a solitude, that the traveller knows not who may be concealed by the innumerable trunks and the thick boughs overhead; so that with lonely footsteps he may yet be passing through an unseen multitude.

"There may be a devilish Indian behind every tree," said Goodman Brown to himself; and he glanced fearfully behind him as he added, "What if the devil himself should be at my very elbow!"

His head being turned back, he passed a crook of the road,

and, looking forward again, beheld the figure of a man, in grave and decent attire, seated at the foot of an old tree. He arose at Goodman Brown's approach and walked onward side by side with him.

"You are late, Goodman Brown," said he. "The clock of the Old South was striking as I came through Boston, and that is full fifteen minutes agone."

"Faith kept me back a while," replied the young man, with a tremor in his voice, caused by the sudden appearance of his companion, though not wholly unexpected.

It was now deep dusk in the forest, and deepest in that part of it where these two were journeying. As nearly as could be discerned, the second traveller was about fifty years old, apparently in the same rank of life as Goodman Brown, and bearing a considerable resemblance to him, though perhaps more in expression than features. Still they might have been taken for father and son. And yet, though the elder person was as simply clad as the younger, and as simple in manner too, he had an indescribable air of one who knew the world, and who would not have felt abashed at the governor's dinner table or in King William's court, were it possible that his affairs should call him thither. But the only thing about him that could be fixed upon as remarkable was his staff, which bore the likeness of a great black snake, so curiously wrought that it might almost be seen to twist and wriggle itself like a living serpent. This, of course, must have been an ocular deception, assisted by the uncertain light.

"Come, Goodman Brown," cried his fellow-traveller, "this is a dull pace for the beginning of a journey. Take my staff, if you are so soon weary."

"Friend," said the other, exchanging his slow pace for a full stop, "having kept covenant by meeting thee here, it is my purpose now to return whence I came. I have scruples touching the matter thou wot'st of."

"Sayest thou so?" replied he of the serpent, smiling apart. "Let us walk on, nevertheless, reasoning as we go; and if I convince thee not thou shalt turn back. We are but a little way in the forest yet."

"Too far! too far!" exclaimed the goodman, unconsciously resuming his walk. "My father never went into the woods on such an errand, nor his father before him. We have been a race of honest men and good Christians since the days of the martyrs; and shall I be the first of the name of Brown that ever took this path and kept—"

"Such company, thou wouldst say," observed the elder person, interpreting his pause. "Well said, Goodman Brown! I have been as well acquainted with your family as with ever a one among the Puritans; and that's no trifle to say. I helped your grandfather, the constable, when he lashed the Quaker woman so smartly through the streets of Salem; and it was I that brought your father a pitch-pine knot, kindled at my own hearth, to set fire to an Indian village, in King Philip's war. They were my good friends, both; and many a pleasant walk have we had along this path, and returned merrily after midnight. I would fain be friends with you for their sake."

"If it be as thou sayest," replied Goodman Brown, "I marvel they never spoke of these matters; or, verily, I marvel not, seeing that the least rumor of the sort would have driven them from New England. We are a people of prayer, and good works to boot, and abide no such wickedness."

"Wickedness or not," said the traveller with the twisted staff, "I have a very general acquaintance here in New England. The deacons of many a church have drunk the communion wine with me; the selectmen of divers towns make me their chairman; and a majority of the Great and General Court are firm supporters of my interest. The governor and I, too— But these are state secrets."

"Can this be so?" cried Goodman Brown, with a stare of amazement at his undisturbed companion. "Howbeit, I have nothing to do with the governor and council; they have their own ways, and are no rule for a simple husbandman like me. But, were I to go on with thee, how should I meet the eye of that good old man, our minister, at Salem village? Oh, his voice would make me tremble both Sabbath day and lecture day."

Thus far the elder traveller had listened with due gravity;

but now burst into a fit of irrepressible mirth, shaking himself so violently that his snake-like staff actually seemed to wriggle in sympathy.

"Ha! ha! ha!" shouted he again and again; then composing himself, "Well, go on, Goodman Brown, go on; but, prithee, don't kill me with laughing."

"Well, then, to end the matter at once," said Goodman Brown, considerably nettled, "there is my wife, Faith. It would break her dear little heart; and I'd rather break my own."

"Nay, if that be the case," answered the other, "e'en go thy ways, Goodman Brown. I would not for twenty old women like the one hobbling before us that Faith should come to any harm."

As he spoke he pointed his staff at a female figure on the path, in whom Goodman Brown recognized a very pious and exemplary dame, who had taught him his catechism in youth, and was still his moral and spiritual adviser, jointly with the minister and Deacon Gookin.

"A marvel, truly, that Goody Cloyse should be so far in the wilderness at nightfall," said he. "But with your leave, friend, I shall take a cut through the woods until we have left this Christian woman behind. Being a stranger to you, she might ask whom I was consorting with and whither I was going."

"Be it so," said his fellow-traveller. "Betake you to the woods, and let me keep the path."

Accordingly the young man turned aside, but took care to watch his companion, who advanced softly along the road until he had come within a staff's length of the old dame. She, meanwhile, was making the best of her way, with singular speed for so aged a woman, and mumbling some indistinct words—a prayer, doubtless—as she went. The traveller put forth his staff and touched her withered neck with what seemed the serpent's tail.

"The devil!" screamed the pious old lady.

"Then Goody Cloyse knows her old friend?" observed the traveller, confronting her and leaning on his writhing stick.

"Ah, forsooth, and is it your worship indeed?" cried the good dame. "Yea, truly it is, and in the very image of my old gossip, Goodman Brown, the grandfather of the silly fellow that now is. But—would your worship believe it?—my broomstick hath strangely disappeared, stolen, as I suspect, by that unhanged witch, Goody Cory, and that, too, when I was all anointed with the juice of smallage, and cinquefoil, and wolf's bane—"

"Mingled with fine wheat and the fat of a new-born babe," said the shape of old Goodman Brown.

"Ah, your worship knows the recipe," cried the old lady, cackling aloud. "So, as I was saying, being all ready for the meeting, and no horse to ride on, I made up my mind to foot it; for they tell me there is a nice young man to be taken into communion to-night. But now your good worship will lend me your arm, and we shall be there in a twinkling."

"That can hardly be," answered her friend. "I may not spare you my arm, Goody Cloyse; but here is my staff, if you will."

So saying, he threw it down at her feet, where, perhaps, it assumed life, being one of the rods which its owner had formerly lent to the Egyptian magi. Of this fact, however, Good-man Brown could not take cognizance. He had cast up his eyes in astonishment, and, looking down again, beheld neither Goody Cloyse nor the serpentine staff, but his fellow-traveller alone, who waited for him as calmly as if nothing had happened.

"That old woman taught me my catechism," said the young man; and there was a world of meaning in this simple comment.

They continued to walk onward, while the elder traveller exhorted his companion to make good speed and persevere in the path, discoursing so aptly that his arguments seemed rather to spring up in the bosom of his auditor than to be suggested by himself. As they went, he plucked a branch of maple to serve for a walking stick, and began to strip it of the twigs and little boughs, which were wet with evening dew. The moment his fingers touched them they became strangely withered and dried up as with a week's sunshine. Thus the pair proceeded, at a good free pace, until suddenly, in a gloomy hollow of the road, Good-man Brown sat himself down on the stump of a tree and refused to go any farther.

"Friend," said he, stubbornly, "my mind is made up. Not

another step will I budge on this errand. What if a wretched old woman do choose to go to the devil when I thought she was going to heaven: is that any reason why I should quit my dear Faith and go after her?"

"You will think better of this by and by," said his acquaintance, composedly. "Sit here and rest yourself a while; and when you feel like moving again, there is my staff to help you along."

Without more words, he threw his companion the maple stick, and was as speedily out of sight as if he had vanished into the deepening gloom. The young man sat a few moments by the roadside, applauding himself greatly, and thinking with how clear a conscience he should meet the minister in his morning walk, nor shrink from the eye of good old Deacon Gookin. And what calm sleep would be his that very night, which was to have been spent so wickedly, but so purely and sweetly now, in the arms of Faith! Amidst these pleasant and praiseworthy meditations, Goodman Brown heard the tramp of horses along the road, and deemed it advisable to conceal himself within the verge of the forest, conscious of the guilty purpose that had brought him thither, though now so happily turned from it.

On came the hoof tramps and the voices of the riders, two grave old voices, conversing soberly as they drew near. These mingled sounds appeared to pass along the road, within a few yards of the young man's hiding-place; but, owing doubtless to the depth of the gloom at that particular spot, neither the travellers nor their steeds were visible. Though their figures brushed the small boughs by the wayside, it could not be seen that they intercepted, even for a moment, the faint gleam from the strip of bright sky athwart which they must have passed. Goodman Brown alternately crouched and stood on tiptoe, pulling aside the branches and thrusting forth his head as far as he durst without discerning so much as a shadow. It vexed him the more, because he could have sworn, were such a thing possible, that he recognized the voices of the minister and Deacon Gookin, jogging along quietly, as they were wont to do, when bound to some ordination or ecclesiastical council. While yet within hearing, one of the riders stopped to pluck a switch.

"Of the two, reverend sir," said the voice like the deacon's,

"I had rather miss an ordination dinner than to-night's meeting. They tell me that some of our community are to be here from Falmouth and beyond, and others from Connecticut and Rhode Island, besides several of the Indian powwows, who, after their fashion, know almost as much deviltry as the best of us. Moreover, there is a goodly young woman to be taken into communion."

"Mighty well, Deacon Gookin!" replied the solemn old tones of the minister. "Spur up, or we shall be late. Nothing can be done, you know, until I get on the ground."

The hoofs clattered again; and the voices, talking so strangely in the empty air, passed on through the forest, where no church had ever been gathered or solitary Christian prayed. Whither, then, could these holy men be journeying so deep into the heathen wilderness? Young Goodman Brown caught hold of a tree for support, being ready to sink down on the ground, faint and overburdened with the heavy sickness of his heart. He looked up to the sky, doubting whether there really was a heaven above him. Yet there was the blue arch, and the stars brightening in it.

"With heaven above and Faith below, I will yet stand firm against the devil!" cried Goodman Brown.

While he still gazed upward into the deep arch of the firmament and had lifted his hands to pray, a cloud, though no wind was stirring, hurried across the zenith and hid the brightening stars. The blue sky was still visible, except directly overhead, where this black mass of cloud was sweeping swiftly northward. Aloft in the air, as if from the depths of the cloud, came a confused and doubtful sound of voices. Once the listener fancied that he could distinguish the accents of townspeople of his own, men and women, both pious and ungodly, many of whom he had met at the communion table, and had seen others rioting at the tavern. The next moment, so indistinct were the sounds, he doubted whether he had heard aught but the murmur of the old forest, whispering without a wind. Then came a stronger swell of those familiar tones, heard daily in the sunshine at Salem village, but never until now from a cloud of night. There was one voice, of a young woman, uttering lamentations, yet with an uncertain sorrow, and entreating for some favor, which, perhaps, it would grieve her to obtain; and all the unseen multitude, both saints and sinners, seemed to encourage her onward.

"Faith!" shouted Goodman Brown, in a voice of agony and desperation; and the echoes of the forest mocked him, crying, "Faith! Faith!" as if bewildered wretches were seeking her all through the wilderness.

The cry of grief, rage, and terror was yet piercing the night, when the unhappy husband held his breath for a response. There was a scream, drowned immediately in a louder murmur of voices, fading into far-off laughter, as the dark cloud swept away, leaving the clear and silent sky above Goodman Brown. But something fluttered lightly down through the air and caught on the branch of a tree. The young man seized it, and beheld a pink ribbon.

"My Faith is gone!" cried he, after one stupefied moment. "There is no good on earth; and sin is but a name. Come, devil; for to thee is this world given."

And, maddened with despair, so that he laughed loud and long, did Goodman Brown grasp his staff and set forth again, at such a rate that he seemed to fly along the forest path rather than to walk or run. The road grew wilder and drearier and more faintly traced, and vanished at length, leaving him in the heart of the dark wilderness, still rushing onward with the instinct that guides mortal man to evil. The whole forest was peopled with frightful sounds—the creaking of the trees, the howling of wild beasts, and the yell of Indians; while sometimes the wind tolled like a distant church bell, and sometimes gave a broad roar around the traveller, as if all Nature were laughing him to scorn. But he was himself the chief horror of the scene, and shrank not from its other horrors.

"Ha! ha! ha!" roared Goodman Brown when the wind laughed at him. "Let us hear which will laugh loudest. Think not to frighten me with your deviltry. Come witch, come wizard, come Indian powwow, come devil himself, and here comes Goodman Brown. You may as well fear him as he fear you."

In truth, all through the haunted forest there could be

nothing more frightful than the figure of Goodman Brown. On he flew among the black pines, brandishing his staff with frenzied gestures, now giving vent to an inspiration of horrid blasphemy, and now shouting forth such laughter as set all the echoes of the forest laughing like demons around him. The fiend in his own shape is less hideous than when he rages in the breast of man. Thus sped the demoniac on his course, until, quivering among the trees, he saw a red light before him, as when the felled trunks and branches of a clearing have been set on fire, and throw up their lurid blaze against the sky, at the hour of midnight. He paused, in a lull of the tempest that had driven him onward, and heard the swell of what seemed a hymn, rolling solemnly from a distance with the weight of many voices. He knew the tune; it was a familiar one in the choir of the village meeting-house. The verse died heavily away, and was lengthened by a chorus, not of human voices, but of all the sounds of the benighted wilderness pealing in awful harmony together. Goodman Brown cried out, and his cry was lost to his own ear by its unison with the cry of the desert.

In the interval of silence he stole forward until the light glared full upon his eyes. At one extremity of an open space, hemmed in by the dark wall of the forest, arose a rock, bearing some rude, natural resemblance either to an altar or a pulpit, and surrounded by four blazing pines, their tops aflame, their stems untouched, like candles at an evening meeting. The mass of foliage that had overgrown the summit of the rock was all on fire, blazing high into the night and fitfully illuminating the whole field. Each pendent twig and leafy festoon was in a blaze. As the red light arose and fell, a numerous congregation alternately shone forth, then disappeared in shadow, and again grew, as it were, out of the darkness, peopling the heart of the solitary woods at once.

"A grave and dark-clad company," quoth Goodman Brown.

In truth they were such. Among them, quivering to and fro between gloom and splendor, appeared faces that would be seen next day at the council board of the province, and others which, Sabbath after Sabbath, looked devoutly heavenward, and benignantly over the crowded pews, from the holiest pulpits in the land. Some affirm that the lady of the governor was there. At least there were high dames well known to her, and wives of honored husbands, and widows, a great multitude, and ancient maidens, all of excellent repute, and fair young girls, who trembled lest their mothers should espy them. Either the sudden gleams of light flashing over the obscure field bedazzled Goodman Brown, or he recognized a score of the church members of Salem village famous for their especial sanctity. Good old Deacon Gookin had arrived, and waited at the skirts of that venerable saint, his revered pastor. But, irreverently consorting with these grave, reputable, and pious people, these elders of the church, these chaste dames and dewy virgins, there were men of dissolute lives and women of spotted fame, wretches given over to all mean and filthy vice, and suspected even of horrid crimes. It was strange to see that the good shrank not from the wicked, nor were the sinners abashed by the saints. Scattered also among their pale-faced enemies were the Indian priests, or powwows, who had often scared their native forest with more hideous incantations than any known to English witchcraft.

"But where is Faith?" thought Goodman Brown; and, as hope came into his heart, he trembled.

Another verse of the hymn arose, a slow and mournful strain, such as the pious love, but joined to the words which expressed all that our nature can conceive of sin, and darkly hinted at far more. Unfathomable to mere mortals is the lore of fiends. Verse after verse was sung; and still the chorus of the desert swelled between like the deepest tone of a mighty organ; and with the final peal of that dreadful anthem there came a sound, as if the roaring wind, the rushing streams, the howling beasts, and every other voice of the unconcerted wilderness were mingling and according with the voice of guilty man in homage to the prince of all. The four blazing pines threw up a loftier flame, and obscurely discovered shapes and visages of horror on the smoke wreaths above the impious assembly. At the same moment the fire on the rock shot redly forth and formed a glowing arch above its base, where now appeared a figure. With reverence be it spoken, the figure bore no slight similitude, both in garb and manner, to some grave divine of the New England churches.

"Bring forth the converts!" cried a voice that echoed through the field and rolled into the forest.

At the word, Goodman Brown stepped forth from the shadow of the trees and approached the congregation, with whom he felt a loathful brotherhood by the sympathy of all that was wicked in his heart. He could have well-nigh sworn that the shape of his own dead father beckoned him to advance, looking downward from a smoke wreath, while a woman, with dim features of despair, threw out her hand to warn him back. Was it his mother? But he had no power to retreat one step, nor to resist, even in thought, when the minister and good old Deacon Gookin seized his arms and led him to the blazing rock. Thither came also the slender form of a veiled female, led between Goody Cloyse, that pious teacher of the catechism, and Martha Carrier, who had received the devil's promise to be queen of hell. A rampant hag was she. And there stood the proselytes beneath the canopy of fire.

"Welcome, my children," said the dark figure, "to the communion of your race. Ye have found thus young your nature and your destiny. My children, look behind you!"

They turned; and flashing forth, as it were, in a sheet of flame, the fiend worshippers were seen; the smile of welcome gleamed darkly on every visage.

"There," resumed the sable form, "are all whom ye have reverenced from youth. Ye deemed them holier than yourselves, and shrank from your own sin, contrasting it with their lives of righteousness and prayerful aspirations heavenward. Yet here are they all in my worshipping assembly. This night it shall be granted you to know their secret deeds: how hoary-bearded elders of the church have whispered wanton words to the young maids of their households; how many a woman, eager for widows' weeds, has given her husband a drink at bedtime and let him sleep his last sleep in her bosom; how beardless youths have made haste to inherit their fathers' wealth; and how fair damsels—blush not, sweet ones—have dug little graves in the garden, and bidden me, the sole guest, to an infant's funeral. By the sympathy of your human hearts for sin ye shall scent out all the places—whether in church, bedchamber, street, field, or forest where crime has been committed, and shall exult to behold the whole earth one stain of guilt, one mighty blood spot. Far more than this. It shall be yours to penetrate, in every bosom, the deep mystery of sin, the fountain of all wicked arts, and which inexhaustibly supplies more evil impulses than human power—than my power at its utmost—can make manifest in deeds. And now, my children, look upon each other."

They did so; and, by the blaze of the hell-kindled torches, the wretched man beheld his Faith, and the wife her husband, trembling before that unhallowed altar.

"Lo, there ye stand, my children," said the figure, in a deep and solemn tone, almost sad with its despairing awfulness, as if his once angelic nature could yet mourn for our miserable race. "Depending upon one another's hearts, ye had still hoped that virtue were not all a dream. Now are ye undeceived. Evil is the nature of mankind. Evil must be your only happiness. Welcome again, my children, to the communion of your race."

"Welcome," repeated the fiend worshippers, in one cry of despair and triumph.

And there they stood, the only pair, as it seemed, who were yet hesitating on the verge of wickedness in this dark world. A basin was hollowed, naturally, in the rock. Did it contain water, reddened by the lurid light? or was it blood? or, perchance, a liquid flame? Herein did the shape of evil dip his hand and prepare to lay the mark of baptism upon their foreheads, that they might be partakers of the mystery of sin, more conscious of the secret guilt of others, both in deed and thought, than they could now be of their own. The husband cast one look at his pale wife, and Faith at him. What polluted wretches would the next glance show them to each other, shuddering alike at what they disclosed and what they saw!

"Faith! Faith!" cried the husband, "look up to heaven, and resist the wicked one."

Whether Faith obeyed he knew not. Hardly had he spoken when he found himself amid calm night and solitude, listening to a roar of the wind which died heavily away through the forest. He staggered against the rock, and felt it chill and damp; while a hanging twig, that had been all on fire, besprinkled his cheek with the coldest dew.

The next morning young Goodman Brown came slowly into the street of Salem village, staring around him like a bewildered. man. The good old minister was taking a walk along the grave-yard to get an appetite for breakfast and meditate his sermon, and bestowed a blessing, as he passed, on Goodman Brown. He shrank from the venerable saint as if to avoid an anathema. Old Deacon Gookin was at domestic worship, and the holy words of his prayer were heard through the open window. "What God doth the wizard pray to?" quoth Goodman Brown. Goody Cloyse, that excellent old Christian, stood in the early sunshine at her own lattice, catechizing a little girl who had brought her a pint of morning's milk. Goodman Brown snatched away the child as from the grasp of the fiend himself. Turning the corner by the meeting-house, he spied the head of Faith, with the pink ribbons, gazing anxiously forth, and bursting into such joy at sight of him that she skipped along the street and almost kissed her husband before the whole village. But Goodman Brown looked sternly and sadly.into her face, and passed on without a greeting.

Had Goodman Brown fallen asleep in the forest and only dreamed a wild dream of a witch-meeting?

Be it so if you will; but, alas! it was a dream of evil omen for young Goodman Brown. A stern, a sad, a darkly meditative, a distrustful, if not a desperate man did he become from the night of that fearful dream. On the Sabbath day, when the congregation were singing a holy psalm, he could not listen be-cause an anthem of sin rushed loudly upon his ear and drowned all the blessed strain. When the minister spoke from the pulpit with power and fervid eloquence, and, with his hand on the open Bible, of the sacred truths of our religion, and of saint-like lives and triumphant deaths, and of future bliss or misery unutterable, then did Goodman Brown turn pale, dreading lest the roof should thunder down upon the gray blasphemer and his hearers. Often, awaking suddenly at midnight, he shrank from the bosom of Faith; and at morning or eventide, when the family knelt down at prayer, he scowled and muttered to himself, and gazed sternly at his wife, and turned away. And when he had lived long, and was borne to his grave a hoary corpse, followed by Faith, an aged woman, and children and grandchildren, a goodly procession, besides neighbors not a few, they carved no hopeful verse upon his tombstone, for his dying hour was gloom.

GLOSSARY

This is not intended to be a complete glossary of literary terms. Such a list would be, rightfully, a book in itself, and adequate reference and source books of that sort are available. The terms given here do, however, appear in the present book—sometimes italicized to call attention to their being glossed here—and have special relevance for the types of literary interpretation that are here discussed.

AESTHETICS. The study of beauty (actually, a branch of philosophy). As the term is used in this book, it refers principally to the combination of feeling and thought stimulated by literary art. It does not concern what is merely "pretty" or picturesque, but what is effective. See ART and ARTIFACT.

ALLEGORY. A narrative that has two meanings, one a literal or surface meaning (the story itself) and one a metaphorical meaning (the characters or actions or even the objects of which have a one-to-one equivalence with those of the literal narrative). Frequently the allegory has distinct moral, political, or philosophical implications embedded in its body of SYMBOLS. (Examples are John Bunyan's *Pilgrim's Progress* and the medieval play *Everyman.*)

ALLUSION. Any reference, direct or indirect, to a person, place, event, or character in history, literature, mythology, or sacred books like the Koran and the Bible.

AMBIGUITY. A vagueness, often intentional, that may enrich an author's MEANING by evoking any or all of a number of possibilities, which, when played off one against the other, heighten the dramatic or aesthetic effect. Sometimes, a deliberate ambiguity may be contained in puns or plays on words (for example, "son" and "sun").

AMBIVALENCE. A paradoxical situation or sensation wherein conflicting forces are experienced simultaneously, as when a person feels both attraction to and revulsion for the same object. (Thus, in Fitzgerald's *The Great Gatsby* Nick Carraway's attitude toward Jay Gatsby might be termed "ambivalent.")

ARCHETYPE. An image, MOTIF, or thematic pattern which has recurred so regularly in history, literature, religion, or folkways as to have acquired transcendent symbolic force. According to Jungian psychology, archetypes or "primordial images" are MYTH-forming structural elements that are always present in the unconscious psyche; they are not inherited ideas but "belong to the realm of activities of the instincts and in that sense . . . represent inherited forms of psychic behaviour" (*Psyche and Symbol* [Doubleday Anchor, 1958], p. xvi).

ART. Generally, any concrete creation of the imagination that so blends FORM and content as to appeal to the emotions and the intellect of the perceiver in an aesthetically satisfying way.

ARTIFACT (literary). The literary work of ART itself: poem, drama, short story, novel; that is, a structure of words that is produced or created, just as a vase, a symphony, or a sculpture is produced.

AURAL IMAGERY. *See* IMAGERY.

CATASTROPHE. The concluding action of a tragedy, wherein the principal character or characters meet death or other significant defeat. By extension the term may also designate an unhappy event in other forms of literature.

CATHARSIS. Aristotle's term for the purgation or purification of the emotions of pity and fear, a purgation that results from the viewing of a tragic drama. The term, itself a metaphor, has had varied interpretations. Perhaps the effect of tragedy would have been better described in terms of the beneficial stimulation of the viewer's total being—moral, emotional, and intellectual.

CLASSICAL. *See* CLASSICISM.

CLASSICISM. That aesthetic temper characterized by an emphasis on rational order, discipline, balance and symmetry, clarity and simplicity, and decorum. Generally, Classicism is conservative, looking to the tradition transmitted from the past, especially from classical Greece and Rome, as a means of knowing man's limitations and the universality of human nature. Unlike ROMANTICISM, Classicism downplays emotion, hyper-individualism, and subjectivism. *See also* REALISM.

CONNOTATION.   An overtone of "evocative" meaning, the suggested or emotional meaning of a word as compared with its "dictionary" or "conceptual" meaning. For example, the connotative values of "home" may in some instances be more important than the denotative values. *See* DENOTATION.

CONTEXT.   The setting or frame of reference in which an event takes place, a speech is made, an idea is conceived, or a word is used.

DENOTATION.   The literal or "conceptual" meaning of a word, more objective than its connotation. *See* CONNOTATION.

DENOUEMENT.   The conclusion of a plot, the unraveling of the mystery, the resolution of various strands of action in a DRAMA or a story. The denouement of a tragedy is often called the CATASTROPHE.

DIALECTIC.   In formalistic criticism, a pattern of opposition between two attitudes, or character traits, or systems of ideas. Like PARADOX and TENSION, dialectic suggests a pull of opposed forces which, nevertheless, move toward synthesis or resolution. (In *Hamlet,* for example, dialectic manifests itself on several levels, as in the disparity between appearance and reality, between things as they are and things as they should be, between the god-like in man and the complex of traits that Hamlet calls the "quintessence of dust.")

DRAMA.   That genre of imaginative literature in which characters act out their roles, conventionally on a stage, although some dramas (called "closet dramas") are meant primarily to be read.

DRAMATIC POINT OF VIEW.   *See* POINT OF VIEW.

EXPLICATION *(explication de texte).*   A critical commentary and interpretation based on a close reading of a literary work.

EXPONENT.   A sign or symbol in a literary work which points toward a pattern of MEANING, a recurrent idea, or an emotion or attitude. It may serve as a clue for a steadily deepening appreciation of a work. (The several allusions to traps, nets, and springes point to the animal IMAGERY in *Hamlet;* in turn, the animal imagery helps suggest and develop the thematic question, "What is a man?")

EXPRESSIVE. A term describing a Romantic theory of criticism that glorifies "self-expression" as a chief function of art.

FIGURATIVE LANGUAGE. A type of expression which achieves aesthetic effect by transcending or by departing from the literal and conventional phrasing. See, for example, METAPHOR, HYPERBOLE, and PARADOX.

FIRST-PERSON NARRATOR. *See* POINT OF VIEW.

FOIL. A character used to compare and contrast with another character, so that the more important character is better delineated. (Thus, Tom Sawyer may be viewed as a "foil" for Huck Finn.) Customarily, the term is used for certain characters in drama, though it may be used in fiction as well.

FORM. See ORGANIC FORM and FORMALISTIC; not to be confused with GENRE.

FORMALISTIC. A term used to describe that type of literary criticism wherein the major concern is with the form of a work of art, ranging from its typography to the STRUCTURE which its ideas build. The interplay of these variations of form results in a totality of effect that INFORMS or shapes inwardly the work and gives its parts a relevance to the whole and vice versa.

GENRE. A literary type: poetry, drama, fiction. To these basic ones may be added others like biography and the personal essay. Sometimes subdivisions of these basic types are also called genres, as with the novel and the short story as the main divisions of fiction, or tragedy and comedy in drama, or epic and lyric in poetry. A genre like ROMANCE may exist in both prose fiction and poetry.

GOTHIC. A term originally used to describe a particularly melodramatic and sensational kind of novel in the eighteenth century. Now used to refer to anything that is ghostly, eerie, mysterious, or horrifying (such as much of Poe's fiction and much of present-day fiction by Southern writers).

GUSTATORY IMAGERY. *See* IMAGERY.

HUMOR CHARACTER. A character, not necessarily "humorous" in the sense of being funny, who is distinguished by some particular trait or dominated by some aspect of his personality. The term derives from medieval physiology, which held that the body consisted of four humors—phlegm, blood, and two kinds of bile—and that a preponderance of any one gave rise to certain personality traits.

HYPERBOLE. A type of figurative language characterized by exaggeration or overstatement for some special effect (for example, John Donne's "Go and catch a falling star, / Get with child a mandrake root . . .").

IMAGERY. Any verbal appeal to any of the senses; a stimulation of the IMAGINATION through sense experience (note that "image" and "imagination" are cognates). The appeal or stimulus need not come through nouns alone. VISUAL IMAGERY, the type most familiar to readers at large, appeals to the sense of sight; thus any object that can be seen can be a visual image. Similarly, AURAL IMAGERY is that which can be heard ("thunderous"). KINESTHETIC IMAGERY —perhaps more strange for the beginning student of literature, since the sense stimulated is not one of the classical five—makes its appeal to the sense of motion and therefore very often introduces a kind of muscular activity; not only words, but prose and verse rhythms can create this effect (as in Browning's "I sprang to the saddle, and Joris, and he . . ."). Other types of imagery that may be perceived are GUSTATORY, TACTILE, OLFACTORY, and THERMAL, which make their appeals, respectively, to taste ("salty"), touch ("velvety smoothness"), smell ("stench"), and sensitivity to temperature ("scorch," "frigid"). Some of these tend to overlap, since what stimulates the taste often stimulates the sense of smell, and what can be heard can also suggest motion, and so on. In some writers (notably the French Symbolist poets of the nineteenth century), the various sense experiences may be associated or mingled in such a way as to produce the effect of synesthesia.

IMAGINATION. That human, mental faculty, distinguished from intellect, will, and memory, which as Coleridge observed shapes and fuses the perceptions brought to the mind; or, more generally, that level of the mind's activity at which things are created or conceived, or from which they begin to rise to consciousness in the mind of the writer, musician, painter, or thinker.

INFORM. To shape inwardly, to present the primary characteristic of an object or idea (not to be confused with the idea of simply presenting information). The term denotes an inner process which gives life to a particular entity. (For example, when we say that Poe's single effect of "the redness and the horror of blood" informs "The Masque of the Red Death," we mean that this quality both pervades the story and gives it its essential MEANING.)

IRONY.   A literary device, a manner of expression, a TONE characterized by a duality wherein what is said or seen or otherwise perceived at one level is at another level either incongruous or misconstrued or diametrically opposed to what is expected. (It is ironic that Oedipus intends to seek the murderer of Laius, since Oedipus himself has, unknowingly, killed him.)

JOURNEY.   In literary analysis, a symbolic action wherein the character involved is not simply taking a trip but rather is experiencing a psychological or moral development or initiation. Not necessarily the same as the journey typical of the picaresque novel.

KINESTHETIC IMAGERY.   *See* IMAGERY.

LIMITED OMNISCIENT.   *See* POINT OF VIEW.

LYRIC.   A major class of poetry, the subject matter of which is usually emotion, often subjectively perceived and presented, and the STYLE of which is highly charged with IMAGERY. Love and nature are two of the subjects with which lyric poets are frequently concerned.

MEANING.   The content, the moral or intellectual or emotional signification, perhaps even the "message," of a given work, which is, however, integral to and inseparable from the work itself. Frequently the "meaning" of a work is stated by the critic in terms of the work's THEME.

MELODRAMA.   A species of DRAMA which lays particular stress on emotion and pays little attention to the probability of action, accurate characterization, or genuine feeling. The typical "western" story and the "mystery" tale offer familiar examples of melodrama. Now, more often than not, melodrama is a term of disparagement in literary criticism.

METAPHOR.   Broadly, FIGURATIVE LANGUAGE used to draw comparisons imaginatively, as opposed to literal STATEMENT. Specifically, a comparison of things essentially unlike, drawn without the use of words such as "like" and "as." (Metaphor occurs when one thing is directly called something else: "John Smith is a snake in the grass"; "Denmark's a prison.")

METAPHYSICAL.   In literary criticsm and history, a type of poetry which flourished in the seventeenth century and the style of which has recurred since then, especially in the twentieth century. It is characterized by bizarre, grotesque, unconventional, even shocking figures of speech, and by wit and IRONY and a kind of detached intellectualism. (The term—actually borrowed from philosophy— received its classic literary definition in Samuel Johnson's *Life of Cowley*.)

MOOD. *See* TONE.

MOTIF. A THEME, an IMAGE, a type of action, or an ARCHETYPE which by its recurrent appearance traces itself through a work and heightens its aesthetic appeal. In literature, it may become a sign or index (see EXPONENT) for the meaning or experience of a work.

MOTIVE. The reason for a character's action (that is, his psychological motivation); the word is sometimes used also for what in this book is called MOTIF.

MYTH. In the traditional sense, an anonymous story reflecting primitive beliefs or explaining the mysteries of the natural universe. In more recent theory, myth is the symbolic projection of a people's collective values—a communal, almost instinctive, articulation of reality.

NEW CRITICISM. A critical position that emphasizes the literary ARTIFACT itself and tends to minimize such matters as the biographical and historical facts about an author and his work. It stresses close analysis of the literary work itself as an entity worthy of attention in its own right.

NOVEL. An extended, fictional, prose narrative which portrays characters in a PLOT. The novel may stress adventure for its own sake or character development or a partisan position on some issue or a blend of these and other emphases. The plot of the novel is more extended than that of the SHORT STORY, having usually many more episodes. In modern fiction it is possible to find novels that treat at length one or a few episodes in psychological depth and with a modified concept of time that plays down sequence and stresses relationship. Especially in our day, the distinction between a novel and a novella becomes difficult.

OEDIPUS COMPLEX. A term used in Freudian psychology to denote the strong attachment, sometimes romantic, of a son to his mother. It may in some cases be sublimated and take conventionally acceptable channels; in others, it may give rise to feelings of jealousy of the father as a rival for the mother's love; in its extreme form it may result in incest. (The term derives from the classical MYTH of Oedipus, who unwittingly killed his father and married his mother.)

OLFACTORY IMAGERY. *See* IMAGERY.

OMNISCIENT NARRATOR (or author). *See* POINT OF VIEW.

ORGANIC FORM. The structural, necessary interrelationship of the parts of a literary work which gives it, as it were, a life of its own that grows from within. The literary work becomes an organism.

PARADOX. A figure of speech containing a contradiction which is, nevertheless, somehow true. It is frequently used to express the complexities of life that do not easily lend themselves to simple statement. (Paradoxes abound, for example, in the Scriptures: "For whosoever will save his life shall lose it: but whosoever will lose his life for my sake, the same shall save it.")

PLOT. The action, that which happens—narratively speaking—in a literary work. Technically, it involves not only a sequence of episodes but their interaction and interrelation in a dynamic STRUCTURE.

POEM. A literary composition characterized by a high degree of verbal compression and FIGURATIVE LANGUAGE, in which pleasure, its primary end, is derived from an appreciation of the parts simultaneously with a perception of the whole. The poem should not be confused with mere verse; although, like verse, it may have a regular rhythm and rhyme, the poem achieves its identity through its heightened and compressed language rather than through mere jingle effects.

POINT OF VIEW. A device used in narration that indicates the position from which an action is observed and narrated. For example, a FIRST-PERSON POINT OF VIEW is that in which the narrator is a participant in the action; he may be a major character, perhaps even the central character; or he may be more of an observer, one who is on the fringes of the action. The OMNISCIENT NARRATOR is a kind of third-person narrator; he speaks with the authority of the creating author who knows all; he is not confined to what he sees or hears; he may even comment on or interpret action or character. Still another point of view, variously called THIRD-PERSON LIMITED or LIMITED OMNISCIENT, presents only that which can be seen or heard; it does not tell what the characters are thinking or feeling, although we may see the action more from the vantage point of one character than another. The SCENIC or DRAMATIC POINT OF VIEW resorts to dialogue even more than is usual with the others, so that the result is the objective reporting of what is said. In all of these there is a possibility of overlap, and sometimes an author will shift from one to another within a story.

PSYCHOANALYSIS. The diagnosis and treatment of mental disorder premised on the Freudian theory that such disorders are caused by repression of desires, desires which the afflicted person may have consciously rejected but which nevertheless persist strongly in his subconscious. In this book, Chapter 3 is predicated in large measure on the psychoanalytic theories of psychology pioneered by Sigmund Freud.

REALISM. A manner of presentation in literature which stresses an accurate, perhaps even factual, treatment of subject matter. The emphasis is on the rational and probable, as opposed, for example, to the romantic.

ROMANCE. A type of narrative fiction characterized by the fanciful, often idealistic, treatment of subject matter; love and adventure are often its principal themes. (The genre is an old one, including, for example, prose and verse from the Middle Ages, such as the Arthurian stories, as well as such later work as Tennyson's *Idylls of the King.*) The romance may be contrasted with the NOVEL. (See, for example, Nathaniel Hawthorne's Preface to *The House of the Seven Gables.*)

ROMANTICISM. That aesthetic temper or philosophy characterized by an emphasis on freedom from restraint; interest in the exotic, the far, the ideal, the past, the picturesque; subjectivism; and individualism. Often opposed to the tenets of CLASSICISM, Romanticism in the critical sense does not concern "romance" in courtship and sentimental love.

SCENIC POINT OF VIEW. *See* POINT OF VIEW.

SEMANTICS. A branch of linguistics and philosophy which concerns itself with the study of meaning, with special consideration for the relationship between a sign and that for which it stands and for the changes that take place in particular meanings over a period of time.

SENTIMENTALITY. An excess of sentiment or emotion beyond what the circumstances seem to call for.

SETTING. A combination of locale; historical period, season, or hour; and spiritual, ethnic, and cultural background.

SHORT STORY. A short, fictional, prose narrative (which, according to Edgar Allan Poe, should work toward a single preconceived effect). As opposed to the TALE, the short story in its most finished form fuses its few characters, its few episodes, and its details into a tightly knit STRUCTURE.

SOLILOQUY. A speech by an actor when he is alone on stage, or at least when he is not speaking to or overheard by anyone else on stage.

SONNET. A fourteen-line LYRIC POEM usually in iambic pentameter; the essential characteristic of most sonnets is the dynamic inter-relationship of their parts—the octave (the first eight lines) with the sestet (the last six) or the three quatrains (four-line STANZAS) with each other and the concluding couplet. With interrelationship in mind, we see that the sonnet can be a good index to a formalistic reading of poems.

STANZA. A grouping of lines in poetry which results in formalized units held together by recurrent patterns of rhyme or sometimes only by thought or by the poet's decision to use units of a given number of lines. See also VERSE PARAGRAPH.

STATEMENT. In literary criticism, a first or surface level of com-munication; a paraphrase of the message or THEME or content of a literary work. The term is often opposed to "suggestion" or subsurface levels of MEANING, and to the AESTHETIC quality of the art object.

STRESS. In metrics, an accented beat in a verse line.

STRUCTURE. A formal pattern of words, images, actions, or ideas. See ORGANIC FORM, FORMALISTIC, and INFORM.

STYLE. The particular way in which an author uses words; it is a manifestation not only of his vocabulary and his rhetorical tend-encies, but also of his personality. It might be influenced in given instances by POINT OF VIEW, SETTING, and other considerations which develop verisimilitude or other desired effects. In the hands of a very skillful writer, style becomes an important key to MEAN-ING (as in much of Hemingway's fiction).

SYMBOL. An image or object or action which is charged with mean-ing beyond its denotative value. Although the term presents difficulty and perhaps should be used with caution and for relatively concrete objects, it is not altogether inaccurate to speak of a character's being a symbol. In its most sophisticated forms, the symbol tends to become more and more indefinite in its meanings in contrast to the fixed meaning of ALLEGORY.

TACTILE IMAGERY. *See* IMAGERY.

TALE. *See* SHORT STORY.

TENSION. Generally, a pull of opposing forces; in criticism, a quality of opposition which gives a kind of inner life to a poem or play or work of fiction by unifying its disparate elements. Thus, we may point out the "tension" between THEME and FORM in a given work. See PARADOX, AMBIVALENCE, IRONY, and FORMALISTIC.

THEME. The underlying idea, relatively abstract, which is given concrete expression by the literary work.

THERMAL IMAGERY. *See* IMAGERY.

THIRD-PERSON LIMITED. *See* POINT OF VIEW.

TONE. A term used, sometimes broadly, to denote the attitude or feeling of the speaker or author as conveyed by the language and its artful arrangement. It may also refer to the atmosphere or MOOD generated by the words in the literary work. Thus a tone might, in the first sense, be urbane, acerbic, sly, ironic; and, in the other, melancholy, joyous, oppressive, tense.

VERSE PARAGRAPH. A grouping of lines in verse primarily on the basis of thought content rather than on rhyme pattern. (*See* STANZA.) Conventionally, the verse paragraph is either indented or separated by some spacing device from preceding and following passages.

VISUAL IMAGERY. *See* IMAGERY.

INDEX

233

68 69 70   11 10 9 8